Cape Town

WHAT'S NEW | WHAT'S ON | WHAT'S BEST

www.timeout.com/capetown

Contents

Don't Miss

Itineraries

Cape Town by Area

Essentials

Published by **Time Out Guides Ltd**
Universal House
251 Tottenham Court Road
London W1T 7AB
Tel: + 44 (0)20 7813 3000
Fax: + 44 (0)20 7813 6001
Email: guides@timeout.com
www.timeout.com

Managing Director Peter Fiennes
Editorial Director Ruth Jarvis
Business Manager Daniel Allen
Editorial Manager Holly Pick
Assistant Management Accountant Ija Krasnikova

Time Out Guides is a wholly owned subsidiary of Time Out Group Ltd.

© Time Out Group Ltd
Director & Founder Tony Elliott
Chief Executive Officer David King
Group Financial Director Paul Rakkar
Group General Manager/Director Nichola Coulthard
Time Out Communications Ltd MD David Pepper
Time Out International Ltd MD Cathy Runciman
Time Out Magazine Ltd Publisher/Managing Director Mark Elliott
Group Commercial Director Graeme Tottle
Group IT Director Simon Chappell

Time Out and the Time Out logo are trademarks of Time Out Group Ltd.

This edition first published in Great Britain in 2011 by Ebury Publishing
A Random House Group Company
Company information can be found on www.randomhouse.co.uk
Random House UK Limited Reg. No. 954009
10 9 8 7 6 5 4 3 2 1

Distributed in the US and Latin America by Publishers Group West (1-510-809-3700)
Distributed in Canada by Publishers Group Canada (1-800-747-8147)

For further distribution details, see www.timeout.com

ISBN: 978-1-84670-180-1

A CIP catalogue record for this book is available from the British Library.

Printed and bound in Germany by Appl.

The Random House Group Limited supports The Forest Stewardship Council (FSC), the leading international forest certification organisation. All our titles that are printed on Greenpeace approved FSC certified paper carry the FSC logo. Our paper procurement policy can be found at www.rbooks.co.uk/environment.

Time Out carbon-offsets all its flights with Trees for Cities (www.treesforcities.org).

Cape Town Shortlist

The **Time Out Cape Town Shortlist** is one of a new series of guides that draws on Time Out's background as a magazine publisher to keep you current with what's going on in town. As well as Cape Town's key sights and the best of its eating, drinking and leisure options, the guide picks out the most exciting venues to have recently opened and gives a full calendar of annual events. It also includes features on the important news, trends and openings, all compiled by locally based editors and writers. Whether you're visiting for the first time, or you're a regular, you'll find the *Time Out Cape Town Shortlist* contains all you need to know, in a portable and easy-to-use format.

The guide divides Cape Town into seven areas, each of which contains listings for Sights & Museums, Eating & Drinking, Shopping, Nightlife and Arts & Leisure; chapters for central areas have maps pinpointing all their locations. At the front of the book are chapters rounding up these scenes city-wide, and giving a shortlist of our overall picks in a variety of categories. We include itineraries for days out, plus essentials such as transport information and hotels.

Our listings give phone numbers as dialled from within Cape Town. The city's area code, 021, must be used for calls both from within and outside Cape Town. South Africa's country code is 27. From abroad, use your country's exit code followed by 27 (South Africa's country code), followed with the number given, dropping the initial '0'.

We have noted price categories by using one to four R signs (R-RRRR), representing budget, moderate, expensive and luxury. Major credit cards are accepted by venues unless otherwise stated.

All our listings are double-checked, but places do sometimes close or change their hours or prices, so it's a good idea to call a venue before visiting. While every effort has been made to ensure accuracy of information, the publishers cannot accept responsibility for any errors that this guide may contain.

Venues are marked on the maps using symbols numbered according to their order within the chapter and colour-coded according to the type of venue they represent:

❶ Sights & Museums
❶ Eating & Drinking
❶ Shopping
❶ Nightlife
❶ Arts & Leisure

Map key	
Major sight or landmark	...... ▉
Railway station	...... ▉
Park	...... ▢
Hospital/university	...... ▢
Pedestrian Area	...... ▢
Motorway	...... ▬
Main road	...... ▭
Airport	...... ✈
Church	...... ✚
Area	...... BO-KAMP

Time Out **Cape Town** Shortlist

EDITORIAL
Editor Lisa van Aswegen
Managing Editor Carla Redelinghuys
Copy Editors Emma Howarth, Patrick Welch
Proofreader Kieron Corless

DESIGN
Art Director Scott Moore
Art Editor Pinelope Kourmouzoglou
Senior Designer Kei Ishimaru
Group Commercial Designer Jodi Sher

Picture Editor Jael Marschner
Acting Deputy Picture Editor Liz Leahy
Picture Desk Assistant/Researcher
Ben Rowe

ADVERTISING
New Business & Commercial Director
Mark Phillips

International Advertising Manager
Kasimir Berger
International Sales Executive Charlie Sokol
Advertising Sales (Cape Town) New Media
Publishing

MARKETING
**Sales & Marketing Director, North America
& Latin America** Lisa Levinson
Senior Publishing Brand Manager
Luthfa Begum
Group Commercial Art Director Anthony Huggins
Marketing Co-ordinator Alana Benton

PRODUCTION
Group Production Manager
Brendan McKeown
Production Controller Katie Mulhern

CONTRIBUTORS
This guide was researched and written by the writers of *Time Out Cape Town*.

PHOTOGRAPHY
Photographyby pages 7, 26, 43 (bottom), 78, 106, 131, 134 Jade Maxwell-Newton; pages 9, 11, 12, 13,17, 19, 24, 46, 48, 53, 54, 61, 68, 71, 81, 87, 97, 101, 114, 121, 122, 140 Jurie Senekal; page 25 Kevin John Winder; page 26 Time Out Cape Town; page 34 Argus Cycle Trust; pages 35, 38, 63, 89, 151 Cape Town Routes Unlimited; page 41 Michael Stevenson Gallery; page 42 Philip Schedler; page 51 Michael Le Grange; page 76 Courtesy of the Cape Town Partnership; page 84 Jazzart/Garth Stead; page 94 Rodger Bosch, MediaClubSouthAfrica.com; page 104 Jackie Caradonio; page 109 Winchester Mansions; page 110 Heather Moore; page 113 Stacy Hardy; page 127 David Lazarus/Cape Town Tourism; pages 137, 139 (top) Andries Joubert/Steenberg Vineyards; page 139 (bottom) David Rogers/Steenberg Vineyards; page 155 Kleine Zalze; page 165 Stellenbosch Wine Route; page 169 Vineyard Hotel & Spa; page 180 (top) Hamish Niven/Cape Villas.

The following images were provided by the featured establishments/artists: pages 10,18, 23, 30, 37, 43 (top), 44, 45, 49, 50, 64, 75, 118, 125, 143, 146, 149, 157,160, 170, 177, 180 (bottom).

Cover Photography by Photolibrary.com

MAPS
JS Graphics (john@jsgraphics.co.uk).

About **Time Out**

Founded in 1968, Time Out has expanded from humble London beginnings into the leading resource for those wanting to know what's happening in the world's greatest cities. As well as our influential what's-on weeklies in London, New York and Chicago, we publish nearly 30 other listings magazines in cities as varied as Beijing and Mumbai. The magazines established Time Out's trademark style: sharp writing, informed reviewing and bang up-to-date inside knowledge of every scene.

Time Out made the natural leap into travel guides in the 1980s with the City Guide series, which now extends to over 50 destinations around the world. Written and researched by expert local writers and generously illustrated with original photography, the full-size guides cover a larger area than our Shortlist guides and include many more venue reviews, along with additional background features and a full set of maps.

Throughout this rapid growth, the company has remained proudly independent, still owned by Tony Elliott four decades after he started Time Out London as a single fold-out sheet of A5 paper. This independence extends to the editorial content of all our publications, this Shortlist included. No establishment has been featured because it has advertised, and no payment has influenced any of our reviews. And, for our critics, there's definitely no such thing as a free lunch: all restaurants and bars are visited and reviewed anonymously, and Time Out always picks up the bill. For more about the company, see www.timeout.com.

Don't Miss

EXPERIENCE A BIG-5 SAFARI
UNDER 2 HOURS FROM CAPE TOWN

DAY TRIP SAFARIS

• Hotel pick-up & transfer • Welcome Drink • 2-3 hour game drive with ranger guide
• Visit San Rock Art site • Lunch in an African boma restaurant
• Free visit to the Karoo Ostrich Farm • Browse our African curio shop • Return to Cape Town

CAPE TOWN — N1 — WORCESTER — AQUILA RECEPTION — TOUWS RIVER — R46

Tel: 0861 73-73-78-3 • Mobile: +27 (0)83 301 9222
E-mail: res@aquilasafari.com • www.aquilasafari.com

Long Street p54

WHAT'S BEST
Sights & Museums

Flanked by blue seas and a towering tabletop mountain, the Mother City (as the locals like to call her) is a sleepy city with a village-like atmosphere. It's clear that her inhabitants would far rather be chilling at the beach or quaffing cocktails than slogging in the office. Things happen at a different pace here, and that's part of the magic – if you're happy to take it slowly, you're bound to be charmed. Cape Town is a cosmopolitan city too. You'll spot Somalians, Nigerians, Xhosas, Zulus, Cape Malay Muslims, English people, Malawians, Germans or Afrikaners going about their daily business (and that's just the locals). Different languages and dialects fill the air and get swept along by the feisty south-easterly wind that puffs up skirts and wreaks general mayhem on the streets in the summer months.

Whatever their culture or creed, the locals here have one thing in common – they adore the flat-topped landmark that is Table Mountain. The ancient granite outcrop watches over the city and is treated like a deity. If you hike all the way to the top, you'll be rewarded with staggering views (just remember to take the necessary safety precautions). One of the most popular routes is Platteklip Gorge, a 2.1-kilometre near-vertical climb. But if time and fitness levels aren't on your side, you can also ride up by cable car (see p63). And if it's your birthday (and you can prove it with your passport), you'll get a free return ride.

Inner-city dreaming

Long Street, Cape Town's lengthy social and cultural hub, sports row upon row of brightly painted Victorian warehouses. Nowadays, however, some are adorned with graffiti murals and flickering bright lights. Shops, bars, boutiques and restaurants are housed inside the warehouses and come Friday night, the street heaves with revellers. Above Long Street, towards the mountain, you'll find trendy Kloof Street, packed with cafés, hip clothing stores and stylish restaurants.

Adjacent to the city centre and nestled under Signal Hill is Bo-Kaap (see p86), the historic Cape Malay suburb where the call of the muezzin and the smell of *koeksisters* (a syrupy local delicacy) waft through the air and colourful building façades beg you to take their picture. Stop by the Bo-Kaap Museum (see p86) to delve into the suburb's rich and varied history. Also visit the city's oldest mosque, the Auwal Mosque (34 Dorp Street, Bo-Kaap, 021 424 8477) and swing by the Noon Gun (see p86), the source of the loud bang that rings through the streets every day at noon.

History & museums

The history of the city – and sometimes the country –is reflected in its many historic sites. Democratic South Africa's first president, Nelson Mandela, was held on Robben Island, infamous for its incarceration of political prisoners, for 18 years (see p91). Ferries leave for the island from the Mandela Gateway on the V&A Waterfront. District Six Museum (see p55), meanwhile, is a tribute to the people who once lived in District Six – a vibrant, multicultural area that was bulldozed to the ground following its declaration as a white area in 1966 under the apartheid Group Areas Act of 1950. There's also the Castle of Good Hope – the oldest extant building in South Africa might not boast any turrets or towers, but the star-shaped fort has many interesting stories and myths attached to it and is home to interesting artefacts. It's also the best place in town to get a glimpse of what life was like in the Cape colony in its earliest days.

The cluster of museums surrounding the Company's Garden (see p55) is collectively referred to as the Museum Mile – these include the Iziko Slave Lodge (see p59), the building where the Dutch East India Company locked up the Cape's first slaves; the Iziko South African Museum (see p60), where you'll find bones, stones and other relics (including an impressive life-size whale), and the Iziko National Gallery (see p59), the Cape's premier art museum, with an

District Six Museum p55

Kalk Bay p124

ever-changing choice of local and international exhibitions and a fascinating permanent collection.

Waterside Cape Town

For shopping, dining and bar-hopping try the quaint and cobbled De Waterkant, with its swanky Cape Quarter shopping precinct (see p88), or trendy Green Point, the city's gay strip and also the location of the impressive new Cape Town Stadium (see p90), built for the 2010 FIFA World Cup.

When you're over this side of town, it's a good opportunity to visit the V&A Waterfront (see p93): this renovated part of the city's old harbour is shopping centre, restaurant hub and also the place from which to take a boat trip.

Next to Green Point, on the Atlantic coast, is its slightly seedier sibling, Sea Point (see p106). As the city's unofficial Chinatown, it's packed with takeaway joints, bars and cheap shops, but it also boasts a pretty three-kilometre-long promenade that's ideal for a stroll.

South of Sea Point, bordering the central city along the Atlantic Seaboard, you'll find the glitzy suburbs of Camps Bay (see p114) and Clifton (see p114), home to bronzed bodies and pristine beaches.

Further south lies the Southern Peninsula, where a string of charming villages dot the coastline. Browse antique shops and sip lattés in bohemian fishing village Kalk Bay (see p124); catch a surf at the Victorian seaside town of Muizenberg (see p124); or follow in the footprints of the famous four-legged seadog, Just Nuisance, on a visit to the historic naval base of Simon's Town (see p124). While you're here you can also see an African penguin colony (see p124).

At the tip of the Southern Peninsula's crooked finger you'll find the jaw-dropping lookout point of Cape Point and the stunning array of fauna and flora of the Good Hope Nature Reserve at Cape Point (see p126). A trip to this side of the world wouldn't be complete without a cruise down Chapman's Peak Drive (p121), a winding toll road squeezed in between mountain and ocean and definitely one of the most beautiful Sunday drives in the world.

Sound of the suburbs

Those who find the time to venture into the heart of suburbia might be surprised at the hidden gems they come across. These include the Constantia (see p137) and Durbanville (see p152) wine routes; the sprawling Kirstenbosch National Botanical Garden (see p144); Rhodes Memorial (a massive shrine to empire builder Cecil John Rhodes (see p147), with bird's eye views over the city; and the Heart of Cape Town Museum (Groote Schuur Hospital, Main Road, Observatory, 021 404 1967, www.heartofcapetown.co.za), which tells the story of the world's first heart transplant. Venture even deeper and you'll come across the sprawling winelands of Stellenbosch (see p155) and Franschhoek (see p162) – a world of sun, wine and leafy vistas.

Get moving

A great way to soak up the sights is to get on the hop-on-hop-off City Sightseeing bus that departs daily from the V&A Waterfront (021 511 6000/www.citysightseeing.co.za/ www.openbus.co.za). Hail a cycle cab (www.cyclecabs.co.za) for a lazy meander through town in a bright yellow cyclist-powered buggy or trot through town in a replica 16-seater horse-drawn Victorian carriage (guided tours depart from the Castle of Good Hope every day). For a view of the mountain from the water, head to Hout Bay (see p121), Simon's Town (see p124) or the V&A Waterfront (see p93). Also look out for MyCiTi buses that service the inner city and the Foreshore for less than R10 a trip.

Noon Gun p86

Olympia Café & Deli p133

WHAT'S BEST

Eating & Drinking

Where to start in a city that is both cultural and culinary melting pot, a bubbling stew of flavours and fragrances? The restaurant scene in Cape Town has exploded in recent years, and visitors are increasingly making their way to these shores with the knowledge that value for money and top-notch dining are givens. Café culture has taken the city by storm too, and finding a good cappuccino is no longer limited to the authentic Italian joints. From the best European blends to local coffees, there's a huge amount of choice, and many lively venues to drink it.

Epitomising this culture are places like Origin Café (28 Hudson Street, De Waterkant, 021 421 1000, www.originroasting.co.za), which sources and roasts all its own beans,

the Atlantic Seaboard's Miss K Food Café (Shop 1, Winston Place, 65 Main Road, Green Point, 021 439 9559, www.missk.co.za), with luscious breakfasts and an equally delicious clientele and Caffé Neo (see p108), where the sea view is an understandable distraction from the Mediterranean-Greek menu.

Down south, Olympia Café & Deli (see p133) sets the bar for quintessential café experiences, from the delightfully down-at-heel interior to its famed loaves of ciabatta, garlicky moules and seriously laid-back atmosphere. And at Birds Boutique Café (127 Bree Street, City Centre, 021 426 2534, www.birdsboutiquecafe.com) you'll find hip planet-loving regulars enjoying organic coffee and wholesome lunch offerings. Noordhoek favourite Café Roux

SPICE
in the heart of the old city

THE TAJ CAPE TOWN BRINGS A NEW SENSE OF SOPHISTICATION TO CAPE TOWN, AND COMBINES LUXURY WITH A TRAVEL AND GOURMET DESTINATION.

The luxurious Taj Cape Town has made its home in the painstakingly restored South African Reserve Bank and old Temple Chambers buildings in the heart of historic Cape Town. The hotel offers three distinct dining experiences. On the ground floor is the **BOMBAY BRASSERIE**, a fine-dining restaurant where chef Harpreet Kaur serves authentic Indian flavours from an extensive à la carte menu.

MINT is an all-day informal restaurant that offers a classic menu of meat, seafood, poultry and vegetarian grills. Take the time to enjoy the urban sights and sounds at alfresco dining on St George's Mall, or unwind in the bright and airy interior with its open-plan kitchen and floor-to-ceiling wine wall.

The aptly named **TWANKEY BAR** is a relaxed seafood, champagne and oyster bar with local Methode Cap Classique and Guinness on tap and is the perfect spot to spend an evening listening to live local music.

AFTERNOON TEA in the tranquil Lobby Lounge is a luxury, with a choice of 20 fine loose-leaf teas and sandwiches, freshly baked scones, Indian petits fours and other irresistible treats.

The Taj Cape Town is a perfect balance between the high standards of a modern hotel and the character of the past. It is the ultimate dining destination in the Mother City and a luxury addition to the hotel scene.

STAY OVER AT THE TAJ CAPE TOWN
Bed and breakfast rates from R2 450.
Taj Cape Town, Wale Street, Cape Town; tel: (021) 819-2000; fax: (021) 819-2001; email: res.capetown@tajhotels.com; Visit our hotel website at www.tajhotels.com/capetown or for more information, please also visit our blog on www.tajcapetown.co.za/blog

 http://twitter.com/tajcapetown
 http://www.facebook.com/tajcapetown

(see p132) is where 'Deep South' locals congregate on weekends for relaxed lunches and live music.

Bistros remain a good bet for good food in down-to-earth surroundings. Be sure to pay the much-lauded Bizerca (see p66), which serves contemporary French food, a visit. Boo Radleys (see p66) is known for old-school favourites, Caveau Wine Bar & Deli (see p67) for tapas and wonderful local wines by the glass and Manna (151 Kloof Street, 021 426 2413)for a stylish take on the city bistro. Meanwhile the revamped River Café (see p142) in Constantia ups the stakes with own-grown produce, hearty dishes and great food and wine pairings.

The Winelands, in particular, are a hub for destination restaurants, such as the award winning La Colombe (see p141) in Constantia and Stellenbosch-based Terroir (see p161), where Michael Broughton and his brigade produce an arsenal of French country-inspired plates of deliciousness.

Top tastes

The Italian accents and well-heeled clientele at 95 Keerom (95 Keerom Street, Cape Town, 021 422 0765, www.95keerom.com) are clues that you're at one of the best Italian restarants in the country. Here, chef-patron Giorgio Nava wears his northern Italian roots and South African locavore badge with pride. At Haiku (see p67) an army of chefs produces pan-Asian treats, each more mouthwatering than the other. At Savoy Cabbage (101 Hout Street, Cape Town, 021 424 2626, www.savoycabbage. co.za), Caroline Bagley makes a particularly memorable mark with her sweetbreads, while at the Roundhouse (see p119) chef PJ Vadas's creations continue to wow diners. Serious foodies keep

DON'T MISS

SHORTLIST

Best new
- Delaire Graff (see p158)
- Jordan Restaurant (see p159)

Best value
- Bread & Wine (see p163)
- Sixteen82 (see p142)
- Wild Woods (see p124)

Seafood stars
- Blowfish (sec p152)
- Chapman's Peak Hotel (see p123)
- Willoughby's (see p100)

Choice cafés
- Café Caprice (see p116)
- Café Roux (see p132)
- Olympia Café & Deli (see p133)
- River Café (see p142)

Cocktail classics
- Murano Bar (see p70)
- Planet Bar (see p72)

Best for nighthawks
- Asoka (see p66)
- De Akker (see p158)

Regional stars
- Bizerca Bistro (see p66)
- The Foodbarn (see p133)
- Kitima (see p123)
- La Bruixa (see p108)

Best views
- Black Marlin (see p132)
- Harbour House (see p133)
- Jonkershuis (see p141)
- Overture (see p159)

Best local flavour
- Africa Café (sce p65)
- Amazink (see p158)
- Catharina's (see p138)
- Fyndraai (see p164)
- Marco's African Place (see p87)

what memory will you choose to bring back?

Use your Visa card for special offers at major attractions around South Africa, including Maropeng, Apartheid Museum, Origins Centre, Liliesleaf, Bayworld and Gold of Africa Museum. Simply mention "Visit with Visa" when making payment.

go to www.visa.co.za to find out more.

staff at Nobu (see p96) busy with their requests for saké menu pairings and the brand's famous miso-marinated black cod, while down south, Peter Tempelhoff's team at the newly refurbished Greenhouse at the Cellars (see p141) marries European sensibilities with local produce beautifully. The tasting menu is a memorable extravaganza. There's a similar African bent and use of local ingredients in the food at the Twelve Apostles (see p178).

Authentic Africa

Ethnically and culturally, Cape Town is an intercontinental smorgasbord, a child with African, European and Asian blood.

For a taste of true Malay cuisine, be sure to stop in at Biesmillah's (2 Upper Wale Street, Bo-Kaap, 021 423 0850) for spicy curries, samosas and chilli bites.

For a pan-African feast, visit Africa Café (see p65) and Mama Africa (178 Long Street, Cape Town, 021 426 1017, www.mamaafrica rest.net). Both take in culinary influences from across the continent and also host live bands. Marco's African Place (see p87) is another vibrant restaurant, with game meat and spiced-up dishes. And for a true taste of the city, visit Miriam's Kitchen (Picbell Parkade, Cape Town, 021 421 9420) for its mean Gatsby, the traditional Cape two-foot-long bread roll crammed with meat, fries, spicy sauces and everything but the kitchen sink.

Meaty eats

From '70s-style steakhouses serving up thick juicy porterhouse steaks to street stalls selling sizzling barbecued *boerewors* (farmer's sausage), there's plenty here for meat lovers to enjoy.

As the name suggests, Carne SA (p66) has meat as its first and almost only menu option; it's always delicious so it's well worth waiting for a table. Expect an array of interesting cuts, simply perfect sides and simple, stylish surrounds. Things continue in a similar vein at Headquarters Restaurant (HQ) (see p69), where seared sirloin, salad and French fries are all that's on the menu, along with meat-friendly wines. Its a formula that really works. At Miller's Thumb (10B Kloof Nek Road, Tamboerskloof, 021 424 3838), chefs make the most famous blackened steak in the city, along with Bordelaise-dressed steak and *espetada*. Don't miss award-winning Waterfront steak restaurant Belthazar (see p95), which carries just about every cut of meat imaginable and a gigantic selection of by-the-glass wines to pair with your choice.

If it's an authentic braai (South African barbecue) experience you're after, check out the now-famous

Keerom p15

Mzoli's (Shop 3, NY 115, 021 638 1355) – this buzzing township tavern boasts a top-notch butchery where diners choose their meat (from steaks to chicken and boerewors), then wait for it to be cooked by the master braaiers. Don't forget your side of pap (mielie-meal), their secret Mzoli's sauce and a bottle of their own-label wine, or better yet a quart of ice-cold beer. Further afield, you'll find yourself in charcuterie heaven at Bread & Wine (see p163), where Neil and Tina Jewell wow guests with superb home-cured meats (his) and fresh artisan breads hers) at their alfresco lunch spot near Franschhoek.

Clink clink

For all the talk of great restaurants in the city, there is just as much to be said for the great bars. From old-school authentic joints that come complete with barflies and barmen who've been there for decades to

Origin Café p13

modish, sexy cocktail haunts, chances are you'll find somewhere to lay your hat in Cape Town. Long Street gets our vote for its good mix of lively spots, such as Neighbourhood Restaurant, Bar & Lounge (see p72), where the city's twentysomethings start or finish their evenings. Julep (see p70) is a tiny space that's got 'hidden gem' written all over it (and great martinis too), while the Waiting Room (see p73) is all about urban hipsters and cool tunes.

Other swanky spots include Planet Bar (see p72) at the Mount Nelson,and Sapphire Cocktail Bar (see p120), with beautiful views and a great list of cocktails. A similar sense of style can be found at the One & Only's Vista Bar (see p179).

Visit Boo Radleys (see p66) or Speedway Café (Tafelberg Tavern, Roodehek Terrace, off Hope Street, Gardens, 084 577 2418) for live music and Perseverance Tavern (83 Buitenkant Street, Gardens, 021 461 2440) or the Fireman's Arms (see p67) for an authentic grubby-pub experience. Finally La Med (see p117) is a guaranteed big night out, especially on Sundays when sun-kissed crowds and live bands make for a lot of fun.

Good to know

For tables of six to eight or more, expect a standard 10 per cent to be added to your bill, otherwise the standard tip is between 10 per cent and 15 per cent. Credit cards are usually accepted except at street vendors, and smoking is banned in all restaurants and some bars. Most restaurants serve lunch from noon to 3pm, while dinner starts at 6pm with last orders generally taken between 10pm and 11pm. Reservations on weekend nights are highlyrecommended.

Church Street p23

Shopping

From hand-crafted wares sold on the city's street corners to glossy imported high-end designer fashion brands, there's no doubt that the spectrum of things to buy in Cape Town is huge.

Get your bearings at the V&A Waterfront (see p89), where you'll find some of the biggest catwalk names in the business (like Paul Smith, Louis Vuitton and Jimmy Choo), rubbing shoulders with local good-quality brands like menswear specialists Fabiani (see p102) and much-loved tableware talent Carrol Boyes (see p100).

If you like the idea of soaking up some of the city's cosmopolitan atmosphere while browsing for unique finds, head for Long Street. Here, specialist stores like Clarke's Bookshop (see p74) carry works by local writers, the fashion scene's

young guns ply their trade at a plethora of independent stores and a new breed of conscious consumers browse at the eco-aware shopping precinct 210 on Long Street (No.210, 021 441 1820, www.210onlong.co.za).

Nearby Kloof Street hosts a strip of trendy fashion stores, including Astore (see p74) and lifestyle emporium Nap (41 Kloof Street, Gardens, 021 422 3781) as well as local furniture and home accessories stalwart LIM (see p77). Meanwhile, the newly completed Cape Quarter extension (see p88) is abuzz with shopping, eating and drinking from early until late.

There are areas with great shopping outside the city centre too, from Cavendish Square (see p148), a hub for smart boutiques, to the pretty vintage-store strip in

My Girl
FOREVER
IN LOVE
FOREVER
IN LOVE

SHIMANSKY

THE ART OF DIAMONDS

Kalk Bay, where shops like Railway House Decor & Collectables (see p136) will keep magpies happy and inspired.

Craft's cool

Part of the joy of a visit abroad is finding that special something to remind you of your time there. For the more predictable African carvings, batik-print textiles, statuettes and colourful beaded jewellery, head for Greenmarket Square (see p54), a centuries-old cobbled marketplace in the city centre where bargaining is part of the deal. The nearby Pan African Market (see p60) is a very African cacophony, with traders jostling for your attention at their mask-and curio-crammed stalls.

For a contemporary take on African crafts visit Heartworks (see p77). Here you'll find quirky, bright and beautiful offerings made by local crafters and sold for fair-trade prices. At Africa Nova (see p88), art meets craft in a carefully chosen display of everything from ceramics to hand-printed fabrics and jewellery, providing Afro inspiration at every turn. Larger collectibles can be found at Imiso Ceramics (Unit A102, The Old Biscuit Mill, 373 Albert Road, Woodstock, 021 447 7668), such as elegant vases and more, while the carefully curated displays at Zulu Azania (56A Church Street, Cape Town, 021 424 4510) showcase the wealth of artists and crafters on this continent, and offer inspiration on how to display these items in your own home.

Afro bling

The African continent is teeming with precious and semi-precious jewels, and if bling's your thing,

S H O R T L I S T

Style buys
- Imagenius (see p77)
- The Space (see p148)

Guy's buys
- A Store (see p74)
- Bluecollar Whitecollar (see p74)
- Poppa Trunks (see p79)

Best bling
- Olive Green Cat (see p79)
- Shimansky (see p103)

Best local
- Blink (see p112)
- Olive Green Cat (see p79)

Best bargains
- Atlas Trading (see p86)
- Pan African Market (see p60)
- Wardrobe (see p79)

Best souvenirs
- African Music Store (see p74)
- Greenmarket Square (see p54)
- Oom Samie se Winkel (see p161)

Best craft
- Bead Merchants (see p74)
- Heartworks (see p77)

Best books
- The Book Lounge (see p74)
- Clarke's Bookshop (see p74)

Must dos
- Canal Walk (see p154)
- V&A Waterfront (see p89)

Cape Town has plenty of excellent jewellers and merchants to choose from. First things first: although prices here offer excellent value for money for precious metals and stones, it's essential you make your purchases through a legitimate business. If a deal seems too good to be true, it probably is.

At Diamond Works (7 Coen Steytler Avenue, 021 425 1970), loose stones and ready-to-wear pieces are specialities and, though diamonds are a focus, tanzanites also feature in every blue hue imaginable. High-end store Shimansky (see p103) prides itself on the ability to make up customised items in lightning quick time, while for a taste of serious luxury pay a visit to Charles Greig (see p100), where Rolexes rub shoulders with multi-carated creations. Contemporary diamond and precious stone creations are a signature at elegant store Christoff (see p102), while Uwe Koetter (see p103) remains one of the city's most popular jewellery designers for both customised and off-the-peg bling. Fans of contemporary jewellery should also pop into the Olive Green Cat (see p79) studio.

Markets & malls

The city's various malls and markets are great for one-stop shopping, and popular with the locals. The V&A Waterfront dominates the pack. The massive complex has smaller satellite shopping precincts surrounding it, including the craft-oriented Blue and Red Sheds. Meanwhile, Canal Walk (see p154) provides enough fashion, jewellery, homeware and grocery shopping opportunities, as well as eating, entertainment and kids' fun, to make a full day's outing for all.

Visit genteel Cavendish Square (see p148) for a taste of local fashion design stores and glossy gift shops, and if you're a fan of design, head for the Willowbridge Lifestyle Centre (39 Carl Cronjé Drive, Tyger Valley, 021 914 7218), where a series of top-notch interior and fashion stores jostle for attention.

Antiques lovers should head for the Church Street Antiques Market. Here, a series of small stores crammed with jewellery, tableware, and vintage clothing are strung together in a delightful hotchpotch. On Fridays, traders show off their latest finds outside in the pedestrian mall.

For the highlight of the social shopping week, head for the Old Biscuit Mill, where the Neighbourgoods Market (Old Biscuit Mill, Albert Road) plays host to purveyors of food, cocktails, organic produce, gourmet goods and a smorgasbord of delicious offerings. The

Africa Nova p88

Designer Goods market is also held here, featuring fashion and accessories by some of the city's most cutting-edge talents.

Fashion forward

From international big-name brands like Gucci, Burberry and Byblos to high-street favourites such as Esprit and Mango, there's much here to satisfy the fashion-savvy shopper. The V&A Waterfront has the best selection of international names and though many shops carry stock from the previous season, some (like Louis Vuitton) release new items in line with the rest of the world, making the rand price great value indeed.

Fashion mavens should visit the Space (see p148) in Cavendish Square and browse the laden rails of up-to-the-minute offerings from local designers, while guys who are looking for something special would do well to visit Bluecollar

Whitecollar (see p74) for an ever-changing selection of shirts.

Traditional Afro-inspired shirts can be made for you by a master tailor at Mali South (see p77), and for leather and suede shoes, head for local success story Tsonga (Shop 48, Constantia Village, 021 794 8827).

The best bet for cool kids is Naartjie (see p102), where the range of cheerful cotton offerings ensures the little people in your life are sartorial success stories.

Epicurean offerings

Foodies should be sure to factor in some time at one or two of the city's delis and food emporiums. Locals love Melissa's the Food Shop (94 Kloof Street, 021 424 5540, www.melissas.co.za) for its superb selection of prettily packaged gourmet gifts, while Giovanni's Deliworld (see p102) remains the store of choice for gourmet cooks, thanks to the plentiful stock of imported products and the freshest produce (takeaway food is excellent too). Newport Deli (47 Beach Road, Mouille Point, 021 439 1538, www.newportdeli.co.za) is a see-and-be-seen spot on the Mouille Point promenade, and its deli counter sells everything from smoothies to sandwiches and freshly baked bread and biscuits by the kilogramme.

Wine lovers should head to Caroline's Fine Wine Cellar (see p74) for one-on-one tastings and to get an idea of what's happening on the local wine front. It ships all over the world.

Finally, for the ultimate reminder of your visit to this melting pot of a city, stop in at Atlas Trading (see p86) and take your pick of fresh curry leaves, powders and mixes to make your own spicy meals when you get home.

Pan African Market p60

Mercury Live & Lounge p29

WHAT'S BEST
Nightlife

There is some debate as to when nightlife in Cape Town actually begins. Is it when the sun goes down or when the laid-back Capetonians finally hit the clubs? If you question locals about their reputation for always being late, they'll either shrug nonchalantly or defend themselves vehemently. But whatever their reaction, this much is true: nothing ever begins on time in this relaxed city.

Most clubs open their doors at around 10pm and many only begin to fill up an hour or two later. In the past, when drinks' licencing restrictions were more relaxed, clubs would stay open well past dawn. Now the 4am close time is strictly enforced, but there are always exceptions and you might be lucky enough to find yourself in a place that dares to bend the rules

a little. Some party spots do open earlier but you'll still find that things only get rocking after that magical hour of 10pm. The venue, the barmen and the band members themselves will swear blind that they'll go on stage not a minute later than 9.30pm. They're all lying. The idea is that the drinks start flowing well before the music starts.

On the whole, the Cape Town club scene is currently in a bit of a slump compared to a decade ago. But even so, there are still plenty of places catering for all tastes in music, style, comfort, and people.

When the sun goes down

So what to do before the 'real' nightlife begins? The city's gorgeous coastline is peppered with sundowner spots, and it's the perfect, and only, way to kick off a night on the town.

Camps Bay is the strip of choice and everywhere here has a view. Sapphire (see p120) works well as a starting point, and the DJs spin tunes that could tempt you into staying later than you had intended. If you need more of a club atmosphere, Karma (see p120) is right next door. There's also Caprice (see p116) and a little further down the road the crowd-pulling La Med (see p117), both with great party vibes that continue well after sunset, with DJs and beautiful people.

Since the city still doesn't have much of a late-night public transport system, it's wise to use a taxi to get from the sunset spots to the late-night haunts and home again. A good option is Rikkis taxis (0861 RIKKIS/745547). Call them early to book your ride; don't drink and drive.

Long Street & around

Long Street is the city's biggest nightlife hub. It's lined with bars, clubs and restaurants and if you keep a close eye and hand on your valuables, it's relatively safe to walk from one end to the other. The top end is the busiest, but there are a few places worth visiting below Wale Street.

Deep house club Deluxe (see p80) is just off Long Street in Longmarket Street and remains one of the last bastions of true quality deep house. If hip hop and R&B are your thing, then Chrome (see p80) is your club; queues often snake around the corner. For alternative and distinctly non-commercial tastes, head up to Fiction (see p82). Some nights it's drum 'n' bass, some nights electro. It also hosts Peroxide, the monthly '80s synth-pop residency that celebrates the decade that taste forgot, but also somehow generated some of the best dancefloor tunes of the century.

Choose your style or substance

For all its mayhem and madness, Long Street actually has few genuine nightclubs – it's more about bars with music, DJs or bands.

Camps Bay p114

Spread your wings a little further and seek out House of Kink (see p77) for a bit of sophistication: it's small and intimate, with sexy decor and eclectic tunes. Another classy venue is 121 (see p79); enjoy drinks and tapas downstairs, dancing upstairs, with regular nights for the ladies and old-school rockers.

You'll find that most places in Cape Town find their identity in both the music they offer, and – inextricably linked – the people they attract. The young girls in heartbreakingly short skirts and killer heels and the guys with gelled hair will be found in the bigger clubs playing commercial house: Fez (see p80) in the city centre; Club 91 (see p150), @mospheer (see p147) and Carnage (see p150) in the Southern Suburbs; and China White (see p154) out north.

The so-called coffin kids, or Goths, along with other tribes from the edgier side of society, will head to Gandalf's (299 Lower Main Road, Observatory, 083 330 0700, www.gandalfs.co.za) and ROAR (above Gandalf's), while trance heads can get their fix at Rhino Room (Green Street, off Long Street, 082 741 8981).

Weekend trippin'

Cape Town is a summer-loving city and it embraces the outdoor dance party season with open arms. It's not just for the psychedelic nuts; anyone can enjoy a weekend camping in the countryside, breathing clean air and stomping on the dancefloor. It's even more fun if you dress up in something outrageous – but it's not a must.

The outdoor season officially begins with Earthdance in mid-September, one of a global series of events with the united mission of 'promoting peace by joining participants worldwide in a

SHORTLIST

Best sound systems
- 121 (see p79)
- @mospheer (see p147)
- The Assembly (see p80)

All night long
- Fez Bar & Club (see p80)
- Tiger Tiger (see p150)

Sunday sessions
- La Med (see p117)
- Polana (see p136)

Perfect for posing
- Jade Champagne Bar & Lounge (see p105)
- Murano Bar (see p70)
- Planet Champagne & cocktail bar (see p72)

Best live gigs
- Boo Radleys (see p66)
- Cape Farmhouse (see p136)
- The Shack (see p73)

Best for old-school style
- Decodance (see p112)
- Julep (see p70)
- Pigalle (see p72)

Best laid-back haunt
- Neighbourhood (see p72)
- Rafiki's (see p73)
- The Waiting Room (see p82)

Best for jazz
- Green Dolphin (see p105)
- Marimba (see p82)

Killer cocktails
- Cubaña Havana Lounge & Latino Café (see p88)
- Sapphire Cocktail Bar (see p120)
- Rick's Café Americain (see p73)
- Vista Bar (see p105)

DON'T MISS

Cape Tourist Guide Connection

Explore the Beauty,
Hear the Stories,
Be Inspired

We will connect you with local passionate, qualified and accredited Tourist Guides.

We provide you with a Tourist Guide who can offer specialised knowledge, speak an array of languages, provide you with safe transport and thereby offer guests unique and informative insight during their visit.

We offer day and overnight private tours and trips and are able to cater to your needs, interests, language requirements and budgets.

Connect with us for the ultimate Tourist experience

Bookings: +27 (0)76 056 7532
bookings@capetouristguide.co.za
www.capetouristguide.co.za
CAPE TOWN, SOUTH AFRICA

DIRECT ACCESS TO QUALIFIED ACCREDITED TOURIST GUIDES FOR PERSONALISED TOURS AND UNIQUE EXPERIENCES

wine

townships

nature

peninsula

adventure

general

synchronised prayer for peace and to support humanitarian causes through the global language of music and dance'. After that, all the way through until at least Easter, there are outdoor parties every weekend. Look out for flyers in coffee shops and funky restaurants like Lola's at 228 Long Street, and at backpackers' hostels. Or check out Facebook groups and websites like www.3am.co.za, www.vortexsa.co.za and www.aliensafari.co.za. Most of these parties take place at venues within an hour or two's drive from the city centre, and transport can usually be arranged.

I'm with the band

Three of the best venues for live music are Mercury Live & Lounge (43 De Villiers Street, City Bowl, 021 465 2106, www.mercuryl.co.za), the Assembly (see p80) and Zula Sound Bar (see p82). They also host other events, like drum 'n' bass nights and comedy, for example. None of them are posh – very much beer and pool table kind of places, but

that's rock 'n' roll for you. All three showcase some of the best bands and musicians in the country across all genres of music, mostly on Fridays and Saturdays but sometimes during the week as well. Keep an eye on the local press for details or join their Facebook groups for regular event invitations.

There are also lots of smaller venues where you can catch live music by solo performers or duos while you sit and enjoy a few drinks. At the other end of the scale there are the big concerts – with local and international artists – at venues like the Grand Arena at GrandWest Casino (see p154). Again, watch the press for details.

In the Mother City, jazz is enormously popular and well supported in clubs like the Rainbow Room (see p82) and West End (College Road, Rylands, 021 637 9132). The weekly jazz nights at Speedway Café 105 (Roodehek Terrace, off Hope Street, Gardens, 084 577 2418) are gaining popularity and respected radio personality and jazz fundi Eric Alan raves about them, as do many jazz musicians.

Vortex p37

City Hall p83

WHAT'S BEST
Arts & Leisure

The city's arts scene is ablaze right now, partly thanks to local set-up Spier and its innovative Africa Centre (www.africacentre. net). As a major investor in the local scene, Spier was behind two of last year's most important cultural events – the Spier Contemporary 2010 exhibition (www.spiercontemporary.co.za) and Infecting the City (www. infectingthecity.com), a cutting-edge annual public arts fest that stages site-specific works in Cape Town's communal spaces.

The Africa Centre also played host to the Badilisha Poetry X-Change (www.badilishapoetry.com), which provided a podcast radio and live event platform for African spoken- and written-word poets. Puppetry is also growing in popularity thanks to the annual Out the Box Festival of Puppetry and Visual Performance (www. unima.za.org).

Cape Town has always been geared to lovers of sports and the outdoors – it hosts major annual sporting events including the J&B Met (www.jbmet.co.za), the Old Mutual Two Oceans Marathon (www.twooceansmarathon.org.za) and the Cape Argus Pick n Pay Cycle Tour (www.cycletour.co.za), the largest individually timed cycle race in the world.

Art

The gritty suburb of Woodstock is the city's new art lung. For a walking tour, a great place to start is Sir Lowry Road where Michael Stevenson Gallery (Ground Floor, Buchanan Building, 160 Sir Lowry

Road, Woodstock, 021 462 1500, www.michaelstevenson.com) and Goodman Gallery Cape (3rd Floor, Fairweather House, 176 Sir Lowry Road, Woodstock, 021 462 7573, www.goodmangallery.com) rub shoulders. Cross the road and you'll see the experimental art project space Blank Projects (113-115 Sir Lowry Road, Woodstock, 072 198 9221, www.blankprojects.com) and new-kid-on-the-block the South African Print Gallery, a small space showcasing prints from some of the country's top artists. Parallel to Sir Lowry Road is Albert Road, where you'll find indie art darling WhatiftheWorld (1st Floor, 208 Albert Road, Woodstock, 021 448 1438, www.whatiftheworld.com).

If you're keen on a peek into the history of the South African art scene, with some international pieces thrown into the mix, try the Iziko South African National Gallery (see p59). Cape Town's premier art museum lies in the heart of the verdant Company's Garden. And if you're interested in buying, head to Camps Bay and pay a visit to esteemed art consultant Rose Korber's suburban home and gallery space, Rose Korber Art (48 Sedgemoor Road, Camps Bay, 021 438 9152, www.rosekorberart.com). Get tips about what's hot on the investment scene and browse the work of respected heavyweights like William Kentridge as well as rising art stars. Meanwhile, photography fans should give the Photographers Gallery ZA a whirl (63 Shortmarket Street, City Centre, 021 422 2762, www.erdmanncontemporary.co.za). And if you've got a soft spot for Damien Hirst and Tracey Emin-style works, pop in to the newish gallery-cum-project space of local art bad boys, Ed Young and Matthew Blackman, YOUNGBLACKMAN (69 Roeland Street, Gardens, 083 383 0656, www.youngblackman69.com).

S H O R T L I S T

Wonderful settings
- Kalk Bay Theatre (see p136)
- Kirstenbosch Botanical Gardens (see p144)
- Theatre on the Bay (see p120)

Best for big productions
- Artscape (see p83)
- Grand Arena (see p154)

Most innovative
- Baxter Theatre (see p147)
- Jazzart (see p83)
- Villa Pascal Intimate Theatre (see p83)

Best bargains
- Baxter Theatre (see p147)
- Endler Concert Hall (see p162)

Best alfresco
- Kirstenbosch Botanical Gardens (see p144)
- Maynardville Open-Air theatre (see p150)
- Oude Libertas (see p162)
- Winchester Mansions (see p112)

Best film venues
- Cine 12 (see p178)
- Cinema Nouveau (see p105)
- Labia on Kloof (see p85)
- Labia on Orange (see p85)

Original creations
- Foxy On Broadway (see p83)

Culture after dark
- Dizzy's (see p120)
- Foxy On Broadway (see p83)
- Green Dolphin (see p105)

i art
g a l l e r y

71 Loop Street, Cape Town / +27 (0) 21 424 5150 / www.iart.co.za
IMAGE – Matthew Hindley, *The Ache of Marriage*, 2010, oil on canvas, 300x200cm

Performing arts

The year 2010 saw the opening of a hot new performance space in the city. Named after celebrated local playwright Athol Fugard, the atmospheric Fugard Theatre (see p83) has firmly wedged itself into the scene as one of the city's top theatre spaces. Its first year included the international premiere of Fugard's new play, *The Train Driver*, and a hugely popular international production of Samuel Beckett's *Waiting for Godot*, starring Sir Ian McKellen.

The city's other two major stalwarts for critically acclaimed works are the Baxter Theatre Centre (see p147) and Artscape Theatre Centre (see p83). For cutting-edge student and independent pieces, try the Intimate (see p83), Little and Arena theatres (Hiddingh Campus, 37 Orange Street, City Centre, 021 480 7129, www.drama.uct.ac.za).

Film

Cape Town is blooming into a popular location for international filmmakers. Touted as one of the biggest commercial production destinations in the world, it now sees many Hollywood stars jetting in for feature film shoots.

Unfortunately, what's dished up on city screens locally doesn't reflect this filmmaking boom, and films by South African filmmakers are still a rarity. To make up for this, the film venues themselves are marvellously diverse and some of them are quirky. The most popular choice for watching indie films is the Labia (see p85) – this retro art deco dame has been around for decades and is much loved by local independent and documentary film buffs.

Classical Music

The country's top orchestra, the Cape Philharmonic Orchestra (www.cpo.org.za), calls the Mother City its home. When not treating audiences to traditional symphony concerts in the historic City Hall (see p83), the orchestra can often be heard accompanying the Cape Town City Ballet or Cape Town Opera at the Artscape Theatre Centre (see p83). The historic St George's Cathedral (see p85), on the fringes of the Company's Garden, plays host to choral and baroque productions, and further afield in the southern suburbs the Cape Town Concert Series (www.ctconcerts.co.za) provides a platform for international artists at the Baxter Theatre Centre (see p147). For an alfresco musical experience, try the Kirstenbosch National Botanical Garden (see p144). Its Summer Sunset Concerts line-up features everything from rock bands to Mozart.

Children

Cape Town is an outdoorsy city packed with kid-friendly excursions. There are plenty of beaches for sandcastle building, sunning and swimming. For a *Finding Nemo* experience, the Two Oceans Aquarium (see p93) is a must. The fun includes a dedicated play area, kid-friendly restaurant, touch pool and animatronic froggy puppet show. Not to mention the abundance of weird and wonderful sea creatures – from seals to sharks and giant crabs. There's even a dedicated clownfish (Nemo) tank.

Other animal encounters in the city include spotting birds and cheeky monkeys at World of Birds (see p123), getting up close and personal with snakes and riding camels at Imhoff Farm (see p128), or watching braying penguins at Boulders Beach (see p124).

For theme park thrills, try Ratanga Junction (Century Boulevard, Century City, Milnerton, 086 120 0300, www.ratanga.co.za) or GrandWest Casino and Entertainment World (1 Vanguard Drive, Goodwood, 021 505 7777, www.suninternational.com). The latter also features two ice-rinks (a grown-up and child-sized version). The Planetarium (see p128) will introduce little ones to the joys of stargazing.

If you're keen on a boat trip around the harbour, why not opt for stowing away on a pirate ship? Kids and kids-at-heart, from six to 60, will love the Jolly Roger Pirate Boat (Quay 5, V&A Waterfront, 021 421 0909). The website Cape Town Kids (www.capetown kids.co.za) is a fabulous resource for travelling parents, while www.tinytourists.com hires out equipment for touring children.

Sport

Good weather, sprawling public spaces and a close proximity to nature makes Cape Town heaven for sports lovers and adventure junkies. Roadrunners, trail runners and cyclists are spoiled for choice when it comes to trails and routes.

The city's biggest annual cycling and running events are the Cape Argus Pick n Pay Cycle Tour and the Old Mutual Two Oceans Marathon. The race sees 40,000 riders annually navigating a 109-kilometre course around the Cape Peninsula while the 'Two Oceans' offers a 56-kilometre race along winding coastal roads; it's often called the world's most beautiful marathon. Trail runners can hit unbeaten paths with Cape Runners Against Gravity (www.crag.org.za) or visit www.trailrunning.co.za for other opportunities. Kite boarders can practise at Blouberg Beach in Table View (see p151), while open-water swimmers can contact CapeSwim (www.capeswim.com) for solo swims in Table Bay, False Bay, Cape Point and Cape Agulhas.

If you prefer watching to participating, the city's major spectator sports are rugby, soccer and cricket. Sahara Park Newlands is a haven for cricket lovers (see p145) while the Newlands Rugby Stadium (see p145) is the traditional home of rugby (although the beautiful new Cape Town Stadium in Green Point has put its future in the balance). Soccer is big (even more so after the FIFA World Cup) and a bright future is predicted for the new Cape Town Stadium venue (see p90).

Cape Argus Pick n Pay Cycle Tour p38

Calendar

Kirstenbosch Sundowner Concerts

Note that event details sometimes change at the last minute, so be sure to keep abreast of things on the various websites. Alternatively, phone the Cape Town Tourism Bureau (021 487 6800/www.cape town.travel). Dates highlighted in bold are public holidays.

December

Dec-Apr **Kirstenbosch Sundowner Concerts**
Kirstenbosch Botanical Garden (see p144)
021 799 8783/www.sanbi.org
Finish off a weekend at one of these awesome open-air sundowner concerts on the lawns of Kirstenbosch botanical garden. Local musos like Arno Carstens and Goldfish light up the stage while you kick back with a glass of wine.

18 **MCQP Festival**
Cape Town Stadium (see p90)
www.mcqp.co.za
Just about as much fun as you can have in your cut-off jeans and construction hat. Previous dress-up themes have included Kitch Kitchen and Tool Box, so put on your most unsensible shoes and come join the pink party.

January

1 **New Year's Day**

1-2 **Cape Town Minstrel Carnival**
City centre
Western Cape's minstrels get decked out in their brightest, shiniest satin suits and swinging parasols, and get the crowd's feet tapping with infectious banjo beats. You'll usually find them on Wale Street.

15 Jan-19 Feb **Shakespeare at the Maynardville Open-Air Theatre**
20 Piers Street, Wynberg
(see p150)
www.maynardville.co.za.
Shakespeare productions are brought to life by some of the country's best directors. Be warned that the weather can get quite nippy at this alfresco affair, so remember to bring a blanket or shawl.

February

24 Feb-6 Mar **Cape Town Pride Festival**
City centre
www.capetownpride.co.za
This absolutely fabulous event sees Cape Town's pink community pulling out all the stops with events like a Pride Pageant and dance-off. The festival culminates in the colourful Pride Parade down Somerset Road.

25-27 **Design Indaba Expo**
CTICC (see p55)
www.designindabaexpo.com
This annual event is hotly anticipated by local creatives. Get clued up on what's hot and not during the lecture series (23-25 Feb), then browse the stalls and take in some fashion shows at the expo.

March

Early Mar **The Labia X-Fest**
Labia (see p85)
www.xfest.org
The line-up includes everything from obscure underground cult hits to commercial slasher movies.

21 Mar **Human Rights Day**

25-26 **Cape Town International Jazz Festival**
CTICC (see p55)
www.capetownjazzfest.com
Jazz extravaganza that has previously seen local improv-legends like Hugh Masekela share the stage with international names like Mos Def.

26 Mar-3 Apr **Out The Box Festival**
Various locations
www.unimasouthafrica.org
Sponsored by The International Union of Puppetry South Africa, this puppet festival will leave you inspired.

Late Mar **Taste of Cape Town**
Location to be confirmed
www.tasteofcapetown.com
Award-winning chefs, food purveyors and wine makers all showcase their wares, offering visitors affordable tasters of their finest exports.

April

22 Apr 2011 **Good Friday**

23 **Old Mutual Two Oceans Marathon**
www.twooceansmarathon.co.za
This scenic run has spectacular views all along the southern peninsula. The 56km ultra marathon is the main mama, but the 21km half-marathon takes place on the same day.

25 Apr 2011 **Easter Monday & Family Day**

27 **Freedom Day**

29 Apr-2 May **SA Agri Expo Cheese Festival**
Franschhoek
www.cheesefestival.co.za
Both boutique and big-name cheese-makers offer their wares for tasting. There are also live cooking shows by local celeb chefs.

May

1 **Workers Day**

4-7 **V&A Waterfront Wine Affair**
V&A Waterfront
www.waterfront.co.za
Some of the Western Cape's best wine producers showcase their stuff in a large communal tent, with plenty of snacks and a live music soundtrack thrown in.

Music notes

Festival and live music dates to put in your diary.

Rocking the Daisies

With glorious landscapes and lots and lots of sunshine, it's not surprising that the area around Cape Town is music festival central. Here's a taste of what you can expect.

Get into the spring swing of things at the hugely popular **Rocking the Daisies** at Cloof Wine Estate, Darling (021 481 1832, www.rockingthedaisies.com), usually taking place in October. Held within easy distance of the quaint little West Coast town of Darling, this fest has become a riotous event, with the country's best bands – in various genres – pulling in the crowds.

Heading into summer, **Up the Creek** at Breede River, near Swellendam (021 510 0547, www.upthecreek.co.za), in February, has gained some notoriety for its no-holds-barred hedonism. Expect revellers to be floating around on the river while watching a comprehensive line-up of South Africa's blues, rock, reggae and indie acts.

RAMfest (021 883 3607/076 416 7230/www.ramfest.co.za), held at Nekkies Resort at Worcester in early March is

the premier alternative music festival in the Western Cape, featuring cutting-edge local and international live acts. There are also metal and electronic stages.

Meanwhile, local tranceheads tend to head for the hills in the summer months to weekend-long **Vortex** parties. The Vortex brand (021 531 2173, www.intothe vortex.co.za) 'embraces the notion of light and love through original Goan trance'. In an attempt to distance itself from 'commercialisation', it has taken things underground. To find out if there is an event going on, you'll have to keep an eye on the website, nab one of the limited tickets and journey out to the secret rural destination.

If you're only in the city for a few nights and want to catch a musical happening, you should know about **Balkanology** parties (072 211 5563/www.balkanology.co.za). They're one nighters, and you should expect Bohemian fiddlers, 'frantic Gypsy electronica' and 'jazzy traditional turbofolk' at these infrequent urban fests, popular with the city's hip twenty- and thirtysomething crowd.

Cape Town Minstrel Carnival p35

13-15 **The Franschhoek Literary Festival**

Franschhoek

www.flf.co.zau

Big names from the local and international literary scenes take part in in-depth interviews, debates and talks.

26-29 **Good Food & Wine Show**

CTICC (see p55)

www.gourmetsa.com

The show has recently featured profanity-prone chef Gordon Ramsay and Italian maestro Giorgio Locatelli, among others, in live demos. There are also myriad food and wine stalls.

June

16 **Youth Day**

End June **Cape Town Book Fair**

CTICC (see p55)

www.capetownbookfair.com

Literary discussions, the chance to meet local and international authors and lots of book-centred events for children.

July

Early July **Pick n Pay Knysna Oyster Festival**

www.oysterfestival.co.za

A host of restaurants offer oyster specials during the festival, which is also known to attract sports fanatics with events like the Argus Rotary Cycle Tour and the Knysna Forest Marathon.

Mid-July **Bastille Day Festival**

Franschhoek

www.franschhoek.co.za/bastille.html

Franschhoek celebrates its French roots by doing up the town in blue, red and white. Francophile activities include a traditional barrel-rolling contest, boules competition and French film festival. And then there's the food and wine.

Late July **Encounters: South African International Documentary Film Festival**

Various venues

www.encounters.co.za

This provocative festival shows award-winning documentaries from South Africa and abroad.

28-31 Stellenbosch Wine Festival

Stellenbosch

www.wineroute.co.za

Home to some of the oldest vineyards (and the first wine route) in the country, Stellenbosch is known for its wine almost as much as for its student populace who so keenly imbibe it. This festival sees over 500 wines up for tasting at various estates in the region; a convenient shuttle service takes visitors between them.

August

Early Aug Cape Town Fashion Week

CTICC (see p55)

www.capetownfashionweek.com

Get clued up on what's hot and what's soooo last season at this fashion extravaganza showcasing haute couture creations from local designers such as Maya Prass, Gavin Rajah and Craig Native.

9 National Women's Day

September

Early to mid Sept Nando's Cape Town Comedy Festival

Baxter Theatre Centre, Rondebosch (see p147)

www.comedyfestival.co.za

The stand-up talent at this funny fest (think locals like Trevor Noah and internationals like Bobby Lee) make for a lot of laughs.

Mid-Sept Out in Africa SA Gay & Lesbian Film Festival

Various venues

www.oia.co.za

A line-up of interesting, often controversial, films and documentaries about gay life in South Africa and abroad. Shows are often preceded by thought-provoking talks by participating film makers.

Mid-Sept The Crazy Store Table Mountain Challenge

Table Mountain

www.crazystore.co.za

Clamber over boulders and wayward dassies on a 35km scramble along Cape Town's iconic mountainscape, in an event brought to you by the store that sells everything from clothes pegs and Tupperware to fake flowers and battery operated ostriches. Sure to be a hoot.

24 Heritage Day

November

Mid Nov Discovery Cape Times Big Walk

www.bigwalk.co.za

Put your cross-trainers to the tar and start walking. You can choose from eight established routes, varying from a laid-back 5km stroll through the Newlands to an 80km powerwalk along the Southern Peninsula. Fun is the name of the game.

December

Early Dec Obz Festival

Lower Main Road, Observatory

www.obzfestival.com

This seriously cool festival sees Observatory's club-lined Lower Main Road closed to cars and swarming with people. Stalls sell clothes, food and drinks, and musicians to entertain.

Early Dec Franschhoek Cap Classique and Champagne Festival

Franschhoek

www.franschhoek.org

Taste some fantastic locally and internationally produced sparklers. The stylish open-air affair also sees Franschhoek Valley's best chefs serving delicacies from a range of restaurant stalls.

16 Day of Reconciliation

25 Christmas Day

26 Day of Goodwill

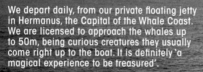

Itineraries

Mount Nelson Hotel p175

Cape of Good Taste

So you've arrived in the Mother City. The city with the largest table in the world – its cloudy tablecloth ready to showcase a smorgasbord of mouth-watering food and wine to the hungry visitor. The sandy white beaches, vibrant culture and exquisite scenery are an integral part of the Cape Town experience, but it's the city's dining scene that ensures it remains South Africa's foodie star. Superb local chefs, a colourful history that marries Malay, European and African influences and a thriving wine industry combine to assure gourmet travellers that they've come to the right place. From sleek and chic five-star restaurants offering exquisitely prepared local cuisine to low-key street vendors selling sizzling specialities for next-to-nothing, Cape Town has it covered.

Those who choose to stay in the city centre or on its fringes are spoilt for choice with a network of streets (easily covered on foot) brimming with delicious restaurants. The Bo-Kaap, a predominantly Muslim area nestled underneath Signal Hill should be one of the first on the list for exploration. Start at the bottom of Rose Street and walk up to Wale Street – check out the candy-coloured homes sandwiched side-by-side as you go – where you'll breathe in the wonderful aroma of slow-cooked biryanis and *boboties* (a sweet and spicy curried mince dish) being prepared for lunch or the evening meal.

At **Biesmillah's** (2 Upper Wale Street, Bo-Kaap, 021 423 0850) you can buy freshly made samosas and chilli bites to take away with a cup of warm, sweet tea (they also do a good lunch of spiced Malay specialities if you feel like swinging by later in the day). Wale Street also plays host to the famous **Atlas Trading** (see p86), one of the city's most popular stops for buying freshly ground spices for

preparing your own dishes at home (they'll tell you exactly how to do it properly too). A popular tourist haunt is the **Noon Gun Tearoom & Restaurant** (273 Longmarket Street, Bo-Kaap, 021 424 0529, www.noonguntearoom.co.za) – it's a fitting place to take a rest after visiting this historic Cape Town neighbourhood. The sweet milk tart is renowned but you can also tuck into a big plate of sweet and spicy lamb curry.

Back down the slope in nearby Loop Street, **Café Zorina** (No.172, 021 424 9301) has been feeding locals at lunchtime with their famous rotis for close to fifty years. Meanwhile, if you're after some authentic African flavour, take a stroll to **Addis in Cape** (41 Church Street, 021 424 5722, www.addisincape.co.za) on Church Street where Ethiopian specialities are the order of the day. Pop into the **Africa Café** (see p65) on Shortmarket Street for a pan-African lunch experience to finish off your morning stroll. Wine enthusiasts should be sure to pop into **Caveau Wine Bar & Deli** (see p67) on Heritage Square too.

The passionate staff here are keen to share their love for local wines and will recommend a by-the-glass choice to partner your lunch.

A leisurely afternoon tea is a fine way to finish off a day of indulgent eating and drinking. Enjoy one of the most famous in the city at the genteel **Mount Nelson Hotel** (see p175) on Orange Street, where

Caveau Wine Bar & Deli p67

Groot Constantia p137

a laden buffet table groans under the weight of sweet and savoury delights and bespoke tea blends are order of the day.

The Sugar High Tea served in the library at the **Cape Grace Hotel** (see p178) at the V&A Waterfront also offers sweet treats. And if you get there a little later in the day, an informed whisky tasting in the hotel's **Bascule Bar** (see p95) makes a pleasing sundowner treat.

Afternoon tea with a view is equally pleasant at the **Winchester Mansions** (see p181) in Sea Point and the **Twelve Apostles' Leopard Lounge** (see p178) on the coastal road towards Hout Bay; both offer different but equally breathtaking views of the sparkling Atlantic waters. And at the **Vista Bar** (see p105) at the One&Only (also at the V&A Waterfront precinct), martinis and petits fours are perfect partners for an afternoon of decadence, while the country's largest cellar means a lot of choice if you're drinking wine.

For an altogether more lively afternoon affair, be sure to pay **La Med** (see p117) near Camps Bay a visit – a popular music venue, bar and restaurant that throbs with activity in the summer months, especially on Sundays.

There's no point in coming to the Cape if you're going to give the glorious wines that are made here a miss. For an on-your-doorstep experience, get to the pretty Constantia Valley where the many estates offer an array of delicious food and wine experiences – from light and lovely Italian at **Constantia Uitsig** (see p137) to French-global at the award-winning **La Colombe** (see p141) and bistro fare at the **River Café** (see p142). Estate and local valley wines are available on each menu here and there's even an on-site wine purveyor so you can shop for South African wine finds after lunch.

Bistro Sixteen82 (see p142) at nearby Steenberg Wine Estate is a seriously sexy new addition to this part of the world – serving brasserie dishes and tapas alongside excellent wines (be sure to stock up on their bubbly at the cellar).

Buitenverwachting (see p137) and **Groot Constantia** (see p137) offer their wines to taste and buy, and provide picnics among the vines too. If you're in the area on a Saturday, be sure to pop on over to the **Porter Estate Market** (see p138, Tokai Forest), a local gathering of stalls in a forest clearing under the Constantiaberg mountain range. The nearby **Earth Fair Market** (South Palms, Main Road, Retreat, 084 220 3856, www.earthfairmarket.co.za) has a slightly less rural setting but is just as serious about its food, with organic specialities, boutique wines and cured meats and cheeses – it's open on Wednesday afternoons and Saturday mornings.

The emerald in the Cape's jewelled crown, the Stellenbosch and Franschhoek wine regions, feature a patchwork of beautifully manicured farms, majestic mountain peaks and some seriously good food and wine destinations. In Stellenbosch, those who love their lunch experience alfresco should book a table under the trees at **Terroir** (see p161), where Michael Broughton combines his love for French country cuisine with the estate's gorgeous liquid offerings.

Visit **Overture** (see p159) for cutting-edge cuisine and a superb view to match or book a table at **Tokara** (p161), where the jaw-dropping vistas of the valley are a suitable backdrop to chef Richard Carstens' artful plates and the sexy winery design. The new Tokara **DeliCATessen** (see p161) at this estate is another must – stock up on olive oils and fill your basket with just-baked breads, delicious cheeses and bottled treats.

Over the hill lies the valley of Franschhoek. For an authentic experience, **Bread & Wine** (see p163) offers handmade own-cured platters of charcuterie from chef and master meathead Neil Jewell, as well as gourmet breads to eat now or take home courtesy of his wife Tina. The menu has plenty of other delicious country-style dishes, while the deli offers such delights as pistachio-studded chicken liver pâté and paprika-scented saucisson to take home.

Le Quartier Français (16 Huguenot Street, 021 876 2151, www.lequartier.co.za) is one of the most famous eating experiences in the valley and also holds cooking courses. For a meal with a view (its tables gaze out across the valley) and boutique wines galore visit **La Petite Ferme** (see p166). And for authentic South African fare teamed with good local wine, check out **Topsi & Co** (7 Reservoir Street West, Franschhoek, 021 876 2952).

For the ultimate foodie buzz, make a beeline for the excellent **Neighbourgoods Market** (Old Biscuit Mill, Albert Road). It's open every Saturday morning and features an open-sided warehouse-like space, with a courtyard annex that's packed to the rafters with stall holders selling everything from Belgian waffles to organic tomatoes and aubergines, pretty iced cupcakes, wedges of cheese, just-ground artisan coffee, handmade pizzas, bottled preserves, biltong, boutique wines, home-made bread, flowers, smoothies… and more. Get stuck in and chat to winemakers about their latest vintages, ask the gardener how he grows his herbs and be sure to try a man-sized steak roll before you leave.

Earth Fair Market p44

ITINERARIES

Greenmarket Square p54

Living History

ITINERARIES

Behind the swanky boutiques, dodgy dive bars and towering office blocks, the Cape of years ago is still visible – you need only know where to look. The first clues to its layered past are bricked into the varied architecture – a mish-mash of building styles trace the city's transformation from Dutch East India Company settlement to British colony and bastion of art-deco architecture in Africa and beyond. But ancient pear trees, hidden plaques, ferry boats and public squares can also provide a peek into the past. Put on your walking shoes and take a scenic stroll for the day.

Day 1: From colony to country

Start your amble through Cape Town's colonial history at the country's oldest building. Built between 1666 and 1679, the **Castle of Good Hope** (see p55) gives the modern visitor an eye into life in the days of the Cape Colony; at that time the building was on the edge of the ocean, with waves lapping against its walls.

After exploring its many nooks and crannies, take a walk to the **Company's Garden** (see p55) – once the scurvy-preventing fruit and vegetable garden of the Dutch East India Company, now a verdant city park. The garden was commissioned by Jan van Riebeeck, who was deployed to the Cape to establish a spice route pit stop between Europe and the East. An ancient pear tree, the last living remnant from Jan's day, still grows next to the gate leading into Victoria Street.

Flanking the garden, along Government Avenue, you'll spy a beautiful historic building known as the **Tuynhuis**, which was home to Dutch and English governors of the Cape for over 200 years. Look out for the company's logo visible in a semi-circular pediment on the façade of the building.

Exit the garden towards Adderley Street and you'll see the big, stocky building on your right where the Dutch East India Company's slaves were housed in cramped conditions. The **Iziko Slave Lodge** (see p59) also served as an informal brothel. Behind the lodge in Spin Street (in the middle of the traffic island) there's a plaque on the ground marking the location of the old fir tree where the slaves were sold.

Across the road is a historic Dutch Reformed church, the **Groote Kerk** (39 Upper Adderley Street, Cape Town, 021 422 0569, www.grootekerk.org.za). The oldest church in South Africa, it boasts an impressive teak pulpit by sculptor Anton Anreith. Inside, eight governors of the Cape lie buried.

Parallel to Adderley Street is St George's Mall, where you can enjoy lunch at any one of the many informal cafés lining this pedestrianised street. Then make your way up to Long Street, also parallel to St George's Mall. Stroll along and admire the rows of **Victorian merchant houses** with their intricate wrought-iron balconies and original street-level shop fronts. Most now house boutiques, bars and restaurants.

Take a turn into Shortmarket Street and visit **Greenmarket Square** (corner of Shortmarket and Burg streets, Cape Town), the country's second oldest public space, flanked by some impressive examples of art-deco architecture. This is also where you'll find the **Old Townhouse** – an 18th-century beauty built in the Cape Rococo style. From this balcony the public declaration of the abolition of slavery was read out in 1834. Today the building houses an esteemed collection of 17th-century Dutch and Flemish art.

From here, head up the slope of Signal Hill on Shortmarket Street to the **Bo-Kaap** (see p86). You'll know you've arrived when you see streets lined with rainbow-coloured Cape Dutch meets Georgian-style cottages. Home to a thriving Muslim Cape Malay community, Bo-Kaap traces its roots back to the 1700s, when it was inhabited by freed slaves, free traders and crafters. Turn left into Rose Street and make your way towards Dorp Street to have a look at the country's oldest mosque – the **Auwal Mosque** (34 Dorp Street, 021 424 8477). On your way, stop at Wale Street and pop in to the **Bo-Kaap Museum** (see p86) for a peek into the district's history.

Day 2: The Mandela years

Start your morning with a call to book your **Robben Island ferry trip** (see p91). Ferries depart at 9am, 11am, 1pm and 3pm, weather permitting, so book for 1pm or 3pm, depending on your schedule. In the busy summer months it's advisable to book a few days in advance. Once you've secured your place, head for the **District Six Museum** (see p55), commemorating the vibrant community of the suburb of District Six, which was bulldozed to the ground. Its residents were evicted from their homes from 1967 onwards, when the area was declared a whites-only zone under the Group Areas Act. If the museum intrigues you, you can also book a walking tour of the site where the suburb once stood at the museum.

Your next stop is close by – the **Grand Parade** and City Hall (see p83). Leave the museum and turn right into Buitenkant Street. Walk down to Darling Street and turn left – the Grand Parade will be on your right and City Hall on your left. The country's oldest public space, the Parade used to be a place where animals grazed and washing was put out to dry. Later it became a military parade ground, gathering space, market and parking lot. One of the biggest multiracial protests against the apartheid regime culminated here on 14 September 1989. The City Hall overlooking the Parade is an elaborately adorned Italian-style building, boasting the only carillon on the continent. Nelson Mandela addressed the country for the first time from this balcony, just hours after being released from prison on 11 February 1990.

The last stop on your tour is a trip via ferry to **Robben Island** (see p91), where the first president of the new Rainbow Nation – Nelson Mandela – was incarcerated for 18 years. To find your way to the departure point at the Nelson Mandela Gateway in the V&A Waterfront, either take a taxi or walk; it's not far and you can easily

Iziko Slave Lodge p59

ask for directions. Used as a prison and place of exile from as early as the 16th century, it once housed lepers and the mentally ill. Many political prisoners, including Robert Sobukwe and Walter Sisulu, were sent here during the Apartheid years. Today the old prison serves as a museum. Trips to the island and back take around four hours. When you get back, toast the setting sun with a cold one at one of the many renovated Victorian warehouses-cum-drinking holes dotting the V&A Waterfront.

Day 3: Get shown around by a pro

A walking tour is a great way to get under the skin of the city and learn what makes it tick. Get an expert to show you around. Ron Viney of Ad Astra Festina Walkabouts (071 141 6005) is an authority on South African history and archaeology and offers set tours as well as tailor-made itineraries on everything from architecture to geology, history and heritage. There's also Wanderlust's Cape Town on Foot and Bo-Kaap City Walking Tour (021 462 4245, www.wanderlust. co.za) to guide you on an amble of the inner city and the Bo-Kaap. Footsteps to Freedom's City Walk (083 452 1112, www.footstepsto freedom.co.za) follows South Africa's path to freedom, while the Lion Walking Tour of the **Gold of Africa Museum** (see p59) tracks the trail of the now extinct Cape Lion and the imprint it left on the city's heritage, architecture and culture. For a Bo-Kaap-only amble contact Bilquees Baker (021 424 3736/074 101 1837) or Tanu Baru Tours (021 424 0719/073 237 3800). Both tours include the chance to sample local Cape Malay delicacies.

Goodman Gallery p50

Woodstock Wander

A few years ago the fraying suburb of Woodstock on the fringes of Cape Town was a no-go zone for the city's upper crust, a 'zone of decay' so to speak. Newspaper headlines shouted gang wars, crack dens and prostitution rings but these days an eclectic buzz permeates the air. Taxis hoot, children play soccer on side streets and residents hang over front gates to chat to their neighbours again. First to spot a lucrative opportunity and migrate here was the creative set that cleverly turned old warehouses and industrial spaces into studios and galleries. Restaurants and quirky shops soon followed and now swanky new loft apartments vie for space next to corner takeaway joints, designer sneaker shops and pavement furniture stores. Local stores see drag queens queue behind art students while first time buyers snap up Victorian fixer-uppers – moving in next door to families who have been calling the suburb home for generations.

Walking through these streets feels much more akin to being in the middle of a heaving multicultural African city than when you're spending time in the suburb's Eurocentric siblings, Camps Bay and De Waterkant. 'For me, Woodstock has always been the Brooklyn (NY) of Cape Town,' muses Justin Rhodes, who, along with partner Cameron Munro, works hard to give life to the new Woodstock with his cutting-edge concepts such as the ever-popular Saturday morning **Neighbourgoods Market** held at the Old Biscuit Mill mixed-use development in Albert Road. 'Woodstock still has a lot of realness and soul about it – an edge that you don't get anywhere else. If you look at cities around the world, it's always the grungy, industrial areas closer to the city that attract the creative types – artists take studios there, galleries open up, a couple of cafés follow and all of a sudden you've got a whole community.'

Start your tour on the bottom end of Sir Lowry Road (on the Cape Town side) with a bout of gallery hopping. Some of the city's best galleries are here – including contemporary art stalwarts like the **Goodman Gallery** (3rd Floor, Fairweather House, 176 Sir Lowry Road, Woodstock, 021 462 7573, www.goodmangallery.com) and the **Michael Stevenson Gallery** (Ground Floor, Buchanan Building, 160 Sir Lowry Road, Woodstock, 021 462 1500, www.michael stevenson.com). The *Art South Africa* magazine (Fairweather House, 176 Sir Lowry Road, 021 465 9108, www.artsouthafrica.com) offices and stop-in gallery shop can be found in this area as well as brand new addition the **South African Print Gallery** (107 Sir Lowry Road, Woodstock, 021 462 6851, www.printgallery.co.za). Although tiny, it showcases prints from some of the country's top contemporary art stars and is worth a visit for well-priced investment purchases.

Having ingested your fill of culture here, stroll down to Albert Road (it's the main road parallel to Sir Lowry Road in the direction of the ocean) where the **Whatifthe World/Gallery** (First Floor, 208 Albert Road, Woodstock, 021 448 1438) is located. This light and airy space has a reputation as a platform for emerging artists, boasting a lot of street cred among creatives. Gallery owners Justin Rhodes and Cameron Munro were the first gallery owners to set up shop here. They also run a quirky café called **Superette** (218 Albert Road, Woodstock, 021 802 5525, www. superette.co.za) next door, and the aforementioned hugely successful Neighbourgoods Market at the Old Biscuit Mill down the street.

Michael Stevenson Gallery

If you're feeling mid-morning hunger pangs or you're itching for some retail therapy, then walk down Albert Road away from the city. You'll come to a red building, The Old Biscuit Mill, on your left. Housing a string of home and gift shops, an old biscuit factory has been restored to its former glory. Swing by **Heartworks** (see p77) and **Imiso Ceramics** (Unit A102, The Old Biscuit Mill, 373 Albert Road, Woodstock, 021 447 7668, www.imisoceramics.co.za) for quirky gifts and collectable ceramics or wander through the sensory overload that is **Plush Bazaar** (Unit A102, The Old Biscuit Mill, 373 Albert Road, Woodstock, 021 447 6495) for gifts, goods and trinkets (from bohemian jewellery to vintage milk jars).

But the real draw here (and one of the main reasons for Woodstock's rising popularity) happens on Saturdays, when the Neighbourgoods Market sets up shop inside an old warehouse within the complex. It's a platform for organic farmers, micro producers and specialty fine food purveyors. Ninety-nine and a half per cent of the produce at the market is local and comes from within a 400-kilometre radius. Long communal tables in the middle of the warehouse proffer the perfect opportunity to kick back and nibble on artisan loaves of bread, Belgian waffles, oysters, sushi, home-brewed coffees, Lebanese delights, organic wines, coffee, veggies, big wheels of handmade cheeses… the list goes on. Apart from a glorious selection of gourmet and organic goodies, there's also the Designgoods market showcasing wares from up-and-coming young designers, from clothes to quirky jewellery, ceramics and handmade shoes. Across the way stands the Kindergoods market with vintage toys and cheeky kiddies wear. When venturing this way on a Saturday it should be noted, though, that the popularity of this venture turns the surrounding streets into a congested hive of activity and finding parking can be quite a feat. It's probably best to walk.

After shopping and feasting your fill at the old mill, you can trawl the many second-hand shops that line the suburb's streets. If you're exploring the suburb on a Sunday, the **Vintage Fair** at the Old Biscuit Mill is also worth a visit for antique finds, from vinyl records to vintage medicine bottles and antique books. Finish off your shopping spree with the lazy lunch at Superette, a refurbished 19th-century corner shop café that now serves as a meeting spot for Woodstock's creative community. The menu brims with fresh, locally sourced fare and the décor and furniture come courtesy of some of the area's hippest emerging artists and designers.

After lunch, it's time to ease into the evening with cocktails on Woodstock's restaurant strip, Roodebloem Road. Although it's not far, it's best to take a taxi there for safety reasons. For dinner, sit down at north Indian foodie favourite, **Chandani** (85 Roodebloem Road, Woodstock, 021 447 7887), and dig into buttery naan breads and favourites like lamb rogan josh. Vegetarians will delight in the stunning selection of veggie-friendly options permeating the menu. If (between October and April) you're exploring the suburb on a Monday, you can opt for a dinner/theatre experience at the **Theatre in the District** (106 Chapel Street, Woodstock, 021 686 2150, www.theatreinthe district.co.za) set inside an old District Six church. Enjoy a Cape Town-themed show, featuring actors from the local community, paired with an authentic Cape dinner that includes local delights like *vetkoek* and *bobotie*.

Chandani

Cape Town by Area

Iziko South African Museum p60

City Bowl

The City Bowl encompasses Cape Town's buzzing Central Business District as well as the mountainside residential suburbs of Vredehoek, Oranjezicht, Gardens and Tamboerskloof. At its west looms Table Mountain. The distinctive and vibrant areas of Bo-Kaap and De Waterkant lie at the eastern base of the mountain.

City Centre

Starting at the foreshore, the International Convention Centre is a world-class conference venue. The nearby pedestrian-friendly **St George's Mall** is studded with coffee spots and shops, taking you past **Greenmarket Square**, a vibrant daily market selling all manner of African curios. **Long Street** starts out pretty seedy at the lower, harbour, end, but evolves into a restaurant-and-club lined hotspot further along.

The **Company's Garden** acts as the city's green lung, with tree-shaded lawns offering lunchtime sanctuary to office workers. Running through it, the oak-lined **Government Avenue** is where you'll find the parliament building, as well as some of the city's most notable museums and galleries.

Kloof Street is the main vein running through the area known as **Gardens**. The lower end is characterised by a cutting-edge crowd and is studded with chic boutiques, record stores and coffee shops, while the upper stretch houses a number of popular restaurants.

By day, the City Centre is generally safe to explore on foot. Night-time is a different story, however, and unless you're in busy upper Long Street, which turns into party central after hours, it's best not to walk the streets alone.

Sights & museums

Cape Town Holocaust Centre

88 Hatfield Street (021 462 5553, www.ctholocaust.co.za). **Open** 10am-5pm Sun-Thur; 10am-2pm Fri. **Admission** free. **Map** p57 D4 ➊

Photos, text, archival documents, artefacts, film footage and multimedia displays tell the story of the Nazi holocaust, and explore its origins in anti-semitism and eugenics. Its events are placed in a South African context with an exploration of racism, colonialism and apartheid. You will also see fascinating personal testimony on film from holocaust survivors now living in South Africa.

Castle of Good Hope

Cnr Buitenkant and Darling Streets (021 787 1249, www.castleofgood hope.co.za). **Open** 9am-4pm daily. **Tours** 11am, noon, 2pm Mon-Sat. **Key ceremony & cannon firing** 10am, noon Mon-Fri. **Admission** R25 adults; R10-R15 concessions; half-price Sun. *Audio guides* R20 (English and Dutch). *Maps* R5 **No credit cards**. **Map** p276 F4 ➋

This pentagonal castle was built in 1666 by VOC commander Zacharias Wagenaer as a place of safety from prospective British raids. It soon became the hub of the Mother City's administrative and military operations. Centuries later, the castle is still the military base of Cape Town, and at 10am or noon every day visitors can witness the marching castle guard and his orange, white and blue liveried entourage perform the ritual key ceremony and firing of the signal cannon. History lovers will be intrigued by the military museum with its original paraphernalia.

The Company's Garden

Government Avenue, enter via Adderley, Queen Victoria or Orange streets. **Open** 7am-7pm daily. **Admission** Free. **Map** p57 D4 ➌

Offering lunchtime respite to office workers and sanctuary to squirrels, the Company's Garden was established by the VOC employee Hendrik Boom in 1652 as a refreshment station for scurvied seafarers. Today it's characterised by its oak-lined avenue, the beautifully scented rose garden and the sprawling lawns. One of the few remaining reminders of its original use is the knobbly pear tree planted by Boom himself. Those keen to find out more about the significance of the historical statues and buildings sprinkled about can get a brochure at the information centre in the middle of the garden.

CTICC – Cape Town International Convention Centre

Convention Square, 1 Lower Long Street (021 410 5000, www.cticc.co.za). **Map** p57 F1 ➍

The imposing Convention Centre was completed by Van der Merwe Miszewski Architects in 2003. As well as hosting prestigious local and international conferences, it has also become associated with events including Cape Town Fashion Week, Design Indaba, The Good Food and Wine Show and the Cape Town International Jazz Festival. Most recently, it saw Oscar-winning actress Charlize Theron make the 2010 Fifa World Cup final draw.

District Six Museum

25A Buitenkant Street (021 466 7200, www.districtsix.co.za). **Open** 9am-2.30pm Mon; 9am-4pm Tue-Sat. **Admission** R20; R5 concessions. **Tours of District Six site** R50 (min 4 people; by prior arrangement only). **Map** p57 F4 ➎

It's hard not to get choked up walking over the street map of the erstwhile District Six painted on the floor here; forcibly removed residents have inscribed their names next to their former addresses. The rest of the two-storey museum is equally emotive and sensitively curated to include personal

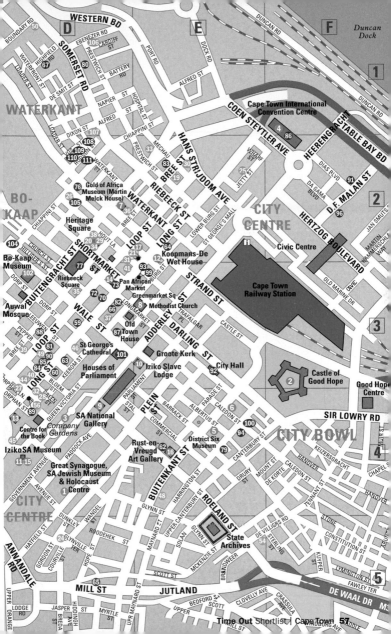

accounts of the evictions of around 60,000 people after District Six was declared a white area in accordance with the apartheid Group Areas Act in 1966. Especially poignant are the upstairs exhibits that include a beautiful mural by Peggy Delport, a display of the community's proud barber-shop heritage and toys left behind after the suburb was razed to the ground.

Fields of Play Museum at the District Six Homecoming Centre

15A Buitenkant Street (021 466 7200, www.districtsix.co.za). **Open** 9am-2pm Mon; 9am-4pm Tue-Sat. **Admission** R20 adults; R5 concessions. *District Six Museum, Fields of Play combo ticket* R35. **Map** p57 E4 ⑥

As much an exposition of South African football history as it is of the consequences of the forced removals from District Six, this cleverly curated museum relies on newspaper clippings, oral history, photographs and video and sound clips to paint a vivid picture of the lives of black and coloured soccer players during the apartheid era. The upper half of the space features an Astroturf-like soccer pitch and cartoon cut-outs of local soccer legends who made it big in Britain, each accompanied by interesting, often heartbreaking profiles.

Gold of Africa Museum

96 Strand Street, Martin Melck House, City Centre (021 405 1540, www.goldof africa.com). **Open** 9.30am-4.30pm Mon-Sat. **Admission** R30 adults; R20-R25 concessions. **Lion Walking Tour** R50. **Pangolin Night Tour** R50 adults; R30-R40 concessions. **Map** p57 D2 ⑦

The permanent 300 piece Barbier Mueller collection of 19th- and 20th-century gold is a trove of artefacts from West Africa's erstwhile gold empires. A timeline details the history of the precious metal from Ancient Egypt to present day. A charming courtyard restaurant adds to the appeal.

Green Market Square

Between Shortmarket and Longmarket streets, off St George's Mall. **Open** 8am-5pm Mon-Sat. **Map** p57 D3 ⑧

Originally a place where Dutch settlers stocked up their shopping baskets with fresh fruit and vegetables, today this buzzing market sells all kinds of African arts and crafts. You'll find curios from around the continent – from Congolese figures to djembe drums and ritual masks – and vendors who are happy to bargain. There are also stalls selling second-hand CDs and books, sunglasses, and clothes.

Iziko National Gallery

Government Avenue, Company's Gardens (021 467 4660, www.iziko. org.za). **Open** 10am-5pm Tue-Sun. **Admission** R15 adults; R5 concessions; free under-16s. **No credit cards**. **Map** p57 D4 ⑨

The permanent exhibition boasts everything from dramatic chiaroscuros by Dutch masters and pre-Raphaelite portraits to audio-visual works by renowned South African artists. Previous temporary exhibitions have been dedicated to the likes of Nicolas Hlobo, William Kentridge, and even Picasso; one of the most recent included an ambitious retrospective on the local art scene called 1910-2010: From Pierneef to Gugulective.

Iziko Slave Lodge Museum

49 Adderley Street (021 460 8242, www.iziko.org.za). **Open** 10am-5pm Mon-Sat. **Admission** R15 adults; R5 concessions; free under-16s. Free to all public holidays and commemorative days. *Audio guides* R20. **Map** p57 E3 ⑩

This building stands as a memorial to the VOC's horrific slave trade history. Between 1679 and 1811 the structure confined over 9,000 slaves imported from regions around the Indian Ocean; their only source of fresh air was the paltry ventilation slats built into the walls. The permanent exhibition documents the suffering experienced at the hands of the Dutch superpower by means of sound clips, short films and installations. Temporary displays have been dedicated to the lives of apartheid heroes Steve Biko and Nelson Mandela, the African slave trade in Brazil, and the struggle against segregated schooling in the US.

Iziko South African Museum

25 Queen Victoria Street (021 481 3800, www.iziko.org.za.sam). **Open** 10am-5pm daily. **Admission** R15 adults; R5 concessions; free under-16s. Free to all public holidays & commemorative days. **Map** p57 D4 **11**

The South African Museum has a certain old-school charm that more technologically advanced and poiltically correct collections lack. There's a vast array of stuffed animals – from a duck-billed platypus to extinct killer sharks, along with models of South Africa's first indigenous peoples. Dinosaur enthusiasts will enjoy the African Dinosaurs exhibition featuring fossils dating back 250 million years.

Koopmans-De Wet House

35 Strand Street (021 481 3935, www.iziko.org.za, koopmans). **Open** 10am-5pm Tue-Thur. **Admission** R10 adults; R5 concessions; free under-16s. **No credit cards. Map** p57 E2 **12**

Wedged between skyscrapers in the cacophony of Strand Street, this elegant structure is South Africa's oldest house museum and shows you what life was like if you were well-to-do in the 18th century. The collection of gleaming silverware and Cape furniture belonged to its last owner, a well-read, wealthy socialite called Marie Koopmans-De Wet, a portrait of whom can be seen in one of the upstairs bedrooms.

Long Street Baths

Corner Long and Orange streets (021 400 3302). **Open** *Pool* 7am-7pm daily. *Turkish Bath* Women 9am-6pm Mon,

Thur, Sat; 9am-1pm Tue. Men 1-7pm Tue; 8am-7pm Wed, Fri; 8am-noon Sun. **Admission** *Pool* R12 adults; R7 children; free pensioners. *Turkish baths* R40 per hr; R80 4hrs. **No credit cards. Map** p57 D4 **13**

This old-fashioned bathhouse offers a welcome retreat in the heart of the city. Beyond the art nouveau façade and old-school turnstiles lie authentic Turkish baths, where you can steam or sauna away muscle aches, as well as a heated 25-metre pool where everyone from teens to retirees can be seen perfecting their strokes from 7am in the morning. Note that during school holidays it can get very busy.

Pan African Market

76 Long Street (021 426 4478). **Open** *Winter* 9am-5pm Mon-Fri; 9am-3pm Sat. *Summer* 8.30am-5.30pm Mon-Fri; 8.30am-3.30pm Sat. **Admission** free. **Map** p57 D3 **14**

This multi-levelled building is crammed with all manner of crafts, most notably Congolese sculptures, macabre masks, fertility figurines and jewellery. If you're looking for something special to wear, a team of nimble-fingered seamstresses who can kit you out in custom-made African attire are ready and waiting to attend to your sartorial needs.

Planetarium

25 Queen Victoria Street (021 481 3900, www.iziko.org.za, planetarium). **Shows** 2pm Mon-Fri (excluding first Mon of month); 8pm Tue; 1pm, 2.30pm Sat, Sun. *Children's show* noon Sat, Sun. **Admission** R20 adults; R10 adults for children's show; R8 pensioners, students; R6 children. **Map** p57 D4 **15**

Looking up at the planetarium's recreated night sky containing exploding balls of gas, moons and planets does give some idea of the vastness of the universe. The customised kids' shows are great – here astronomy is explained in fun, bite-sized increments.

CAPE TOWN BY AREA

Castle of Good Hope p55

Mountain high

How to experience the city's favourite landmark.

Table Mountain makes her presence felt at every turn. At 1,067 metres above sea level her summit is the city's highest point, and some 20 million visitors have been here via the Table Mountain Aerial Cableway (*see p65*).

It goes without saying that the views of the city, the sea and the Cape Peninsula from here are spectacular. You'll find various viewing decks as well as a popular eatery from which to enjoy them. And don't forget to look out for the little rock hyraxes, or dassies, that make this mountain their home.

If you're feeling energetic, consider a walk up to the top of the mountain and a ride down in the cable car – the challenging Platteklip Gorge is a steep two- to three-hour hike that takes you up and through a massive 'crack' in the mountain. Or if you're in the market for an adrenalin rush, why not try an abseiling experience with Abseil Africa (021 424 4760, www.abseilafrica.co.za)?

Table Mountain is the 'anchor tenant' of the Table Mountain National Park, which stretches all

the way down to Cape Point. Walkers could consider booking a two- to five-day Hoerikwaggo Trail (021 782 9356, www.capepoint route.co.za) that traverses the park down to Simon's Town in the south. Walkers sleep in custom-built chalets and enjoy all the benefits of a fully portered and catered mountain walking experience. For a short walk, join the locals at full moon as they climb nearby Lion's Head (between Table Mountain and Signal Hill) to watch the moon rise from the peak. And runners should contact CRAG (Cape Runners Against Gravity, www.crag.org.za), who meet at various points across the peninsula (many of them in the Table Mountain National Park) every Wednesday evening.

Of course, the Table Mountain is just as impressive on its lee side, as the pristine Kirstenbosch National Botanical Garden (021 799 8782, www.sanbi.org) is home to thousands of plant species. It hosts a popular series of alfresco Sunday concerts – a great way to end a week in the Mother City.

Gold of Africa Museum p59

Rust & Vreugd

78 Buitenkant Street (021 464 3280, www.iziko.org.za, rustvreugd). **Open** 9am-4pm Tue-Fri. **Admission** free, donations appreciated. **Map** p57 E4 ⓲

Rust en Vreugd (rest and joy, or peace) is what you'll find when you step out of the unglamorous clamour of Lower Buitenkant Street and through the gate of this inner-city secret garden. It's something straight out of a BBC period drama, what with its manicured lawns, lollipop shrubs, pristinely pruned rose-bushes and the odd Egyptian goose. Towering over the serene scene, the peach-coloured Edwardian building houses the William Fehr collection of valuable lithographs and aquatints depicting scenes from rural KwaZulu-Natal and 18th-century Cape Town.

South African Slave Church Museum

40 Long Street (021 423 6755). **Open** 9am-4pm Mon-Fri; 9am-noon during school holidays. **Admission** free, donations appreciated. **Map** p57 E2 ⓱

Walk a tad too fast and you might miss this inner-city place of worship. It's the oldest South African slave church building and was completed in 1804 under the auspices of the South African Missionary Society. The tiny interior boasts long teak balconies, intricately carved oak pews and an organ with beautifully decorated pipes. The structure was the first in the city to be built in the form of a basilica, and has the only remaining lime-concrete pitch roof in the country.

Table Mountain Aerial Cableway

Lower cable station, Tafelberg Road (021 424 8181, www.tablemountain.net). **Open** (weather permitting) *Oct-Apr* 8am-9.30pm daily. *May-Sept* 8.30am-6pm daily. **Tickets** (return) R180; R95 under 18s; free under 4s. **Online** R170; R90 under-18s. **Map** off p56 B1 ⓳

Good news to all South Africans old enough to drive: if it's your birthday and you've had the presence of mind to remember your ID, you can get a free cable-car ride up and down Table Mountain. If you're a tourist, the experience is great value for money. It takes about five minutes to get to the top and once you're there you can meet the mountain's furry little mascot, the dassie (also known as the rock rabbit) and explore the vantage points looking out on to Robben Island, Table Bay and Cape Point.

Eating & drinking

&Union

St Stephen's Church, 110 Bree Street (021 422 2770). **Open** 7am-11pm Mon-Thur; 7am-12am Fri. **RR**. **Bar**. **Map** p57 E2 ⓳

Artisan beer and sausages are the cornerstones of this sexy city spot where a good-looking bunch of locals congregate on a daily basis. Make sure you partner your beer with one of the famous spicy Prego rolls. There is a covered outdoor area, and regular live music by edgy city talents.

Africa Café

108 Shortmarket Street (021 422 0221, www.africacafe.co.za). **Open** 10am-4pm, 6-11pm Mon-Sat. **RR**. **Pan African**. **Map** p57 D2 ⓴

This place celebrates Africa as a continent and an experience, and serves delicacies from South Africa, Botswana, Morocco, Nigeria, Malawi, Tanzania and other countries. Staff are hospitable and there are hand-washing ceremonies and African drumming. Very popular with tour groups.

Airstream Penthouse Trailer Park

Grand Daddy Hotel, 38 Long Street (021 424 7247, www.daddylonglegs. co.za). **Open** 9am-8.30pm daily. **RR**. **Bar**. **Map** p57 E2 ㉑

This small bar with lowslung couches hosts guests lucky enough to be staying in one of the vintage Airstream caravans on the roof of the hotel, as well as members of the public. On weekend nights, especially in summer, the crowds flock to chill to the sounds of blues harmonica magician Dave Ferguson and other indie musicians. It's truly one of a kind.

Arnolds

60 Kloof Street (021 424 4344, www. arnolds.co.za). **Open** 6.45am-late Mon-Fri; 8am-late Sat-Sun. **R. Café**. **Map** p56 C4 ②
Legendary among City Bowl residents for the enormous easy-going menu and especially the value-for-money breakfasts. A daily happy hour, location with view of Table Mountain and a casual, friendly atmosphere ensure its continued popularity.

Asoka

68 Kloof Street (021 422 0909, www. asokabar.co.za). **Open** 5pm-2am daily. **RR**. **Bar**. **Map** p56 C5 ②
Famous for, among other things, the olive tree around which it is built, Asoka is a tranquil and restful place. This, however, is not to say it doesn't provide a fun and often raucous night out. The tapas are moreish, and so are the cocktails. There is music almost every night of the week, from laidback lounge beats played by DJs to live jazz.

Aubergine

39 Barnett Street (021 465 4909, www.aubergine.co.za). **Open** 7-10pm Mon- Sat; noon-2pm Wed-Fri. **RRR**. **Contemporary**. **Map** p57 D5 ②
The ever-changing and seasonal menu here is a reflection of chef Harald Bresselschmidt's personal culinary journey, creativity and imagination. With impeccable service and a well thought-out wine list, this is the perfect special occasion restaurant, There's a pretty courtyard for alfresco summer dining.

Bizerca Bistro

15 Anton Anreith Arcade, Jetty Street (021 418 0001, www.bizerca.com).

Open noon-3pm Mon-Fri; 6.30-10pm Mon- Sat. **RRR**. **French bistro**. **Map** p57 E2 ②
Run by French chef Laurent Deslandes and his South African-born wife Cyrillia, this bistro burst on to the local restaurant scene two years ago and has been consistently scooping up awards ever since. Laurent's focus is on traditional French bistro fare, which changes seasonally. He is famous for his signature dish of pig trotters, shredded and parcelled in phyllo. The minimalist interior is warmed up by individualistic service.

Boo Radley's

62 Hout Street (021 424 3040, www.booradleys.co.za). **Open** 10.30am-2am Mon-Fri; 5.30pm-2am Sat. **RR**. **Contemporary comfort food**. **Map** p57 D2 ②
You'll find a menu of homely and comforting food here, from mac & cheese to steaks and a great Caesar salad. The decor is reminiscent of the 1920s, with black and white tiled floors, black and white photographs, leather-covered booths and a bar serving cocktails. There's live music two or three nights a week. A stylish city crowd calls this their regular.

Café Mojito

265 Long Street (021 422 1095). **Open** 10am-midnight Mon-Sat; 5pm-late Sun. **R. Bar, café**. **Map** p57 D3 ②
Dine on Latin-inspired food accompanied by beer or cocktails. There's a fireplace inside for cold winter nights, but in summer take an outside table and sit and soak up the atmosphere of the Mother City's party street; Mojito is a popular haunt with the city's twentysomethings, especially on Friday evenings.

Carne SA

70 Keerom Street (021 424 3460, www.carne-sa.co.za). **Open** 6.30 10.30pm Mon- Sat. **RRR**. **Meat**. **Map** p57 D4 ②

Vegetarians might want to avoid Carne, but for carnivores, the show-and-tell platters of the different and more unusual cuts available, like hanger steak, are helpful and could lead to you ordering something other than the usual fillet or sirloin. The giant T-bone, a whopping 1.2kg beast served off the bone for two, is fantastic, as is the lamb ravioli. A grappa trolley adds to the fun.

Caveau Wine Bar & Deli

Heritage Square, 92 Bree Street (021 422 1367, www.caveau.co.za). **Open** 7am -10pm Mon-Sat. **RR**. **Wine bar/bistro**. **Map** p57 D2 ㉙

Despite having a restaurant and deli on site, Caveau has always been about the wine. With more than 500 local wines and bubblies on the list, many available by the glass, it's a one-stop tour of the winelands. There are tables inside, on the veranda or in the pretty courtyard. Tapas favourites include beef cubes and béarnaise, lamb samosas with tzatziki or tempura prawns; a blackboard menu lists more substantial dishes. Service can be scatty when it's busy.

Col'caccio

No.2 Spearhead, 42 Hans Strijdom Avenue, Foreshore (021 419 4848, www.colcacchio.co.za). **Open** noon-11pm daily. **RR**. **Pizza/pasta**. **Map** p57 E2 ㉚

The Col'Cacchio chain has become synonymous with a range of crisp thin-based pizzas with more toppings than you can shake a wedge of parmesan at, as well as an impressive variety of freshly prepared salads and pastas. The gourmet pizza selection is impressive as is the commitment to offering healthy menu options – many of which have been approved by the Heart and Stroke Foundation South Africa.

Daddy Cool

Grand Daddy Hotel, 38 Long Street (021 424 7247, www.daddylonglegs. co.za). **Open** 3-11pm Mon-Thur; 6pm-1am Sat. **RR**. **Bar**. **Map** p57 D2 ㉛

Decorated in opulent gold and white upholstery, this is a classy place to hang out. When it's quiet you can sit sedately in a corner sipping champagne or a cocktail. But on weekend evenings it can turn into quite a party, when the DJs get going with their dance music. A small bar menu is available too.

Dubliner @ Kennedy's

251 Long Street (021 424 1212, www.thedubliner.co.za). **Open** 11am-4am daily. **R**. **Pub**. **Map** p57 D4 ㉜

This Irish-style pub is one of the most popular, busy and crowded places in Long Street every night of the week, despite the fact that drinks are on the pricey side. Guinness and Pilsner are on tap, and there's usually live music of the singalong cover variety.

Fireman's Arms

25-27 Mechau Road, corner Buitengragt (021 419 1513). **Open** 11am-midnight Mon-Sat & Grand Prix Sun. **R**. **Pub**. **Map** p57 E2 ㉝

With more than a dozen beers on tap and grub like meaty pies, bangers and mash or wood-fired pizzas, The Fireman's Arms is your traditional, old-fashioned pub, frequented by both local barflies and well-clad 'suits'. It's one of the oldest in Cape Town and defiantly holds out against all the high-rise stainless steel and glass developments going up around it. It's also a sports supporters' pub with TV screens showing all the matches, whether rugby or football. Quiz nights on Thursdays are great fun.

Fork

84 Long Street (021 424 6334, www.fork-restaurants.co.za). **Open** noon-11pm Mon- Sat. **RR**. **Tapas**. **Map** p57 D2 ㉞

Fork embraces the spirit of sharing with its contemporary tapas. Although there is a long-running lunchtime special (which includes a glass of wine and coffee), the best way

CAPE TOWN BY AREA

Carne SA p66

to sample the menu is at a leisurely pace with a group of friends. It is divided according to price categories and includes things like crispy asparagus and parmesan rolls, sweet honey potatoes, pan-seared ostrich fillet with sweet and sour chutney, grilled sardines, and roast pork belly with mustard and parsley crust. There are lots of vegetarian options too.

Fuji Yumi

Glaston House, 110 Loop Street (021 422 3660, www.fujiyumi.co.za). **Open** 10am-10pm Mon-Fri; 6.30-10.30pm Sat. **R. Japanese**. **Map** p57 D3 ㉟

Traditional and modern Japanese dishes are on the menu in this slightly stark, contemporary restaurant – sushi, of course, as well as noodles, stir-fries and more. Prices are reasonable and look out for the value-for-money buffet specials that are offered from time to time.

Gold

96 Strand Street (021 421 4653, www.goldrestaurant.co.za). **Open** 6.30pm-11pm Mon- Sun; 10am-11pm Mon-Sat. **RRR. Cape Malay**. **Map** p57 D2 ㊱

Gold is one of South Africa's most precious natural resources and the women behind this restaurant are surely worth their weight in it.The set tasting menu is the perfect way to sample Cape Malay cuisine as well as many traditional African-inspired dishes from countries like Cameroon, Côte d'Ivoire, Ghana, Nigeria and Algeria. Adjoining the Gold Of Africa Museum, the experience begins with interactive *djembe* drumming, followed by a hand-washing ceremony and a 15-course feast in the magical courtyard. There's entertainment throughout the evening.

Haiku

58 Burg Street (021 424 7000, www.haikurestaurant.com). **Open** noon-3pm, 6pm-11pm daily. **RRR. Pan Asian**. **Map** p57 D3 ㊲

Dim sum, sushi, noodles, robata grills and wok dishes are meant to be ordered in abundance and shared, so ideally you should go with a group of friends and get as much as possible out of the extensive menu. This includes soups, hot pots, sizzlers and more, all prepared by imported chefs in the open-plan kitchen. The surroundings are dark and sultry, and this restaurant really comes into its own at night.

HQ

Heritage Square, Shortmarket Street (021 424 6373, www.hqrestaurant. co.za). **Open** 11.30am-10.30pm Mon-Sat. **RRR. Meat**. **Map** p57 D2 ㊳

Salad, steak, chips. That's it. Oh, and Café de Paris butter. If you're going to do something this simple, and nothing else, you'd better make sure you do it well, and HQ does exactly that. Take the vegetarians somewhere else. There is a good wine list, with everything available by the glass, loads and loads of cocktails, delicious desserts and a fireplace. And at weekends, there's a buzzing party vibe with DJs playing.

Jardine

185 Bree Street (021 424 5640, www.jardineonbree.co.za). **Open** 7-10pm Mon-Sat; noon-2pm Wed-Fri. **RRR. Contemporary**. **Map** p57 D3 ㊳

With multiple accolades under its belt, Jardine has been a heavy hitter on the local food scene since opening in 2006. While co-owner and chef George Jardine now focuses on his delicious new venture at Jordan winery in Stellenbosch, diners are in the capable hands of bright young executive chef Eric Bulpitt. On offer are exciting, experimental dishes (the West Coast rock pool is a must) as well as robust, comforting mains like suckling pig, presented in three ways and served on a rustic wooden board. Or try a multi-course tasting menu with some interesting wine pairings.

Joburg

218 Long Street (021 422 0142,
www.joburgbar.com). **Open** 5pm-4am
Mon-Sat; 6pm-4am Sun. **RR**. **Bar**.
Map p57 D3 ⓵

Loud and noisy, with hip hop blaring
and a mix of immigrants hailing from
every corner of the African continent,
Joburg remains one of the stalwart
favourites of Long Street, filling to
overflowing later in the night and in
the early hours of the morning. There's
a small dance floor, a pool table at the
back. The neighbouring Pretoria,
accessed by a secret side passage or
from the street, keeps its dancefloor
pumping all night.

Julep

2 Vredenburg Lane (off Long Street)
(021 423 4276, www.julep.co.za).
Open 5pm-2am Mon-Sat. **RR**. **Bar**.
Map p57 D3 ⓵

The days of Julep being one of Cape
Town's best-kept secrets are long gone.
This small, intimate bar, which feels
like a home from home, has become one
of the city's most popular hang-outs.
Sample the huge range of classic and
modern cocktails, and listen to live
music from the likes of Dave Ferguson
and Jack Mantis. Vintage movie
posters decorate the walls, and bare
brick and comfy couches add to the
rustic atmosphere.

Kyoto Garden Sushi

11 Lower Kloof Nek Road (021 422
2001). **Open** 5.30-11pm Mon-Sat.
RR. **Japanese**. **Map** p56 C4 ⓵

For the sushi road less travelled, visit
this tranquil little place in the heart of
the City Bowl. Water features and
Zen-inspired decor have a calming
effect, and the menu may include sea
urchin, farmed abalone, conch from
Mozambique, giant Alaskan king
crab, tender sweet squid and fresh
wasabi root, flown in from the far-off
mountains of Japan, to be grated at
your table. The crayfish miso soup
has legions of fans.

Mason's Café & Grill

64 Kloof Street (021 422 5325).
Open 9am-11pm daily. **R**. **Café/
meat**. **Map** p56 C5 ⓵

A very reasonably priced selection of
all-day breakfasts is just what City
Bowl dwellers love, along with great
brunch options, light meals and salads, as well as Wi-Fi. This cosy
restaurant leans more towards the
grill side of its name by night, offering a host of meaty options like sirloin, rib-eye, T-bone, and ribs.
Specialities include châteaubriand,
lamb rump, cracked pepper fillet and
a *boerewors* plate.

Minato Sushi Restaurant

4 Buiten Street (021 423 4712).
Open noon-2.30pm Mon-Fri; 6.30-
10.30pm Mon-Sat. **RR**. **Japanese**.
Map p57 D3 ⓵

The sushi joint for aficionados in the
know, Minato is reached down a long
narrow passage through a nonde-
script door in a side road off Long
Street. It's worth the effort for the generous portions of fresh sushi, with no
fuss and frills. Ingredients can be
swapped, sometimes at a price for the
trouble, sometimes not. The mixed
tempura can be a light meal on its
own, and the big wooden boats brimming with fresh pink sashimi may
be a bit cheesy but they're a sushi
addict's dream come true.

Murano Bar

15 On Orange Hotel, cnr Grey's Pass
& Orange Street (021 469 8000,
www.africanpridehotels.com). **Open**
11am-11pm daily. **RRR**. **Bar**.
Map p57 D4 ⓵

More than 10,000 individual Murano
glass links were imported from Italy
to create the two-storey glass chandelier that encircles an intimate 12-
seater VIP lounge suspended above
the bar. What's more, the backdrop of
floor to ceiling glass provides exquisite views of Table Mountain. This is
understated class at its best.

Fork p67

Neighbourhood Restaurant & Bar

163 Long Street (021 424 7260, www. goodinthehood.co.za). Open noon-late Mon-Sat. RR. **Bar**. Map p57 D3 ⓐ

A large selection of local and imported beers, a games room with a foosball and pool table, as well as LCD screens for sports and a projector for all major fixtures and a full menu of gourmet pub food makes this a great late-night hang-out. It's spacious, but with a number of interleading rooms the place retains a feeling of intimacy. The vast balcony overlooking Long Street is always packed, even on so-called quiet nights.

Nonna Lina

64 Orange Street (021 424 4966, www.nonnalina.com). Open 6-10.30pm Mon-Thur; 10am-3pm, 6-11pm Fri-Sun. . RR. **Italian**. Map p56 C4 ⓐ

Created in loving memory of Antonello Scamuzzi's granny, Nonna Lina aims to keep her memory alive through her style of robust and authentic Italian and Sardinian food. Thin-crust pizzas, gorgeous summer salads and hand-made pastas are a must. Ask about the specialities, which include cured tuna roe, 'fire and ice' hot pasta with cold salsa or *culurgiones* – classic Sardinian pasta pockets filled with fresh mint, potato and pecorino served with minty tomato sauce.

Perserverance Tavern

83 Buitenkant Street (021 461 2440, www.perseverancetavern.co.za). Open noon-late Mon-Sat. R. **Bar**. Map p57 E4 ⓐ

Nearly 200 years old, Percy's – as it's affectionately known – is the oldest pub in Cape Town. Steeped in history and old-world charm, this is a pub in the true sense of the word, where you can sit and reflect on the generations of drinkers who came before. Tuck into hearty old-fashioned pub grub, rub shoulders with the resident bar flies and compare notes on the sport on the telly.

Paparazzi

Pepper Club Hotel, cnr of Loop and Pepper streets (021 812 8888, www. pepperclub.co.za). Open 8am-4am daily. RRR. **Bar**. Map p57 D3 ⓐ

Influenced by some of New York's most stylish after-hours haunts, this bar combines international elegance with a uniquely South African feel. Its following already includes legendary jazz musician George Benson, who frequented the bar during last year's Cape Town International Jazz Festival. Its regular jazz evenings are popular with many of Cape Town's elite who start their weekends here sipping on champagne and indulging in fresh oysters.

Pigalle

57A Somerset Road, Green Point (021 421 4848, www.pigallerestaurants. co.za). Open 7pm-late Mon, Tue; noon-3pm, 7pm-late Wed-Sat; noon-3pm Sat. RR. **Portuguese/grills**. Map p57 D1 ⓐ

Finding the elusive entrance to this popular restaurant takes a little patience, but it's worth it. Decorated in grand fashion with ornate chandeliers, large-scale prints of sensual ladies, and ubiquitous velvet-red, the restaurant is based on the popular American supper-club format, and is the only place in the city that offers dinner and dancing. The fare has a distinct Portuguese bent, and favourites include peri-peri chicken livers, Mozambiquan prawn curry and veal scallops Madeira.

Planet Champagne & Cocktail Bar

Mount Nelson Hotel, 76 Orange Street (021 483 1000, www.mountnelson. co.za). Open noon-midnight daily. RRR. **Bar**. Map p56 C5 ⓐ

For a dash of class but without the pretentiousness, head to this beautiful bar situated in one of Cape Town's oldest hotels. It's just a stone's throw from the city centre but you'd never realise when you are sitting on the terrace overlooking the manicured garden with its pretty fountain. Inside it's comfort and style for your cocktail- or champagne-sipping, and it's a favourite hang-out for celebs and locals alike.

Rafiki's

13B Kloof Nek Road (021 426 4731, www.rafikis.co.za). **Open** 11am-2am daily. **R**. **Bar**. **Map** p56 C4 ⑤②

It's all about location – this corner spot with its wraparound balcony is the perfect place for afternoon-into-evening drinks, although you're going to struggle to find parking in the area. Inside there are several small, intimate rooms with fireplaces for cosy winter nights. The food is cheap and easy – pizza and prawn specials are often available – and there's often live music too.

Rick's Café Americain

2 Park Road (021 424 1100, www.ricks cafe.co.za). **Open** 11am-late Mon-Sat (no children after 6pm). **RR**. **Bar**. **Map** p56 C4 ⑤③

Inspired by the city of Casablanca and the movie of the same name, the decor here is gorgeously colonial and warm, with wicker chairs, bare bricks, brass lamps, potted palms, movie posters on the walls. And there are three fireplaces in winter, something Capetonians love during the cold, wet season. It's a great venue for drinks but the menu of global tapas, seasonal salads, gourmet burgers, Moroccan specialities, seafood and Mediterranean grills is worth exploring too.

The Shack

45 De Villiers Road (021 461 5892). **Open** 1pm-4am Mon-Fri, 6pm-4am Sat, Sun. **R**. **Bar**. **Map** p57 E5 ⑤④

When all else fails there is the Shack. Play pool or foosball, order a snack from the kitchen, which is open till 3am, or just hang at one of the five bars chatting to your mates or the friendly barman. Drinks are still among the cheapest in town, and the bathrooms are a lot better than they used to be.

Societi Bistro

50 Orange Street (021 424 2100, www.societi.co.za). **Open** noon-11pm Mon- Sat. **RR**. **Café**. **Map** p56 C4 ⑤⑤

The owners of this popular city spot have gone out of their way to create a friendly local. Most starters are under R40, mains less than R100, and all wines (wine list and off-menu specials) are available by the glass; you can now get a 450ml carafe for just R30. The menu changes seasonally, although certain bistro classics like fillet au poivre are regular fixtures. Societi Bistro also lives up to its name with several daily chalkboard specials. The small adjoining bar is a welcoming pre- or post-dinner venue.

The Waiting Room

273 Long Street (021 4224536). **Open** 6pm-2am Mon-Sat. **RR**. **Bar**. **Map** p57 D4 ⑤⑥

A top-storey bar in the heart of Cape Town, this venue switches with ease from lounge room in the evening to club by night. As well as a stylish interior, it has enviable views of Table Mountain, best appreciated while sharing sundowners with friends on the roof-top terrace. Come for band nights on Monday and Tuesday, or shake it on the dancefloor to the DJs' tunes every Wednesday to Saturday.

Yindees

22 Camp Street (021 422 1012, www.yindees.com). **Open** 12.30-3pm, 6-10pm daily. **RR**. **Thai**. **Map** p56 C5 ⑤⑦

Whether it's spring rolls, satay, fish cakes, stir fries, curries, noodle dishes, deboned duck or chicken medallions with seven secret spices, the best way to enjoy the Thai cuisine here is to sample several dishes, so round up a crowd. Many dishes on the vast menu have flexible options to cater for palates fond of chillies or garlic. Yindees has been around for 14 years and in Cape Town restaurant-speak that's a lifetime, and means it's doing everything right.

Shopping

Astore

Shop 2, Mooikloof Centre, 34 Kloof Street (021 422 2888, www.astoreis good.com). **Open** 9am-6pm Mon-Fri; 9am-3pm Sat; 10am-2pm Sun.
Map p56 C4 ⓝ

The place to find the latest sneakers from Japan, cult tees and itty bitty items of cool for the edgy urbanite. There are also cosmetics in a kaleidoscope of colours, along with interesting art books and a host of contemporary jewellery items.

African Music Store

134 Long Street (021 426 0857, www.africanmusicstore.co.za). **Open** 9am-6pm Mon-Fri; 9am-2pm Sat.
Map p57 D3 ⓝ

For a taste of the sounds that shape the continent, head for this fascinating store that celebrates South African music, along with that of artists from all around the continent. A great stop if you're looking for a souvenir that won't take up a lot of space.

Bead Merchants

223 Long Street (021 423 4687, www.beadmerchantsofafrica.com). **Open** 8.45am-5pm Mon-Fri; 8.45am-2pm Sat. **Map** p57 D3 ⓝ

Shoppers are given a tray and encouraged to fill it with all the sparkly baubles their hearts desire. Bead Merchants also stocks all the paraphernalia you'll need to make your own jewellery at home and has off-the-peg pieces for sale too.

Bluecollar Whitecollar

Shop G21, Lifestyles on Kloof, 50 Kloof Street (021 426 1921). **Open** 9.30am-6pm Mon-Fri; 9am-3.30pm Sat; 10am-2pm Sun. **Map** p56 C4 ⓝ

It is said that a well-tailored shirt is the mark of a well-styled man – and this is the place to find it. This store specialises in out of the box, off-the-peg styles. Choose from the popular signature cut, the ultra slim fit, or perhaps opt for a panel style or classic cut if you're broader shouldered.

The Book Lounge

71 Roeland Street (021 462 2425, www.booklounge.co.za). **Open** 8.30am-7.30pm Mon-Fri; 9.30am-6pm Sat; 10am-4pm Sun. **Map** p57 E4 ⓝ

Book lovers and literati agree: this underground-though-accessible bookstore is deserving of all its accolades. From the period building exterior to the wood-clad interiors and downstairs lounge complete with coffee machine, comfy chairs and an owner and staff in love with books, this one is a winner. A great stop for South African fiction, and their regular readings are a great way to meet like-minded souls.

Clarke's Bookshop

211 Long Street (021 423 5739, www.clarkesbooks.co.za). **Open** 9am-5pm Mon-Fri; 9am-1pm Sat. **Map** p57 D3 ⓝ

A bastion of political, art and current affairs information, books and catalogues, this Long Street shop is both library and retail set-up, with owner Henrietta Dax and her enthusiastic team pointing visitors in the right direction. Wander upstairs and ask to see the Africana collectibles.

Caroline's Fine Wines

Shop 44, Matador Centre, 62 Strand Street (021 419 8984, www.carolines wine.com). **Open** 9am-5.30pm Mon-Fri; 9am-1pm Sat. **Map** p57 E2 ⓝ

Owner Caroline Rillema is an industry stalwart and an inspiration to both her passionate wine-loving staff and the people who cross the threshold of her city and Waterfront stores. An enormous selection of mostly South African wine awaits – with both boutique and big-name bottles. Formal tastings are a staple in the Strand Street store while Thursday and Friday evenings at the Waterfront store (Shop KWH 8, Victoria Wharf,

Astore

Outdoor art

Discover the Mother City's creativity in public spaces.

Africa.

Start your public art tour in Cape Town's foreshore. Jetty Square, the area between Pier Place and Thibault Square, hosts artist Ralph Borland's shiny 'swimming' skeleton shark sculptures.

Nearby, in St George's Mall, you'll discover a bronze sculpture studded with yellow Bart Simpson heads. Called *Africa*, the piece is by acclaimed contemporary artist Brett Murray. In neighbouring Church Street, Johann van der Schiff's *Arm Wrestling Podium* offers a platform for the settling of 'disputes'.

Standing next to the Cape Town Civic Centre, a short distance away, is a postbox-red sculpture by Italian-born sculptor Edoardo Villa. This famous steel piece, officially entitled *The Knot* (1981), is often referred to by locals as 'the bent paper clip'.

Head next to the V&A Waterfront, where, next to the Musica Megastore, you'll find Noble Square, home to four bronze sculptures by South African artist Claudette Schreuders, commemorating South Africa's Nobel Peace laureates: the late Chief Albert Luthuli, Archbishop Desmond Tutu, and former presidents Nelson Mandela and FW de Klerk. Across the quay is the mammoth 18-metre-tall *Crate Fan*. Artist Porky Hefer used a skeleton of steel scaffolding and 42,000 recycled red Coca-Cola crates to create the work, which will remain in place for a full year after the World Cup.

Behind Prestwich Memorial in Green Point, you'll also spy a cluster of sculptures commissioned by the City of Cape Town for the FIFA World Cup. Six pieces interpret the theme 'A trophy for Cape Town as the best city in the world'.

Also look out for artworks at the city's various IRT stations, such as Sue Williamson's sandblasted work *A Random History of Cape Town (1499-1994)* at Cape Town International Airport.

Meanwhile, the country's young democracy is represented along Sea Point promenade in work by Marieke Prinsloo-Rowe. This comprises 18 sculptures entitled *Walking the Road* (www.walking theroad.com). The story unfolds as you walk from the direction of the public swimming pool along a 1.1km stretch. The sculptures will be removed in June 2011.

021 425 5701) are devoted to casual sampling. Will ship all over the world.

Heartworks

Shop 51, Gardens Centre, Mill Street (021 465 3289, www.heartworks.co.za). **Open** 9am-7pm Mon-Fri; 9am-5pm Sat; 9am-2pm Sun. **Map** p57 D5 ⑥⑤
Owner Margaret Woermann is a tireless campaigner for empowerment of local craftsmen and women through sound business practice. Her charming stores are colourful spaces crammed with everything from hand-woven basketry, painstakingly painted ornaments, exquisitely detailed cushion covers, bags and the most beautiful collectible embroidered teddies. The perfect pit stop for something unique, colourful and quirky to take home as a reminder of your visit to Cape Town.

Imagenius

117 Long Street (021 423 7870, www.imagenius.co.za). **Open** 9.30am-4.30pm Mon-Fri; 9.30am-1.30pm Sat. **Map** p57 D3 ⑥⑥
This through-the-looking-glass type space is crammed full of owner Jacqui Hunter's delightful finds – from turn-the-key collectable tin animals to hand-hewn ceramics, Tord Boontje flatpack metal garlands, jewellery by top local talents and kitsch and quirky toys and objects to make you smile. A good bet for unusual gifts.

Kids Emporium

18 Somerset Square, Highfield Road (021 418 7636, www.kidemporium. co.za). **Open** 9am-5pm Mon-Fri; 9am-2pm Sat. **Map** p57 D1 ⑥⑦
From the latest, greatest pram, to baby monitors, nursery accessories, educational toys and clothing. A one-stop shop for people with little people and a must-visit if you're looking for something for a baby shower.

Kink

3 Park Road (021 424 0758, www. kink.co.za). **Open** 10am-6pm Mon;

10am-midnight Tue-Fri; 10am-3pm, 7pm-midnight Sat. **Map** p56 C4 ⑥⑧
Home of saucy knickers, bustiers and imported lingerie to raise eyebrows and bedroom temperatures, this emporium of naughtiness really is nice. Along with gorgeous pieces to bring out the vixen in even the most shy and retiring soul, there are also plenty of gizmos that go buzz in the night. The sexy little bar has become a hip hangout for urbanites.

LIM

86A Kloof Street (021 423 1200, www.lim.co.za). **Open** 9am-5pm Mon-Fri; 9.15am-1pm Sat. **Map** p56 B5 ⑥⑨
LIM is an acronym for Less is More, and it's all about subtle, pared-down style. Owner Pauline Mutlow designs much of her own furniture and accessorises her creations perfectly with global wares. Team these with capsule collections of classic-contemporary tableware, bath and body accessories and you have one of those stores you wish you could use as a template for your life.

Mali South

90 Long Street (021 426 1519). **Open** 7am-6pm daily. **Map** p57 D3 ⑦⓪
If a taste of Africa is what you want to inject into your wardrobe, then make a beeline for this authentic store where bespoke suits and shirts and Afro chic ensembles for both men and women are made up for you in a slew of Malian fabrics by Meiga Abdulaye and his team. Plain shirts take 24 hours to complete, while you're looking at around two or three days if you'd like one embroidered.

O.live

Shop 2, Buitenkloof Studios, 8 Kloof Street (021 426 5773). **Open** 10am-5pm Mon-Fri; 10am-2pm Sat. **Map** p56 C4 ⑦①
Talented owners Rupert Smith and Warren Matthee have the merchandising gift down pat. With everything

Imagenius p77

from colour-coordinated cabinets holding vintage tea sets, to Delft-look jugs and jars of candles, this is a space to get lost in for a while. You'll find gifts for the girl who has everything, glassware for cushions in contemporary fabrics and pretty, fragranced bits and bobs. The modern retro appeal is infectious.

Olive Green Cat

Ground Floor, Holland House,
76 Church Street (021 424 1101,
www.olivegreencat.com). **Open** 8am-5pm Mon-Fri; Sat by appointment.
Map p57 D3 ⑫
Co-creator Ida-Elsje is a wh.iz at engagement and dress rings while her business partner and fellow local talent Philippa Green has garnered a reputation for her resin and Perspex diamond combinations. Both have a big following among Cape Town's cutting-edge jewellery lovers and design-savvy set.

Pan African Market

76 Long Street (021 426 4478).
Open *Summer* 8.30am-5.30pm Mon-Fri; 8.30am-3.30pm Sat. *Winter* 9am-5pm Mon-Fri; 9am-3pm Sat.
Map p57 D3 ⑬
Snatches of different African languages can be heard up and down the corridors, and stall upon stall of carved masks jostle for attention at this indoor market, which also sells fabrics and jewellery. Bargaining's a must, and so is a bite to eat at the on-site café.

Poppa Trunks

45D Kloof Street (021 424 3504).
Open 10am-6pm Mon-Fri; 10am-4pm Sat; 10am-2pm Sun. Winter closed Sun.
Map p56 C4 ⑭
This edgy urban store oozes street style – from the speaker-clad wall to the bright young things browsing the rails of on-trend offerings. You'll find the sneakers of the season, a kaleidoscope of one-of-a-kind tees and jeans galore. Look out for labels such as

Lundun and Evol, and shop for retro classic Casio watches while you're at it.

Wardrobe

45B Kloof Street (021 422 2885).
Open 9am-5pm Mon-Fri; 10am-4pm Sat. **Map** p56 C4 ⑮
Vintage fiends and fashion followers pay regular visits to this trendy raw-wood clad store where edgy street style rubs shoulders with classics and fabulous vintage finds. This one's for everyone, from twentysomethings with that deconstructed chic thing to savvy 40-somethings on the hunt for something special. Look out for offerings from a range of upcoming young designers.

Nightlife

121

121 Castle Street (021 422 2175,
www.121castle.co.za). **Open** 3pm-2am Tue-Sat. **Map** p57 D2 ⑯
This double-storey venue is a cocktail and tapas bar by day and party hotspot by night. Downstairs you'll find a clean-lined, modern bar with mirrored walls. The upstairs section is more plush with couches and splashes of red, and this is where the dancing happens. The club is home of the resurrected and insanely popular Flava R&B nights as well as The L-Way (for the ladies).

&Union Beer Salon & Charcuterie

Shop 7, St Stephen's Church, 110 Bree Street (021 422 2770, www. andunion.com). **Open** 7am-11pm Mon-Thur; 7am-midnight Fri, Sat.
Admission free. **Map** p57 D2 ⑰
If you're something of a beer connoisseur, try this venue from the original creators of Vida e Caffè. With solo artists on Friday evenings and a smashing display of original hard bop quartets in the Puma Early Session every Saturday from 7pm, this is set to become a firm favourite among Cape Town's jazz lovers.

Asoka

*68 Kloof Street (021 422 0909,
www.asokabar.co.za).* **Open** 5pm-2am
daily. **Admission** free. **Map** p56 C5 **78**
Every Tuesday at this intimate venue
you can catch post-bop strategists the
Restless Natives, a funky jazz quintet
who bring a gonzo undertone to canonical Blue Note-era material. This is a
popular spot among urban hipsters,
and you can also get a bite to eat.

Assembly

*61 Harrington Street (082 856 7438,
www.theassembly.co.za).* **Open** 9pm-
4am Fri, Sat. **Admission** R40-R50.
Map p57 E4 **79**
Once dedicated to live music, over time
The Assembly expanded to include
regular DJ nights, covering genres like
trance and minimal – this is where
you'll find regular music night Killer
Robot these days. On the live music
side you'll still hear some of the top
names in the industry, from Just Ginjer
to Flat Stanley and Taxi Violence, and
every style of music: from indie to
punk, rock, jazz, ska, blues, electronica,
rockabilly and more. This is also
where you're likely to catch Afro-pop
sensations such as Freshlyground,
Mozambican dub fusionists 340ml or
electro-jazzy house hipsters Goldfish.
And as a venue goes it's a winner, with
plenty of space, an adjacent bar, and a
raised perimeter with soft seats and a
good view of the madness.

Beefcakes Burger Bar

*Shop 7 Sovereign Quay, 40 Somerset
Road (021 425 9019, www.beefcakes.
co.za).* **Open** 11am-11pm Mon-Sat; 5-
11pm Sun. **Drag night** 9pm
Thur. **Map** p57 D1 **80**
This delicious camp new '50s-style
diner brings 'a touch of madness and
Miami chic' to the area around Green
Point. Beefy waiters dish up moreish
burgers (try Buffy the Hamburger
Slayer) and if you book a table, it'll get
pre-adorned with a selection of porno
pink, red and purple cowboy hats.

Come for Thursday's drag night or on
Monday when local drag legend Miss
Lola Fine hosts Bitchy Bingo. The pint-
sized downstairs club, Studio 54, plies
old-school disco and '80s classics.

Chrome

*6 Pepper Street (083 700 6078, 9,
www.chromect.com).* **Open** 9pm-4am
Wed; 10pm-4am Thur-Sun. **Admission**
R60; R120 VIP. **Map** p57 D3 **81**
Expect to queue here, even on a week-
night; at weekends it's even more popular. The smart city spot attracts R&B
and hip hop enthusiasts, and boasts
state of the art lighting and sound.

Deluxe

*Unity House, corner Long and
Longmarket streets (021 422 4832).*
Open 10pm-4am Fri, Sat. **Admission**
R50. **Map** p57 D3 **82**
In a dance music world increasingly
taken over by commercial house, R&B
and hip hop, this remains one of the last
true deep house clubs in Cape Town. It's
been around for years. It's comfortable
and unpretentious and a place to appreciate music and dance without worry-
ing about your hair or make up.

Fez Bar & Club

*11 Mechau Street (021 419 7000,
www.vaudeville.co.za).* **Open** 10pm-
4am Mon-Sat. **Admission** R50.
Map p57 E2 **83**
Once a legendary club back in the hey-
day of Cape Town clubbing, the Fez is
back with a vengeance, retaining all the
feel and glory of the former club in a
brand-new space. You'll even hear
some of the DJs from the past – like
Dino Moran, Dean Fuel, Richard
Marshall and Rob Taylor – laying
down today's freshest beats. The venue
offers a winning combination, namely
the biggest, crispest sound system in
town, a downtown location in the
Bohemian Vaudeville Theatre, pleasant
doormen and beautiful people. Book a
table at Vaudeville and your entrance
to the club is thrown in for free.

Assembly

Fiction DJ Bar & Lounge

*226 Long Street (021 424 5709,
www.fictionbar.com).* **Open** 9pm-
4am Tue-Sat. **Admission** R40.
Map p57 D3 ❽

Still as popular as ever, Fiction has to be
one of the coolest places in Cape Town.
It's small and intimate, and the dancefloor tends to get packed, especially
when sounds are drum 'n' bass, minimal
or indie. The monthly Peroxide ('80s
synth pop) nights are brilliant, with
guests dressing the part. There's a wide
wraparound balcony from which to look
down on the Long Street action.

Jo'burg Bar

*218 Long Street (021 422 0142,
www.joburgbar.com).* **Open** noon-4am
Mon-Sat; 6pm-4am Sun. **Admission**
varies. **Map** p57 D3 ❽

At the very hub of the Long Street
strip, this old timer is a popular and
often packed favourite for a slightly
older crowd content with smaller acts.
Pop in for a spot of rockabilly, frac-
tured folk or simple singer-songwriter
strummers on Sundays.

Marimba Restaurant

*CTICC, Heerengracht (021 418 3366,
www.marimbasa.com).* **Open** 8.30am-
11.30pm Mon-Fri; 4-11.30pm Sat;
music from 7.30-10.30pm Thur-Sat.
Admission free. **Map** p57 F1 ❽

'When marimba rhythms start to
play, dance with me…' The musicians
here hail from the Congo, Mozambique
and South Africa, and offer recognis-
able tunes with an African slant,
including African interpretations of
songs from Broadway and the Great
American Songbook.

Rainbow Room

*Mandela Rhodes Place, Church Street
(021 422 1428, www.therainbow
experience.co.za).* **Open** 8pm-2am
Mon, Fri, Sat. **Admission** R50-R100.
Map p57 D3 ❻

The Rainbow Room is a lovely little
underground – literally – jazz club in

the heart of the city centre. Since opening a year ago it has built a reputation
for hosting some of the hottest local
and international jazz acts, as well as
providing a platform for new, up-and-
coming bands and musicians. It's
part of the Rainbow Experience at
Mandela Rhodes Place, which is a
place to eat, drink, socialise, shop and
enjoy events like book and poetry
readings and art exhibitions.

Vudu Lounge

*165 Bree Street (021 426 0275,
www.vudulounge.co.za).* **Open** 8pm-
4am Thur-Sat. **Admission** varies.
Map p57 D3 ❽

Upmarket decor and Afropolitan chic
make this cosy hip hop and kwaito-
house hotspot the city-centre choice for
album launches and glam big brand
sponsored bashes. Expect plenty of visiting performers from up north, who
keep the booties shaking on the
crammed dancefloor.

The Waiting Room

273 Long Street (021 422 4536).
Open 6pm-2am Mon-Sat. Live
music Tue. **Admission** varies.
Map p57 D4 ❻

Fast becoming one of Cape Town's
hippest spots, what started as a waiting room for Long Street's Royale
Eatery has become a venue to visit for
its own sake, featuring a selection of
new and established local artists.
Expect originals rather than cover
versions, with the emphasis on folk
and funky jazz. The spectacular sundowner deck and edgy design make
this a memorable venue.

Zula Sound Bar
& Restaurant

*196 & 188 Long Street (021 424
2442, www.zulabar.co.za).* **Open**
10pm-late daily. **Admission** varies.
Map p57 D3 ❾

Since owners Zofi and Vusa Mazula
took over this laid-back venue four
years ago, it has become something of

a favourite on the Long Street strip, with queues sometimes stretching halfway down the block. It's a friendly hang-out for travellers and locals with a taste for original rock, reggae, dub, ska, funk, slam poetry and acoustic folk. In other words, anything goes.

Arts & Leisure

Artscape Theatre Centre

DF Malan Street (021 410 9812, www.artscape.co.za). Bookings also on Computicket. **Map** p57 F2 **①**

This imposing grey edifice might not be the prettiest building around, but it's played host to some impressive productions over the years and continues to be a major venue for big productions. Behind the revolving glass doors lies a regal opera house, a 540-seater theatre and a tiny arena for more intimate shows. Productions range from contemporary dance shows to ballet, opera, circus spectaculars and plays.

City Hall

Darling Street, opposite Grand Parade. (bookings 021 421 7695, Computicket). **Concerts** 8pm Thur. **Map** p57 E3 **②**

The home of the Cape Philharmonic Orchestra, City Hall's concert hall has superb acoustics. From Bach to Shostakovich, the range complements the calibre of visiting conductors and soloists. If you don't mind the startling proximity of the timpani and tuba, opt for the cheap seats under the impressive organ. Also, a little tip: while shows start at 8pm, come at 7.15pm and, with your glass of wine from the bar in hand, enter the hall for a free, informal and informative talk by Fine Music Radio host Rodney Trudgeon. He's a fount of entertaining titbits about the symphony to be performed.

Foxy at On Broadway

44 Long Street, corner Hout Street (021 424 1194, www.onbroadway. co.za, bookings also on Computicket). **Map** p57 E3 **③**

This brand-new retro bioscope is run by the organisers of the annual Out in Africa Gay and Lesbian Film Festival. Located in a stunning Victorian building, upstairs from the newly relocated On Broadway theatre, this loft-style space, with its blood-red chairs, black velvet curtain and wooden ceiling, is set to become a haven for alternative cinema-lovers.

The Fugard

Cnr of Harrington & Caledon streets, District 6 (021 461 4244, www.the fugard.com). **Map** p57 E4 **④**

The Fugard has become one of the Mother City's top theatre spots since opening in 2009. Named after internationally renowned South African playwright Athol Fugard, it is home to the award-winning Isango Portobello Theatre Company. Aside from the company's productions, the theatre has also staged works like the world premier of Fugard's play, *The Train Driver*, and Sean Mathias's box-office record-breaking international production of Samuel Beckett's *Waiting for Godot*, with an international cast that included Sir Ian McKellen.

Intimate Theatre

Hiddingh Campus, 37 Orange Street (021 480 7129, www.intimate theatre.net). **No credit cards.** **Map** p56 C4 **⑤**

On the campus of the University of Cape Town's Drama department, this petite spot was originally a student working space but nowadays it hosts professional productions. The theatre has staged some pretty pioneering pieces, showcased the work of stalwarts and launched the careers of many young performers. The speck-sized bar is great for a post-show mingle.

Jazzart Dance Theatre

Artscape Theatre Complex, DF Malan Street (021 410 9848, www.jazzart. co.za. Bookings Computicket, Dial-a-Seat, Artscape, Baxter). **Map** p57 F2 **⑥**

This award-winning contemporary dance company is known for its groundbreaking repertoire, which incorporates a unique fusion of African and Western dance styles. The oldest contemporary dance company in the country, it started out in 1973 as a modern jazz dance studio, soon ballooning into a celebrated multicultural company. One of the first integrated dance companies in the country, Jazzart was never afraid to air its anti-apartheid views and employed dance as a form of protest during the struggle years.

Labia on Kloof

Lifestyles on Kloof Centre, 50 Kloof Street (021 424 5927, www.labia.co.za). **Tickets** R30; R25 concessions. **Map** p56 C4 **37**
Smaller and without the vintage charms of its big sister, but the tickets are still dirt cheap, the movie deals still apply and this branch too has a well-stocked bar. In general, movies shown here are slightly more mainstream than those at Orange Street.

Labia on Orange

68 Orange Street (021 424 5927, www.labia.co.za). **Tickets** R30; R25 concessions. **Map** p56 C4 **98**
The oldest independent arthouse cinema in the country, this Cape Town cultural icon started life as an Italian embassy ballroom and owes its name to Italian princess Labia, who, in 1949, converted it to a theatre. A vintage barred ticket booth adds a touch of retro grandeur, while four screens show the latest art-house releases and documentaries, with regular film festivals. The on-site coffee bar and chocolate bar are popular.

On Broadway

44 Long Street (021 424 1194/5, www.onbroadway.co.za, bookings also on Computicket). **Shows** 8.30pm (6.30pm for dinner) daily. **Map** p57 E3 **99**

When the New Space Theatre closed down last year, musical and supper theatre stalwart On Broadway packed its bags and moved to its vacated premises on party-central Long Street. It still offers dinner: theatre-goers now have a choice between eating here or next door at retro prohibition-style haunt Boo Radleys. You can still expect the regular mix of stand-up comedy, musical revues and queer cabaret, but the New Space's atmospheric vintage theatre space, with its red velvet seats, black walls and gorgeously ornate windows, now provides a suitably stylish backdrop.

Que Pasa Latin Lounge

15 Caledon Street, below Dias Tavern (074 199 0918, 021 465 0225, www.quepasa.co.za). **Classes** 6.30-7.30pm Tue-Thur; 9.30-10.30pm Sat (free party afterwards). **Admission** R50. **No credit cards.** Map p57 E4 **100**
Set your sights on learning the sexy salsa. Que Pasa is the city's only club dedicated to this dance form. Learn the moves at one their group salsa classes and have fun on the dancefloor with your newfound Latin prowess at the party afterwards. On Saturdays things really heat up; the doors stay open until the wee hours of the morning.

St George's Cathedral

5 Wale Street, City Centre (021 424 7360, www.stgeorgescathedral.com). **Bookings** Computicket; 1 hour prior to performance. **No credit cards.** Map p57 D3 **101**
The spiritual seat of Archbishop Desmond Tutu, this beautiful Anglican cathedral on the edge of the Company's Gardens hosts many a choral or Baroque production, aided by an impressive new Hill organ. The acoustics are fantastic, and the venue also hosts some pretty avant-garde events throughout the year – recently the pews were packed to capacity for a performance of Tibetan Buddhist overtone chanting from a group of monks.

CAPE TOWN BY AREA

Bo-Kaap

The multicoloured rectangular houses lining Bo-Kaap's steep cobbled streets have become a symbol of this predominantly Muslim suburb, but they were actually only painted this way about 20 years ago, thanks to one adventurous resident.

This historic area dates back to the 1700s, when it was known as the Slave Quarter and was home to freed slaves and exiles from the east. The Muslim heritage is evident in its beautiful mosques, among them the **Auwal Mosque** (43 Dorp Street), which is South Africa's oldest.

Walking tours can be arranged with companies such as Cape Capers (021 448 3117, www.tour capers.co.za) or Cape Fusion Tours (021 461 2437, www.capefusion. co.za). Factor in some time for lunch or a snack at one of the area's authentic eateries.

Bo-Kaap Museum

71 Wale Street (021 481 3939, www.iziko.org.za, bokaap). **Open** 10am-5pm Mon-Sat. **Admission** R10 adults; R5 concessions. **No credit cards.** **Map** p57 D3 **102**

On the slopes of Signal Hill, the Bo-Kaap was initially named Waalendorp after Jan de Waal, the man who spearheaded the development of the area in the 1760s. Later it became known as the Malay quarter or Slamse buurt, after its predominantly Muslim population, of which many were former slaves and exiles from India, Malaysia and Indonesia. Set in the only remaining unaltered Jan de Waal structure left in the hilly suburb, the Bo-Kaap Museum was established in 1978 and casts a spotlight on the fascinating history of the area and its people. Start your tour of this postcard pretty mountainside suburb at the museum.

Noon Gun

Military Road, follow the signs from cnr Bloem Street and Buitengragt (www.bokaap.co.za, attractions, noongun.html). **Map** p56 C1 **103**

Cape Town's noon gun has been booming away steadily atop Signal Hill since 1902. The twin cannons were in the Castle of Good Hope until the British occupation in 1806, when they moved them to what was then the much less populated part of the city.

Shopping

Atlas Trading

94 Wale Street (021 423 4361). **Open** 8am-noon, 2pm-5pm Mon-Fri; 8.30am-12.45pm Sat. **Map** p57 D2 **104**

Looking for something small and significant to take home as a souvenir of Cape Town? Look no further than this old-school spice store where giant sacks of turmeric, cardamom and curry leaves beckon. Pre-mixed curry spice packs are available en masse and kilograms of salted or raw nuts (including, almonds, cashews and pistachios) are offered at the best prices in the city.

Nightlife

Marco's African Place

15 Rose Street (021 423 5412, www.marcosafricanplace.co.za). **Open** noon-late Tue-Sat; 3pm-late Sun. **Admission** R15 (for those also dining); R30 (without dinner). **Map** p57 D2 **105**

Marco's is a 220-seater restaurant and bar in the Bo-Kaap area that has become a favourite stop for tour buses – but don't let that put you off. You're guaranteed a memorable African party experience, with some exotic all-African cuisine included. Tuesdays and Wednesdays it's a lively marimba party, with the rest of the week dedicated to an eclectic mix of jazzy African sounds.

Bo-Kaap

De Waterkant

Eating & drinking

Beluga

The Foundry, Prestwich Street (021 418 2948). **Open** noon-11pm daily. RR. **Sushi and grills**.
Map p57 D1 **106**

Beluga means half-price sushi. Or at least that's what this restaurant's many fans have in mind when they arrive in the buzzing courtyard. Equally popular are the cocktails – a big hit with the area's office workers who descend in great numbers on Friday nights. In addition to the main menu (the signature dish is the aply named Fillet of Luxury, with a creamy duck-liver parfait, balsamic roasted baby onions and a bordelaise jus) there's one dedicated to Pacific Rim dishes. A sexy, popular spot.

Cubaña Havana Lounge & Latino Café

9 Somerset Road, De Waterkant Centre (021 421 1109, www.cubana.co.za).
Open 7am-4am daily. RR. **Bar**.
Map p57 D1 **107**

This vibey bar is lavish and opulent and sets the tone for glam entertainment and hot-blooded socialising. Think hip-shaking Latin beats, decadent cocktails, Caribbean cuisine, and real-deal Cuban cigars. The dress code is smart casual, and there's a no under-23s door policy.

Shopping

Africa Nova

C3, Cape Quarter, Waterkant Street (021 425 5123, www.africanova.co.za).
Open *Summer* 9am-5.30pm Mon-Fri; 10am-5pm Sat; 10am-2pm Sun. *Winter* 9.30am-5.30pm Mon-Fri; 10am-3pm Sat.
Map p57 D2 **108**

Owner Margie Murgatroyd is a passionate purveyor of local crafts and handiwork. Look out for own print textiles available by the metre (perfect for making cushions when you get home), jewellery with a contemporary ethnic edge, an extensive range of ceramics, authentic artefacts and a range of contemporary goods that reflect the 'Afro-urban' context.

Cape Quarter & Cape Quarter extension

72 Waterkant Street (021 421 1111, www.capequarter.co.za). **Open** 10am-6.30pm daily. Map p57 D2 **109**

This glossy new spot, over the road from the original Cape Quarter, plays host to a piazza lined with smart eateries and places to enjoy a drink or two, as well as boutiques whose stock ranges from fashion to stationery and leather accessories and jewellery – the perfect merchandise for the well-heeled clientele who frequent it. The original Cape Quarter offers eateries and eclectic homeware at Baraka (021 425 8883).

Loading Bay

30 Hudson Street (021 425 6320, www.loadingbay.co.za). **Open** 7am-6pm Mon-Fri; 8am-4pm Sat.
Map p57 D2 **110**

Discerning fashion design followers head for this urban haven of cool – where brands like Acne and cult denim label Naked & Famous beckon. Check out the beautifully cut coats, jackets and everyday quality basics. The on-site café offers post-shopping sustenance for weary spenders.

Private Collections

66 Waterkant Street (021 421 0298).
Open 8am-5pm Mon-Fri; 9am-3pm Sat.
Map p57 D2 **111**

Larger-than-life antiques and Indian collectibles set the scene at this magnificent store – from gates and doors sourced from Rajasthani villas, solid silver chairs reminiscent of the Raj and trinkets to add to the exotic atmosphere. The camphor wood kists and beautifully carved beds are reminiscent of another era.

Clock Tower Precinct p90

V&A Waterfront & Green Point

The Atlantic Seaboard starts its journey at the Cape's consumer capital, the **V&A Waterfront**.

Named after Queen Victoria and her second son Alfred, the V&A Waterfront is situated in the city's working harbour and the country's most visited destination. Its main lure is the high-end V&A Mall, with its slew of international designer shops, the Two Oceans Aquarium, several upmarket hotels, as well as the Clock Tower Precinct shopping centre. The Waterfront is also the site from which many of the city's sightseeing buses and the **Robben Island** ferry depart.

As the place where South Africa's first post-apartheid president, Nelson Mandela, was incarcerated for 18 years by the country's apartheid governments, Robben Island is one of Cape Town's most well-known and important sights. It has been declared a museum and a national heritage site.

This stretch of beach-dotted seaboard then heads west to **Green Point**, home of the giant 2010 **World Cup Stadium** and a smattering of clubs, coffee shops and restaurants. Green Point has a colourful history, dating back to the 18th century. Originally the area was much larger, stretching all the way from Signal Hill to the ocean, and various sporting pursuits have taken place here, including some of the country's earliest cricket and rugby matches.

Sandwiched between Three Anchor Bay (see p106) and the V&A Waterfront, Mouille Point is at the western tip of Green Point. Its main tourist attractions include an outdoor putt-putt course, a small kiddies' train and a square, red-and-white lighthouse (see p108).

Sights & museums

Cape Town Stadium

Granger Bay Boulevard (021 430 7346, www.stadiumcapetown.co.za). **Open** Tours 10am, noon, 2pm Tues, Thur, Sat. **Admission** R30 adult; R15 reductions. **Map** p90 C4 ❶

Since the advent of the successful 2010 Fifa World Cup, the magnificent Cape Town Stadium has become an iconic part of the city's landscape. The graceful bowl (called the toilet bowl by some) takes up around six neighbourhood blocks and stands 15 storeys tall and cost an astonishing USD 600 million to complete. Its pièce de résistance, a 4 500-ton glass roof, was modelled on a bicycle wheel, and when illuminated, becomes a glowing halo suspended in front of the city and her mountain. A fascinating tour of the stadium and its inner sancta is a highlight for architecture enthusiasts and soccer fans alike.

Clock Tower Precinct

V&A Waterfront (021 408 7600, www.waterfront.co.za). **Map** p91 E4 ❷

A Gothic-style, red octagonal clock-tower forms the centre of this V&A Waterfront retail complex. Built in 1882, it served as the port captain's office so he could check on the comings and goings of the harbour from his first-storey mirrored office. The ground floor still houses the erstwhile tide-gauge mechanism used to determine the water levels, whilst the original clock can be viewed on the top

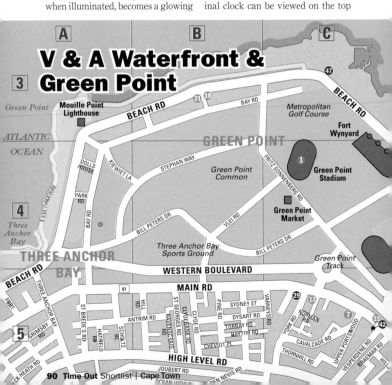

V & A Waterfront & Green Point

floor. Connecting this satellite precinct of the V&A to the 'mother ship', there is a bridge that swings open every so often to let large ships pass through.

Iziko Maritime Centre

Union Castle Building, V&A Waterfront (021 405 2884, www.iziko.org.za/maritime). **Open** 10am-5pm daily. **Admission** Free, donations appreciated. **No credit cards**. **Map** p90 D4 ❸

A must-visit for those with a penchant for sailing and the sea, this museum houses a comprehensive collection of maritime artefacts and associated ephemera. Its permanent exhibition includes an 1885 model of Table Bay Harbour, made by prisoners and warders of the defunct Breakwater

Prison, pictures depicting the evolution of the harbour between the 17th and the 20th centuries, as well as the largest collection of model ships in the country. As an optional extra, visitors can step on to the *SAS Somerset*, the coal-fired steam tug permanently moored outside.

Robben Island Museum

Ferries depart from Nelson Mandela Gateway, Clocktower Precinct, V&A Waterfront (021 4220/1, www.robben-island.org.za). **Open** *Office hours* 7.30am-6pm daily; closed 1 May. *Ferries* 9am, 10am, 11am, 1pm, 3pm (2pm in winter) daily, weather permitting; book in advance. **Admission** R200 adults; R100 under-18s. **Map** p91 E4 ❹

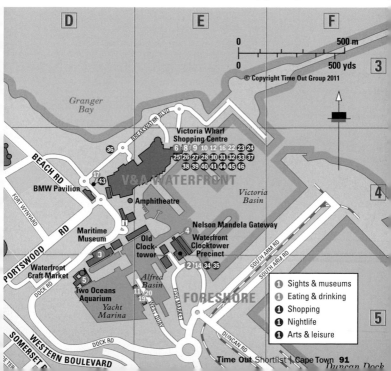

MYATT

CAFÉ & CHOCOLATIER

SHOP 6244 • V&A WATERFRONT • CAPE TOWN • SOUTH AFRICA • TEL: +2721 4188844 • WWW.MYATTCAFE.COM

Welcome

Myatt Café & Chocolatier receives an encore with the opening of their doors at the new fashion wing of the V&A Waterfront.

Delicious gourmet sandwiches, pastries, cakes and chocolates are but a few of the choices you will be faced with. With a variety of coffees and teas you could be tempted to stay all day and, with names such as Kenyan Black, Ceylon Petiagala and Blooming Show Tea you could be forgiven for thinking you are seated at the front row of a High Fashion Award in Paris.

Our retail counter offers you a wide range of these Myatt products and MARY chocolates. These are imported from Belgium and crafted especially for Myatt Café & Chocolatier. Why not take a little of the Myatt flavour home with you? Indulge in excellence.

For an afternoon of pure indulgence, our High Tea is a must. The menu includes pastries, cakes, mini croissants and finger sandwiches prepared by our renowned confectionary chef.

Should you be doubly tempted, these works of art can be made to order for corporate gifts or private functions. In fact we are pleased to be at your service for any of the above.

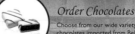

Order Chocolates

Choose from our wide variety of Mary chocolates imported from Belgium.

Order Macaroons

Come and indulge in excellence with this exclusive treat.

Order Cakes

Choose from our delectable range of cakes including everything from Carrot Cake rolled in Coconut, to Lemon Meringue.

VIEW OUR FULL MENU AND ORDER ONLINE. WWW.MYATTCAFE.COM

Robben Island was once a place of banishment for society's pariahs, including lepers, the mentally insane and prisoners, but today stands testament to the power of hope and forgiveness. The island is most infamous for its incarceration of political prisoners during the apartheid era, most notably Nelson Rolihlahla Mandela, who spent 18 years in its confines. It was declared a national heritage site and museum three years after the country's first democratic elections, during which Mandela was appointed president. Today visitors can experience the blinding white light of the lime quarries in which the prisoners toiled, as well as Mandela's claustrophobic cell.

Two Oceans Aquarium

Dock Road, V&A Waterfront (021 418 3823, www.aquarium.co.za). **Open** 9.30am-6pm daily. *Feeding times General* 3pm Tue, Thur, Sat. *Sharks* 3pm Sun. *Kelp Forest Exhibit* Noon Sat. *Penguins* 11.30am, 2.30pm daily. **Admission** R94 adults; free-R73 reductions. **Map** p91 D5 ❺

Space might be the final frontier, but life on the ocean floor isn't any less mysterious, as you'll realise wandering the ethereally lit corridors of this popular family attraction. There are terrifying and oversized spider crabs, jellyfish that light up like trance-party paraphernalia, groups of anemones participating in a perpetual Mexican wave and blue stingrays jetting about. Not to mention a couple of scary-looking sharks: Should you have the inclination and a scuba licence, you can ogle them up close during a diving session. The daily penguin feeding is a highlight for young and old while the shark tank, with its resident ragged- tooth inhabitants, slowly trawling through the kelp forest, will make you stop and rethink your fear of these majestic creatures (or not). For the peckish, there's an on-site café and the downstairs activity room is a boon for parents.

V&A Waterfront

Dock Road, Foreshore (021 408 7600, www.waterfront.co.za). **Open** *Shops* 9am-9pm daily. *Craft Market & Wellness Centre* 9.30am-6pm daily. *Restaurants & bars* until late. **Map** p91 E4 ❻

When Queen Victoria's second son Alfred tipped a ceremonial bucketload of stones into the ocean in 1860 to signify the start of the Cape Town harbour construction, he couldn't possibly have imagined the multi-million rand conglomeration as it stands today. It isn't one of the Mother City's top tourist sites for nothing: the harbour-side development encompasses child-friendly destinations like an aquarium, indoor golf arena and semi-precious gemstone scratch patch, while adults can choose how to spend their money between its swanky malls (the V&A and the Clocktower, filled with hundreds of smart shops and eateries) and hotels (the One&Only and Cape Grace, among others). The Red and Blue sheds are havens of small local business development for local crafters and stallholders who sell everything from hand carvings to beaded jewellery, curio knick-knacks and artworks. It's also the site from which the popular City Sightseeing Bus and the Robben Island ferry depart. From here it's a short walk to the Cape Town Stadium and the buzzing Green Point restaurant strip.

Eating & drinking

1800° Grill Room

Cape Royale Hotel, Main Road, Green Point (021 430 0506, www.18hundred degrees.com). **Open** 6.30-10.30am, noon-3.30pm, 6.30-11.30pm daily. RR. **Grills**. **Map** p90 C5 ❼

Referring to the eponymous grill in the open-plan kitchen which reaches 1800°F, this sophisticated grillhouse is dedicated to serving the perfect steak. Situated in the swish Cape Royale Hotel on the buzzing Green

Fair game

Cape Town Stadium – a new city icon.

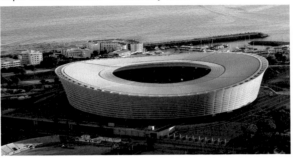

The year 2010 saw the world shift its focus to South Africa for the FIFA World Cup, The legacy of this unforgettable chapter in local history remains in the city with the new and improved facilities created for the hordes of local and visiting enthusiasts. Cape Town Stadium (P0) is one of these. Built on the original site of the Green Point Stadium, an 18,000-seater sports arena constructed in the 1940s and the home ground for many a city soccer team, the new, smarter, 68,000-seater stadium began to emerge from the partially demolished old stadium in 2007. The stadium as we see it today took just 33 months to complete, at a cost of some US$600 million. The design is the work of German stadium specialists GMP Acrhitects and two local firms, Louis Karol and Associates and Point Architects. Designed to 'float' against the city and mountain backdrop, the multi-level stadium was constructed with an external 'skin' to allow for natural ventilation and to reduce glare and thermal radiation to the surrounds, with a complex series of glass roof panels protecting spectators from the sometimes unpredictable Cape Town weather.

For those wishing to get up close and personal with the stadium, a tour is the way to go – visitors are escorted through the stadium's spectator and VIP areas, via the media zones and into the player facilities, offering an insiders' view of how the stadium must look to those whose job is to make magic on the pitch. The stadium is withing walking distance of the V&A Waterfront and the Sea Point promenade and, in time, a 12.5-hectare Green Point Park surrounding the stadium will ensure it becomes a backdrop to continuing leisure activity in the city. Jokingly dubbed 'the toilet bowl' by some, there's no denying the impressive mark that this magnificent piece of architecture has made on the Cape Town landscape and in the hearts of sports fans and players alike.

■ Stadium tours: 10am, noon, 2pm Tue, Thur, Sat.

Point mile, the 72-seater features a spacious courtyard and polished interior accented with dark woods and starched whites. The sauces accompanying the steaks vary according to the chefs' whims, but can include anything from Argentinian chimichurri and Madagascan pepper to English mustard and creamy béarnaise, served of course with suitably crispy fries on the side.

221 Waterfront

Shop 221, V&A Waterfront (021 418 3633, www.221waterfront.co.za). **Open** Noon-11pm daily. **RR**. **Modern global**. Map p91 E4 ⑧

This spot boasts a killer view of the busy V&A Waterfront harbour with the toing and froing of boats as well as Table Mountain. The menu is globally representative, including a spectacular 600g prime rib and a Cape Malay trio of traditional chicken curry, lamb *bredie* and fish *bobotie* (served with all the traditional sambals). If you have a sweet tooth, dip into the handmade nougat ice cream topped with berries and halva, or the decadent chocolate chilli ganache.

Baia Seafood Restaurant

Victoria Wharf, V&A Waterfront (021 421 0935, http://baiarestaurant. co.za). **Open** Noon-3pm, 6.45-10.30pm daily. **RRR**. **Seafood & grills**. Map p91 E4 ⑨

Adorned by Egon Schiele prints and hued in accents of black, purple and silver, this sophisticated Waterfront restaurant is hot property for its uninterrupted sea view (courtesy of four glass-sheltered terraces) and comprehensive menu showcasing the ocean's bounty. The renowned seafood laden platters are epic in size and variety, featuring your choice of specialities such as prawns, crayfish and langoustines while Portuguese dishes like *trinchado*, *langoustine nacional* and Mozambiquan curry also have a steady following.

Balducci's

Shop 6162, Lower Level, V&A Waterfront. (021 421 6002/3, www.balduccis.co.za). **Open** noon-11pm daily. **RR**. **Café**. Map p91 E4 ⑩

Set in a contemporary-comfy, wood-accented venue in the Waterfront, this is the place to visit for hearty Italian fare and people-watching, thanks to the throngs of well dressed regulars who think of it as their local coffee, lunch and sushi spot. The thin-crusted gourmet pizzas are the real deal, topped with the likes of salmon, grapefruit, cream cheese and caviar on the one side of the spectrum and fall-off-the-bone oxtail on the other. Laidback and cosmopolitan.

Bascule Whisky, Wine & Cocktail Bar

Cape Grace, West Quay, V&A Waterfront (021 410 7082, www. capegrace.com). **Open** 10am-late daily. **RR**. **Whisky bar & Café**. Map p91 E5 ⑪

Bascule is a delightful combination of intimate interiors and a sun-drenched deck with a spectacular view of the international yacht marina. It is the perfect setting to take in the sights and sounds of the busy waterfront surrounds and the luxury pleasure craft that are moored here. There are more than 400 whiskies from around the world and an impressive selection of the finest Cape wines on offer – book a berth on one of the bespoke whisky tastings and savour the flavours of top whisky offerings from around the world.

Belthazar

Shop 153, V&A Waterfront (021 421 3753/6). **Open** Noon-10pm daily. **RRR**. **Steaks & grills**. Map p91 E4 ⑫

Listing a selection of 250 wines by the glass, the choice in this place is so vast that surplus crates are literally stacked in the rafters. Another claim to fame is the meat: it has won numerous 'best steakhouse' awards over the years for their meaty efforts. On the menu expect to find everything from perfectly seared rib-eye steak served with a choice of sauces including chocolate chilli and Madagascan green pepper sauce to house specialities like flame-grilled lamb chops and luxury burgers topped with deep-fried onions and guacamole. Slick service and knowledgeable wine staff enhance this experience.

Doppio Zero
81 Main Road, Green Point (021 434 9581). **Open** 8am-2am daily. **R.** **Italian café.** Map p90 C5 ⓭
The menu at this urban chic hangout leans heavily towards the Italian and is extensive to say the least: there are breakfasts, light meals, soups, salads, antipasti, meat, fish, poultry, vegetarian dishes, gourmet sandwiches, croissants and toasted tramezzini and of course, pizza and pasta. And don't forget the artisan bakery, which churns out a range of fresh breads and pastries every day. The secret to the best bread and pizza bases is the fine stone ground Italian 00 flour, which is double zero, or 'doppio zero'.

Emily's
Suite 202, Clock Tower Centre, V&A Waterfront (021 421 1133, www.emily-s.com). **Open** noon-2.30pm, 6.30-10pm Mon-Sat. **RRR. Contemporary South African.** Map p91 E4 ⓮
Run by dynamic dining duo Johan Odendaal and Peter Veldsman, this charming Afri-Victorian spot is the perfect place for a romantic get-together, thanks to its views out across the Waterfront basins. The extensive menu sees modern interpretations of local and North African cuisine with plenty of twists in between. Traditional denningvleis, for example, is made with tender, deboned lamb and served atop spicy lentils with a pineapple and sour-fig sambal,

whilst malva pudding is turned onto its head (literally) and baked with apples to create a newfangled tarte tatin called skinderpoeding ('gossip pudding'), which is then balanced with a scoop of Amarula ice cream.

Mano's
39 Main Road, Green Point (021 434 1090, www.mano.co.za). **Open** noon-late daily. **RR. Modern café.** Map p90 C5 ⓯
Adorned by authentic art deco windows and John Lennon prints, this bright, effortlessly cool restaurant has been going strong for 14 years now thanks to its consistently good food and amiable service. Pre-dinner drinks at the sprawling, sexy bar counter are a must before you sidle in at one of the brown-paper topped tables to tuck into succulent fresh fish or spicy Prego rolls – typical of the menu that's peppered with no fuss easy-to-eat food (the burgers are great).

Meloncino
Shop 259, Upper Level, Victoria Wharf, V&A Waterfront (021 419 5558, www.meloncino.co.za). **Open** 9.30am-10.30pm daily. **RR. Contemporary Italian.** Map p91 E4 ⓰
The patio area overlooking the harbour is a prime spot on a good day and the perfect setting from which to relish the contemporary Italian fare – get here early to bag a good table. Favourite bites include homemade pastas like the *spaghetti scoglio in carta fata* (pasta with mixed seafood, cherry tomatoes and chilli served in a cellophane wrapping), wood-fired pizzas and traditional dishes like Milanese-style veal. A favourite with Atlantic Seaboard glossy posses who come for lunch and linger until its time for cocktails.

NOBU
One & Only Cape Town, Dock Road, Victoria & Alfred Waterfront

V&A Waterfront p93

Lip-smacking local food

Your glossary to a gamut of homegrown dishes.

Beskuit (Rusks): Bone-dry rectangular biscuits that are best enjoyed dipped intoa piping hot cuppa and then slurped in a style that eludes sophistication.

Biltong: The preferred snack of sports enthusiasts, these dried, salty strips of beef are perfect when washed down with liberallashings of beer.

Bobotie: This fragrant, slightly spicy Cape Malay dish is comprised of curried mince with dried fruit such as raisins, topped with an egg custard, which is then baked.

Boerewors: No self-respecting braai should be without this spiced beef sausage. Slap on a long bread roll, slather with tomato sauce or chutney, and hey presto, you have a boerewors-roll.

Bunnychow: Hollow out half a loaf of white bread, fill with curry and dig in. Elegant it ain't, but damn, it's good.

Chakalaka: Ranging from a bit-of-a-bite to hot-as-hell, this tomato-based vegetable relish is usually served with pap (mealie-meal porridge) and meat dishes.

Koeksisters: Sinfully sweet plaits of dough, which are deep-fried before being drenched in a cinnamon-sugar syrup. Not a healthy snack.

Koeksister: Not to be confused with *koeksisters*, this sweet Cape Malay snack is more like a small, fragrant doughnut, soaked in syrup and then dipped in coconut.

Potjie: The key components to preparing the perfect *potjie* stew are simple enough: you need a castiron pot known as a potjie, a decent fire, a little stirring and a whole lot of patience. The choice of ingredients relies very much on the *potjie* master, but stews usually includes meat and vegetables.

Smiley: Describing this township delicacy as an acquired taste would be a definite understatement. We're actually talking about a boiled sheep's head here.

(021 431 5111, www.capetown.one andonlyresorts.com). **Open** 6pm-10.30pm daily. **RRRR**. **Japanese**. Map p91 D4 🅘

World-class master chef Nobuyuki 'Nobu' Matsuhisa has expanded his eponymous empire with the debut of his first restaurant in Africa. No stranger to worldly culinary influences, Nobu gives classical Japanese cuisine a contemporary twist. Diners can indulge in fresh South African seafood and indigenous spices in mesmerising dishes such as sake roast whitefish with jalapeno or the chocolate bento box – a dark chocolate fondant with green tea ice cream and a sesame seed tuile. If overwhelmed by the extensive choice, let your server select for you – it's a guaranteed flavour fest.

Pepenero

Shop 1, Two Oceans Beach, Bay Road, Mouille Point (021 439 9027). **Open** 9am-11pm daily. **RR**. **Contemporary Italian**. Map p90 B3 🅘

Pepe, as it's referred to by its adoring fans, sits right on the Atlantic and is a good bet for relaxed afternoon wine sipping or a more upmarket evening affair. The cheery outside seating area is kitted out in wicker chairs, potted plants, blue and red scatter cushions and blankets in case of a chill, whilst the interior lets its streamlined furniture and sea view do the talking. The food is Italian with a contemporary bent, starring mains like prawn linguine with fennel and parmesan, avocado tagliata, and grilled sole with basil pesto and lemon, and desserts such as the fried choc and banana beignets with honeycomb ice cream.

Sevruga

Shop 4, Quay 5, V&A Waterfront (021 421 5134, www.sevruga.co.za). **Open** 11.30am-11pm daily. **RRR**. **Sushi and Modern International**. Map p91 E5 🅘

The upmarket ambience at this caviar-themed restaurant is maintained with an impressive wine collection and polished interior details like the velvet love couches in the bar. The menu features a generous sprinkling of sevruga caviar along with a plethora vegetarian, seafood, shellfish, poultry and meat options, with everything from aubergine parmigiano to seared tuna fillet and extra large langoustines to roast duck and braised springbok loin. Half-moon portholes offer a great view of the Waterfront for those seated inside – if it's a balmy, an outdoor table is a must.

Signal

Cape Grace Hotel, West Quay, V&A Waterfront (021 410 7080, www. capegrace.com). **Open** 6.30am-late daily. **RRR**. **Contemporary South African**. Map p91 E5 🅘

With panoramic views of Signal Hill, Signal restaurant at the world class Cape Grace Hotel on Quay 5 provides a welcoming setting on the water's edge. Here you can enjoy fresh, local ingredients, not only when the noon cannon signals lunchtime, but at any time of the day. The menu is a unique combination of flavours incorporating influences from the many cultures that called upon this region during its history, namely French, British as well as Dutch and Asian.

Wakame

Cnr Surrey Place and Beach Road, Mouille Point (021 433 2377). **Open** Noon-3pm, 6-10.30pm Mon-Thur; noon-2.30pm, 6-11pm Fri, Sat; noon-2.30pm, 6-10pm Sun. **RR**. **Asian**. Map p90 B3 🅘

Upon entering this swish seaside restaurant you're greeted by the sight of a metre-long wooden reproduction of a tilapia swimming in mid-air above the sushi counter, and a wander up the stairs to Wafu will reveal a school of fish happily finning about in the aquarium built in under the bar. If the hint didn't take, this outfit is big on seafood and Asian dishes, serving everything from sake-and-miso-cured salmon to lemongrass-steamed Alaskan crab. Other favourites include confit Peking duck and the beef wing rib, which is dished up with either shiitake mushroom or green pepper sauce. The homemade wasabi ice cream is the perfect palate cleanser.

Willoughby & Co

Lower Level, Victoria Wharf, V&A Waterfront (021 418 6115, www.willoughbyandco.co.za). **Open** 11.30am-10.30pm daily. **RR. Sushi and Seafood. Map** p91 E4 ㉒

This is the place to go for fresh sushi in the Mother City. Wait for a seat at one of the tables or slip into a stool at the counters (there are many of them) to order your sushi or à la carte favourites. They're famous for their out-of-the-box sushi offerings like the mouthwatering Rainbow Roll Reloaded, the prawn tempura rolls and authentic snacks (edamame and dim sum) to get you started. If you're feeling flush, order a bento box to go, or tuck in and savour.

Shopping

Cape Union Mart

Quay Four Adventure Centre, V&A Waterfront (021 425 4559, www.cape unionmart.co.za). **Open** 9am-9pm daily. **Map** p91 E4 ㉓

Sibling to the massive Canal Walk Adventure Centre (021 555 4692) where you can test drive their ice chamber and climbing wall, this two-floored store has a number of departments – from adventure and hardworking footwear to camping gear, leisure wear (that straddles fashion and function perfectly) and all the goodies for the outdoor lover. A ladieswear section plays host to the popular Poetry brand – expect pretty offerings in natural fibres that are right in line with stylish leisurewear trends.

Carrol Boyes

Shop 6180, Lower Level, Victoria Wharf, V&A Waterfront (021 418 0595, www.carrolboyes.com). **Open** 9am-9pm daily. **Map** p91 E4 ㉔

This South African pewter and silverware stalwart has fans all over the globe thanks to its weighty, organically influenced tableware creations – from letter openers and wine coolers to Carrol's ever-popular carving knife, serving spoons and sugar bowls that make a distinctive style statement in any home. Her store glitters with these handmade creations.

Caviar Fine Foods

Shop 6102, V&A Waterfront (021 418 0909, www.caviar.co.za). **Open** 9am-9pm daily. **Map** p91 E4 ㉕

This little gourmet emporium in the heart of the V&A Waterfront does a roaring trade in lunchtime sushi but if you look at the fridges a little more closely you'll also see posh pantry choices – foie gras, caviar, of course, and salmon for impromptu soirées. They'll cook anything to order – and you can pick anything from homecooked bolognaise to aged slabs of fillet and sushi to go.

Charles Greig

Shop U6224, Victoria Wharf, V&A Waterfront (021 418 4515, www.charlesgreig.co.za). **Open** 9am-9pm daily. **Map** p91 E4 ㉖

Looking for some bespoke bling to add to your repertoire? Owned by the country's leading jewellery dynasty, this five-star jewellery is a haven of beautiful gems – its seasonal collections never fail to wow those who are fortunate enough to get up close and personal with them, and moneyed enough to buy them. Greig is a great bet for classics that'll stand the test of time, and their innovation ensures they're always ahead in the trend stakes too. They are also purveyors of some of the world's biggest timepiece brands – from Chopard to Rolex.

Robben Island Museum p91

Christoff Fine Jewellery

Shop 7217, V&A Waterfront (021 421 0184, www.christoff.co.za). Open 9am-9pm Mon-Sat; 10am-9pm Sun. Map p91 E4 ㉗

The perfect destination for classic and contemporary jewellery lovers – this elegant boutique plays host to bespoke suites of precious jewels, often in myriad colours. Discreet and knowledgeable service ensures a loyal clientele. The understated interior makes the place popular with design-savvy diamond shoppers.

Fabiani

Shop 272, Upper Level, V&A Waterfront (021 425 1810, www.fabiani.co.za). Open 9am-9pm daily. Map p91 E4 ㉘

This super-smart local label is a must-visit for fashion-conscious men. Browse the rails of colourful stripy shirts, pop on a Liberty print trilby or Panama hat, or take the time to try on one of the well-cut suits. The linen shirts stand the test of time while the leisurewear range (which includes pieces from the likes of G Star and Seven for All Mankind) will serve you well on those relaxed days off. The store offer a complimentary alterations service for their garments.

Giovanni's Deliworld

103 Main Road, Green Point (021 434 6893). Open 7.30am-9pm daily. Map p90 C5 ㉙

The city's most authentic Italian deli is the real deal – and then some. Customers can jostle for attention at the lunchtime takeaway counter (which serves everything from curries to schnitzels), rub shoulders with regulars as they pick up their bagel orders and compare notes with fellow food lovers as they eye out patanegro ham, the olives, cheese and pots of foie gras. There are pantry basics galore too, as well as delicious prepacked salads, picnic goodies and heat-and-eat suppers.

Zoom

Shop 6178, Lower Level, Victoria Wharf, V&A Waterfront (021 418 8719, www.universalfootwear.com). Open 9am-9pm daily. Map p90 C5 ㉚

Unlike almost every footwear retailer in South Africa, Zoom shoes designs almost all of its own collections. Expect all the hottest high street styles at impressively low prices – and don't worry if you're not a major slave to the trends, they're a good bet for classic styles that have a sprinkle of the season's latest look.

Naartjie

Shop 136, Victoria Wharf, V&A Waterfront (021 421 5819). Open 9am-9pm daily. Map p91 E4 ㉛

Looking for quintessential SA gear for little people with style? This SA success story brings out several ranges of seasonal coordinates in their trademark cottons and great looking prints. It's quality that's supremely comfy.

Pastimes

Shop 120, Lower Level, Victoria Wharf, V&A Waterfront (021 421 1191). Open 9am-9pm daily. Map p91 E4 ㉜

Older kids and men who're still into toys will love this shop that's filled with things to make, break, bounce, ride and cause havoc with. From cheap and cheerful practical joke paraphernalia to giant puzzles, telescopes, Jboards, model ship kits and the latest must-have gizmo, this one's your best bet.

Red Square

Shop 6206, Upper Level, Victoria Wharf, V&A Waterfront (021 419 8766, www.edgars.co.za). Open 9am-9pm daily. Map p91 E4 ㉝

The shiny, happy department-store style set-up inside one of the country's biggest fashion chains has an excellent selection of big-name brand cosmetics and fragrances.

Shimansky Collection

Shop 210-212, Clocktower Precinct,
V&A Waterfront (021 421 1488,
www.shimansky.co.za). **Open** 9am-9pm
Mon-Sat; 10am-9pm Sun. **Map** p91 E4
34

This local success story is a leading
seller in the diamond and precious jewellery stakes. Look out for the signature My Girl cut that's in a class of its
own and the near perfect Hearts and
Arrow diamond. Tanzanite pieces are
also available, and clients can order off-
the-peg and bespoke pieces with a
quick turnaround time.

Tanzanite International

Shop 118, Clocktower Precinct,
V&A Waterfront (021 421 5488,
www.tanzanite-int.com). **Open** 9am-
9pm daily. **Map** p91 E4 **35**

Precious stones in an unmistakable
blue hue are what this store is about.
As the assistants will tell you –
Tanzanite is a limited resource (some
say likely to become more precious
than diamonds) that is unique to
Africa. Whether you opt for brilliant
blue statement pieces or closer-to-pur-
ple coloured items, there's no doubt
you'll be making a style statement.

Toy Kingdom

Shop 005, Lower Level, Breakwater
Parking Garage, Breakwater
Boulevard, V&A Waterfront (021 421
1192, http://toykingdom.co.za). **Open**
9am-9pm daily. **Map** p91 D4 **36**

Don't think you'll walk out of this fabulous emporium empty-handed – from
dress-up clothes for little princesses to
soft and cuddlies, the latest, greatest
Lego offerings, Hello Kitty, Barbie and
their friends, games, action figures,
trains sets …you get the picture. A
treasure trove for young and old.

Uwe Koetter

Shop 14, V&A Arcade, V&A
Waterfront (021 421 1039, www.uwe
koetter.co.za). **Open** 9am-9pm Mon-Sat;
10am-9pm Sun. **Map** p91 E4 **37**

Uwe and Magda Koetter are the industry's power couple and their sets and
individual pieces have been snapped
up by many a visiting celebrity. Aside
from their bold diamond pieces, their
African-influenced creations (like their
precious stone bangle range) are a
sight to behold.

Uzzi

Shop 269, Upper Level, Victoria
Wharf, V&A Waterfront (021 418
0334/www.uzzi.co.za). **Open** 9am-9pm
daily. **Map** p91 E4 **38**

A must for the twenty- and thirtysomething stylemonger – this bou-
tique-style store is filled with edgier
Italian-inspired high-street styles than
its mainstream sibling stores in the
Truworths stable. Bomber jackets,
great going out shirts and a well-cut
range of trousers for work and play are
their signatures.

Victoria Wharf

V&A Waterfront (021 408 7600/
www.waterfront.co.za). **Open**
9am-9pm daily. **Map** p91 E4 **39**

With a seemingly never-ending list of
places to swipe that plastic, this enormous mall is a shopping, eating and
entertainment destination on the harbour's edge, linked to a number of mini
malls and shopping precincts within
the V&A Waterfront.

Wordsworth

Shop 7103, Lower Level, Victoria
Wharf, V&A Waterfront (021 425
6880, www.wordsworth.co.za). **Open**
9am-10pm Tues-Sun; 10am-9.30pm Sun,
Mon. **Map** p91 E4 **40**

This popular chain of stores is a comfortable marriage of commercial success and corner store management
style. The difference is their staff – well
read, interested folk who are encouraged to share their opinions with customers. You'll find gorgeous gift books,
all the bestsellers and an in-store travel book shop that's a boon for those
with wanderlust.

CAPE TOWN BY AREA

Vista Bar

Nightlife

Jade Champagne Bar & Lounge

39 Main Road, Green Point (021 439 4108/www.jadelounge. co.za). **Open** 8pm-2am Wed-Sat. **Map** p90 C5 ㊷

The lounge bar is where you can relax in comfort, especially if you find yourself an artful little nook, and the dance floor is the place to boogie, giving you the best of both worlds. The crowd is slightly older (over 23), smart and stylish.

Vista Bar

One and Only Resort, Dock Road, Victoria & Alfred Waterfront (021 431 5888/www.oneandonly resorts.com). **Open** 6.30am-1am daily. **Map** p91 D4 ㊸

Vista Bar at One&Only Cape Town is the ideal party spot for the more discerning reveller. By day, the venue offers great views of Table Mountain as well as an excellent high tea, featuring a choice of 35 delicious brews and a selection of good snacks. Once night falls, the space comes into its own, as hotel guests and visitors alike congregate for cocktails around the circular bar or in front of the floor-to-ceiling windows. Come Friday nights the place is transformed into an elegant end of week party venue with local DJs.

Arts & Leisure

Cinema Nouveau

Lower level, Kings Warehouse, V&A Waterfront (082 16789/www.ster kinekor.com). **Map Map** p91 E4 ㊹

Ster Kinekor's alternative option in the world of cinema brings you the latest arthouse releases as well as ballets, operas and the odd film festival. Its handy free magazine, *Film Finesse*, available in the foyer, gets you clued up on current shows and coming attractions. For folks who prefer a shot of java with their daily dose of culture there's also coffee and shortbread.

Green Dolphin

Victoria & Alfred Arcade, V&A Waterfront (021 421 7471). **Map** p91 E4 ㊺

The Green Dolphin undoubtedly falls under the city's top five jazz venues, with live performances every night and a side order of exceptional dining thrown in too (expect continental, seafood and pasta specialities). It even has its own three-volume CD collection and has hosted big names such as Herb Ellis, Natalie Cole and Jim Galloway. Also look out for award-winning African diva Judith Sephuma and, if you're visiting during the winter, the Johnnie Walker Jazz Sessions.

Nu Metro

Shop 223, Victoria Wharf, V&A Waterfront (021 419 9700/www. numetro.co.za/www.waterfront.co.za). **Map Map** p91 E4 ㊻

Although mainstream fare is the name of the game here, the country's second largest cinema chain also has a few surprises up its sleeve.

OneWellness Spa

The Radisson Hotel, Beach Road, Granger Bay (021 441 3000, www. radisson.com). **Open** 8am-8pm daily. **Map** p90 C3 ㊼

With an ideal location close to the V&A Waterfront and the rest of the Atlantic Seaboard, this quality spa is perfect for visitors who want to get in some pampering during their stay. Aside from the expected beauty offerings, this spa also carries the Pevonia range of products and offers various body treatments (such as the Pevonia Tropicale deageing experience) that rejuvenate and revitalise. Enjoy your après spa time by ordering a cocktail at the hotel's terrace bar overlooking the ocean.

Sea Point Promenade

Three Anchor Bay to Bantry Bay

Set between Sea Point and **Mouille Point**, the seaside area of **Three Anchor Bay** is home to **Signal Hill**, the site of the city's booming noon gun and a popular picnic place due to its show-stopping view over the harbour and Cape Town Stadium. The seaside enclave encompasses a small beach and starfish-filled rock pools, and is a popular destination for kayakers and surfers.

Sea Point, Cape Town's most densely populated suburb, is home to a large sector of the city's gay and Jewish communities. Sea Point is known for its miscellany of seafront high-rises (some glamorous, others looking rather worse for wear), a buzzing promenade, and an Olympic-size seawater pool complex. Its buzzing Main Road is a little bit run-down in patches and houses the city's unofficial Chinatown; it has

generous sprinkling of Chinese takeaway joints, as well as a burgeoning restaurant sector.

Headed towards Clifton side, **Bantry Bay** is hot property among moneyed holidaymakers and those fortunate enough to live here full-time, given that it's the most wind-free area in the city, enjoying an average of just less than 300 gust-free days per year. Swanky penthouse apartments atop multi-storey blocks and sprawling properties built at the turn of the last century rub shoulders with five-star and boutique hotels on this smart stretch of the Atlantic Seaboard, all of them safe in the knowledge that theirs is possibly the best view of the sea in the city. Enjoy a stroll along this picturesque stretch of coastline and perhaps pop in to one of the hotels for a cheeky sundowner while you're at it.

Three Anchor Bay
to Bantry Bay

0   300 m
0   300 yds
© Copyright Time Out Guides 2011

A T L A N T I C

O C E A N

Graaff's Pool

SEAPOINT

Saunders
Rocks

QUEENS RD

Bantry Bay

BANTRY
BAY

1st Beach
Clifton

LION'S HEAD WALK
Lion's Head
669 m

Green
Point

Mouille Point
Lighthouse
Dolls House

Three Anchor
Bay

THREE ANCHOR
BAY

❶ Sights & museums
❶ Eating & drinking
❶ Shopping
❶ Nightlife
❶ Art & leisure

Time Out Shortlist | Cape Town **107**

Sights & museums

Mouille Point Lighthouse

100 Beach Road, Mouille Point (021 449 5172). **Open** 10am-3pm Mon-Fri. **Admission** R16 adults; R8-10 reductions. **No credit cards.** **Map** p107 C1 ❶

This rectangular, red and white striped beacon on the water's edge was erected in 1824 and the name descends from the Dutch, who commissioned the construction of a breakwater (*moilje*) as a defence against the Atlantic's havoc-wreaking waves. The task proved more difficult than anticipated and the project was abandoned after three years. In 1781 the French built a battery near the breakwater and named it Mouille. Some 43 years later, the lighthouse was completed, and two score ago, it was declared a national monument – today it is an ever present fixture on this pretty promenade and a regular backdrop for bridal party shoots.

Sea Point Promenade

Beach Road, Sea Point (swimming pool 021 434 3341). **Open** *Winter* 9am-5pm daily. *Summer* 7am-7pm daily. **Admission** R15 adults; free-R7 reductions. **Map** p107 B2 ❷

Snaking its way along the Atlantic, The Promenade or 'Prom' as it's known by locals, is a favoured destination for early morning jogs, after-work walks and all the ice-cream eating you can manage in between. While the adults do their tai chi and stretching exercises on the lawns, kids can work off excess energy running around and scrambling over the jungle gym. On Sundays, informal soccer games provide entertainment aplenty. Water babies can get in their day's worth of strokes at the Sea Point swimming pool complex which includes an Olympic size saltwater pool and its share of regulars come winter or summer weather. Of course, one of the best promenade activities remains sitting on a bench and staring out at the ocean.

Eating & drinking

La Bohème & La Bruixa

341 Main Road, Sea Point (021 434 8797, www.labohemebistro.co.za). **Open** 7.30am-10pm Mon-Sat. **RR**. **Tapas/café**. **Map** p107 B3 ❸

Stepping off Main Street into the canopied *stoep* on Sea Point's ever-buzzing main strip, the door on the left hand side is for La Bohème and the one on the right for La Bruixa, but if you prefer to dine from the menu of the first in the second locale, or vice versa, you're more than welcome. La Bruixa is the smaller and more relaxed of the pair, with a deli menu including authentic Spanish tapas staples like white anchovies on bruschetta or chorizo with homemade gnocchi, whereas La Bohème sports a more upmarket, roomier dining area with an open-plan kitchen which whips up ribsticking bistro fare like slow-roasted pork belly with mustard mash and apple, and roasted duck with caraway cabbage.

Caffé Neo

129 Beach Road, Mouille Point (021 433 0849). **Open** 9am-11pm daily. **RR**. **Café**. **Map** p107 C1 ❹

For Greek food in a contemporary setting, beautiful sea views and an achingly cool local crowd, head for this comfortable Mouille Point fixture that's situated diagonally across from the Mouille Point lighthouse. Mezze platters, generous sandwiches and laden breakfast plates ensure an all-day crowd who natter away over cappuccino's while drinking in the views.

The Cedar

The Courtyard Building, 100 Main Road, Sea Point (021 433 2546). **Open** 11am-2pm, 5pm-late Mon-Sat. **R**. **Lebanese**. **Map** p107 C2 ❺

Run by David and Marlene Davids, this unfussy eaterie serves up authentic Lebanese comfort food with aplomb. Apart from the regular menu, with veggie-friendly staples like baba ghanoush

Harvey's at the Mansions p111

Blink p112

and houmous, as well as kibbeh balls, falafel and lamb shwarma, the Davidses also prepare at least one off-the-menu item, which can include anything from malfouf (cabbage stuffed with a lamb mince and rice filling and served with tart pomegranate syrup) to sugar beans and chicken in a tomato, garlic and coriander sauce. Make sure to ask them what's cooking – they'll be sure to offer you a taste of whatever's on the stove.

Duchess of Wisbeach

The Courtyard Building, 3 Wisbeach Road, Sea Point (021 434 1525).
Open 6.30-10.30pm Mon-Sat. **RR**.
Comfort Food. Map p107 C2 ⑥
Two classic cameos face each other on opposite sides of a bright red door, setting the scene for the humorous grand-meets-grotty ambience inside. The main dining room is kitted out in a miscellany of classical and kitsch apparel (think Victorian chairs and white starched table cloths accented with twee porcelain doggies). The food, though it doesn't take itself too seriously either, is comfort fare at its best, featuring fillet with mustard béarnaise and chips, classic cottage pie and roasted baby peri-peri chicken. The hot sticky apricot pudding with fudge sauce is the perfect way to end your meal.

Harvey's at the Mansions

Winchester Mansions, 221 Beach Road, Sea Point (021 434 2351, www.winchester.co.za). **Open** 7am-10pm daily. **RR**. **Modern Global**.
Map p107 B2 ⑦
The sunny courtyard of this grand Cape Dutch manor house is definitely where you want to spend a languid boozy lunch, whilst the classic interior overlooking gently swishing palms and Sea Point's snippet of the Atlantic makes for a soothing dinner experience. Starters include the signature Harvey's salad niçoise with dukkah-spiced tuna, while a dinner must-have is the beef fillet with pesto-potato gratin, baby-marrow flan and tomato-and-Pernod jus. Something

of a grande old dame on the Sea Point strip – the air of gentility is intoxicating.

La Mouette

78 Regent Road, Sea Point (021 433 0856, www.lamouette.co.za). **Open** Noon-3pm Tue-Sun; 6pm-10pm Tue-Sat. **RRR**. **Modern international**.
Map p107 A4 ⑧
The gentle trickle of a four-tiered fountain set in the palm-tree-lined courtyard (a coveted seating area in summer) welcomes you as you step out of the din of Main Road. The grand Tudor-style structure houses several hearthed dining areas, opulently dressed for the occasion in damask wallpaper. Chef Henry Vigar is at the helm, and since he has worked with culinary luminaries like Gordon Ramsay, you can bet your bottom dollar the food will be good. Expect contemporary fare like duck confit with red cabbage, gnocchi with mushrooms, shallots and gorgonzola, and beef sirloin with mash and bordelaise sauce. For dessert dip into the deconstructed G&T, composed of gin syrup, tonic jelly and lime ice-cream.

La Perla

Beach Road and Church Street, Sea Point (021 434 2471, www.la perla.co.za). **Open** 10am-late daily.
RR. **Italian**. Map p107 B3 ⑨
Nestled up against the sparkling Atlantic, this Sea Point institution's doors slide right open on sunny days to let the fresh sea breeze inside. Its been going for decades now and still the vast verandah with its mosaic fountain is swamped with Chardonnay- quaffing regulars on fair-weather days, whilst the interior beckons diners with a superb collection of local artworks on loan from Stellenbosch's SMAC Gallery. Authentic Italian food is on the menu, featuring crowd-pleasers like the always delicious sirloin tagliata on rocket leaves drizzled with olive oil, chilli and garlic, veal saltimbocca, crumbed sole and epic seafood platters. Old-school

CAPE TOWN BY AREA

seafood and steaks with a dash of style – the waiting staff, in their traditional coats, are equally old-school.

Posticino

3 Albany Mews, 323 Main Road, Sea Point (021 439 4014). **Open** 12.30-10pm daily. **RR. Italian.** Map p107 B2 ⓾

Fronted by friendly stripy awnings and green umbrellas, this Italian mainstay enjoys a special place in many a Capetonian's heart thanks to its authentic, always-excellent, offerings. The first thing that strikes you is the smell of the prized thin-based pizzas baking in the wood-burning oven. Favourites include panna (smoked salmon, cream cheese and caviar) and strega (chicken livers and onion fried in wine and peri peri sauce). Home-made pasta is also excellent, and you can customise it with your choice of sauce. Booking is advised.

Salt

The Ambassador Hotel, 34 Victoria Road, Bantry Bay (021 439 7258). **Open** 12.30-3pm, 6.30-10pm daily. **RR. Modern Global.** Map p107 A4 ⓫

Elegant simplicity is king at this venue, which is revered for its amazing view over Bantry Bay. The menu is chic and contemporary. Start off with something like endive, pear and smoked rosa tomatoes with aubergine caviar, or rilette of pork with apple purée, then move onto mains like duck confit with miso broth or springbok loin with white cabbage and cherry jus. The adjoining vodka and champagne bar serves up a menu of quality liquid offerings.

Shopping

Blink

71 Regent Road, opposite Checkers, Sea Point (021 434 0541). **Open** 9am-5pm Mon-Fri; 9am-2pm Sat. **Map** p107 B4 ⓬

Blink majors on contemporary, locally made handcrafted and designer wares. Some of the country's finest producers are represented here – you'll find tea towels by much-loved textile talent

Heather Moore, tableware by cult brand Wonki Ware and nature-inspired napery by Veldt.

Slick

359A Main Road, Sea Point (021 433 1050, www.slickonline.co.za). **Open** 9am-5pm Mon-Fri; 9am-noon Sat. **Map** p107 B3 ⓭

Expect all the perfect fashionable basics, and all the trimmings too (like the perfect slouchy handbag or gladiator sandals). There's lots of cotton stretchy finds and plenty of comfortable essentials that don't skimp on style - great prices for on-trend fashions without losing out on class.

Nightlife

Decodance Underground

120B Main Road, Sea Point (079 608 9855,www.decodance.co.za). **Open** 8.30pm-2am Wed-Thur. **Admission** Free before 10pm, R30 after. **No credit cards.** Map p107 C2 ⓮

This club, specialising in 1980s and alternative music, has a new home in Sea Point. There are now two dancefloors (one for non-smokers) and facilities for live music, comedy and karaoke. The vibe is still the same, with the best party music, themed dress-up parties, and great music and decor. It's for the more mature – no under-22s, and all-dressed-up is a mode that's appreciated.

Arts & Leisure

Winchester Mansions

221 Beach Road, Sea Point (021 434 2351, www.winchester.co.za). **Open** 11am-2pm Sun. **Map** p107 B2 ⓯

Daytime jazz is something of a rarity in Cape Town, but the big Sunday brunch here is a great alternative for music lovers who aren't night owls. Eat in the beautiful courtyard and enjoy a complimentary glass of champagne and the Sunday paper while the live band pumps out Afro-influenced, laid-back standards.

Bejazzled

The cream of the crop of Cape Town's jazz musos.

South African music has always been revolutionary. As legendary pianist Abdullah Ibrahim remarks in the documentary *Amandla!* the toppling of apartheid was the first revolution ever to be conducted 'in four-part harmony'. Years after apartheid's demise, the Mother City jazz scene that birthed the world famous Ibrahim (formerly known as Dollar Brand) has lost none of its revolutionary edge... but it has reinvented the harmony. A new generation of musical freedom fighters is aggressively reclaiming jazz as the future sound of South Africa's urban youth. Leading the charge are post-bop strategists the Restless Natives, whose home-grown sound adds a funky gonzo undertone to canonical Blue Note-era bop material. They're joined by improvisational engineers Closet Snare, whose bitching brew of trumpet, guitar, bass and drums chased with turntable wizardry unites past and future, making music that's both fun and forward-looking. Elsewhere Afro-Indo fusion crew Babu synchronises ambient Indian guitar ragas with increasingly progressive jazz-rock rhythms in a global gang of sheer talent that keeps the crowds coming back time and time again. There is a restless intensity to all this music, but the performers never lose the collective thread. As drummer Kesivan Naidoo, who plays for all three combos, explains, 'We're just a funky bunch of guys who really love the jazz tradition. We respect the past, but we're also trying to forge a South African sound into that.' Sassy sax man Rus Nerwich, who combines acid jazz with urban rap, agrees. 'It's a collective imagination. The whole point is a musical collective of artists that have a diverse set of influences.' For those who prefer the comfort of old-school scatting, there are jazz bars and clubs scattered across the city – from **Brio 1893** (ABC Building, 130 Adderley Street 021 422 0654/ www.brio1893.com) where owner Skippy, a passionate jazzman, breaks into song on a whim, to much loved fave the **Green Dolphin** (see p105), a longstanding stalwart on the city jazz scene, with different bands, singers and saxophonists doing their thing every night.

Clifton

Clifton & Camps Bay

Home to some of the most expensive stretches of seaside property in South Africa, the wealthy mountainside suburb of **Clifton** – referred to by some as the Monaco of Cape Town – is renowned among locals and tourists both for its sophisticated and glamorous beachfront apartment buildings and high design homes as well as its four adjacent beaches that are separated by clusters of granite boulders. Each of these beaches has a distinct personality. Towards the north (closest to Sea Point) lies **First Beach**, the largest of the four and with the strongest surf should you be brave enough to swim in these icy waters. **Second Beach** is known for the strutting of the muscled gay set who religiously frequent it. **Third Beach** is a great family beach and the preferred destination for those who come armed with beach bats and frisbees while **Fourth Beach is** the busiest and most elite of the lot, with many a yacht throwing anchor in its calm, turquoise waters (it's also the shortest climb up to the road).

Along from swanky Clifton lies its equally affluent neighbour **Camps Bay**. This hive of activity is the city's Copacabana. Hugging the shoreline, Victoria Road is the main hub. The palm-fringed beach and tidal pool is always buzzing with sun worshippers on pleasant days, as are the glitzy pavement cafés, restaurants and clubs that have been graced by celebrities such as Leonardo DiCaprio and Robbie Williams. Hotspots like Caprice and Baraza remain the places to be seen quaffing cocktails. South of here and also worth mentioning for its glam factor is the Twelve Apostles Hotel & Spa (see p178), which contains a noteworth restaurant and bar and even a cinema.

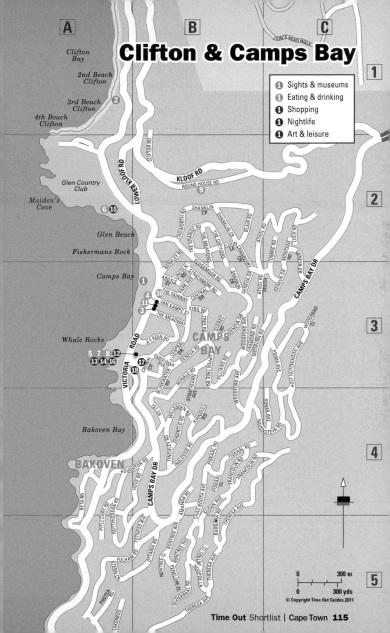

Clifton & Camps Bay

Clifton Bay

2nd Beach Clifton

3rd Beach Clifton

4th Beach Clifton

- ① Sights & museums
- ① Eating & drinking
- ① Shopping
- ① Nightlife
- ① Art & leisure

LION'S HEAD WALK

A | B | C

1

2

3

4

5

CLIFTON RD

LOWER KLOOF RD

KLOOF RD

ROUND HOUSE RD

Glen Country Club

Maiden's Cove

Glen Beach

Fishermans Rock

Camps Bay

Whale Rocks

Bakoven Bay

BAKOVEN

VICTORIA ROAD

CAMPS BAY DR

CAMPS BAY DR

CAMPS BAY

SHANKLIN CR

SHANKLIN CR

CHILWORTH RD

THE GRANGE RD

THE MEADWAY

THE CHEVIOTS

SEDGEMOOR RD

STRATHMORE RD

SHANKLIN

BLAIR RD

ELDON LA

CRANBERG RD

GENEVA DR

ATHOL RD

COMRIE RD

MONTAGNE RD

LOCH RD

GENCALDA

CAMPS BAY DR

BERKLEY RD

LINCOLN RD

ARGYLE ST

PARK AVE

CENTRAL DR

THE FAIRWAY

SYBIL RD

QUEBEC RD

TREE RD

GENEVA DR

WOODFORD AVE

OAKHURST AVE

WOODHEAD CL

A K KEEN RD

CENTRAL DR

FAROUHAR

GENEVA AVE

FIELD RD

FILTRACE RD

PRELLER RD

PRIMA AVE

HOLY HUTCHINSON AVE

CROWN

BLINKWATER

ROMALD RD

RONDALD RD

STRATHMORE AVE

WOODFORD AVE

HORAK AVE

RAVENSTEIN RD

LISTER RD

WILLSDEN RD

RUNNEFELD RD

KINNOULL

INGLESIDE RD

FINCHLEY RD

HOUE RD

FISKAAL RD

FISKAAL RD

FISKAAL RD

FRANKLLIN RD

FRANCOLIN RD

FISKAAL

BARROWE AVE

HOUGHTON RD

BETA RD

PITLOCHRY RD

ROTTINGDEAN RD

OTTNESS AVE

FULHAM RD

ST NELLS RD

PROTEA RD

UKEMBOS

THERESA AVE

OLDERKRAAL RD

PETREL CL

THERESA CL

THERESA AVE

PENELOPE CL

RONTREE RD

RONTREE CL

OTTWIL RD

RONTREE AVE

AMANDA RD

CHAS BOOTH AVE

SUSAN AVE

THERESA AVE

② ⑥ ⑮ ⑨ ① ④ ⑩ ⑪ ③ ⑤ ⑦ ⑧ ⑫ ⑬ ⑭ ⑯ ⑰ ⑱

0   300 m
0   300 yds

© Copyright Time Out Guides 2011

Sights & museums

Camps Bay
Victoria Road, Camps Bay.
Map p115 B3 ❶
This flush stretch overlooking the Atlantic isn't called Cape Town's Copacabana for nothing. Besides the palm-flanked, shimmery beach and tranquil tidal pool, it's known for its collection of swanky restaurants, cocktail bars and clubs, which attracts a perfectly tanned, hair-straightened, designer-sunglass-wearing crowd. Easily accessible, with no stairs, it's popular from early – with morning walkers – until late, when the Capetonians make their way from work for supper and sundowners on the beach. Note that alcohol is banned on beaches throughout South Africa; so make sure your beverage is of the non-alcoholic variety.

Clifton
Victoria Road, Clifton. **Map** p115 A1 ❷
The city's most famous four beaches are dotted along a sparkling piece of Atlantic Seaboard coastline and each has its own unique atmosphere and set of regulars who think of it as their summery home from home. Park up on the road (warning: parking's a nightmare in these parts in summer, so you'd do well to come by taxi) and make sure you've got all your beach essentials before making your way down the steep stairs to reach your beach of choice. First and second beach are the quietest of the lot, popular with families and, on the rare days when wind threatens to ruin things, the most sheltered. Weave your way through the boulders to third beach, unofficial gay beach where throngs of bronzed boys eye each other up. Fourth beach is the one closest to Camps Bay and the stretch of sand most popular for ball sports and frisbee games. It's also closest to La Med if an après-beach sundowner is what you have in mind.

Eating & drinking

Bayside Café
51 Victoria Road, Camps Bay (021 438 2650). **Open** 9am-11pm Mon-Sat, 9am-10pm Sunday **RR**. **Steaks & grills**.
Map p115 B3 ❸
This old-school steak house with its signature dark-green tablecloths is a Camps Bay institution, thanks to the always outstanding grills (try the memorable ribs and steaks) and selection of seafood temptations. Crammed with locals young and old, conveniently situated across the road from the beach and offering generous two-for-one specials in the winter months, when it comes to ribsticking fare, this one's a surefire winner.

Café Caprice
37 Victoria Road, Camps Bay (021 438 8315, www.cafecaprice.co.za). **Open** 9am-late daily. **RR**. **Café**.
Map p115 B3 ❹
For years now this has been one of the coolest hang-outs in Camps Bay. Busy pavement café and restaurant by day but after another of those magnificent sunsets, it's all about cocktails and partying with the beautiful people. There are queues and bouncers, lithe young things eyeing each other up, a mix of local and international DJs, and some dancing too. Great cocktails soothe parched throats and they're as famous for their giant burgers as for the glossy posses parking their smart cars outside.

Kove
Shop 2B, The Promenade, Camps Bay (021 438 0004, www.thekove.co.za). **Open** Noon-10.30 daily. **R**. **Grills**.
Map p115 B3 ❺
Autumn-coloured vines and an ivy-clad wall set the scene at this otherwise monochromatic and streamlined restaurant in the heart of the action in Camps Bay. The wood-smoked *braai* is quite a local-flavoured novelty, resulting in lip-smacking eats such as

venison-rich Kove kebab, crayfish with your choice of lemon or peri-peri butter and succulent baby-back ribs basted in a secret sauce. If barbecue isn't your bag, opt for signature dishes like the laden seafood platter or the châteaubriand steak.

La Med

Glen Country Club, Victoria Road, Clifton (021 438 5600, www.lamed. co.za). **Open** 11am-late Mon-Fri; 9am-late Sat-Sun. **RR**. **Bar/Restaurant**. **Map** p115 A1 ➏

With the ocean on one side and the magnificent Table Mountain and Twelve Apostles on the other, sports bar cum nightclub and live music venue La Med has one of the best locations in Cape Town. In summer, it's easy to go from beach to cocktail hour, and on Sunday nights the gigantic bar transforms itself into a heaving nightclub crammed with twentysomethings partying the night away. In winter it's a warm and cosy venue, with roaring fires and comfy lounges; rugby is the sport of choice on the big screen TV's. Enjoy delicious pizzas, DJs playing sundowner sets and an all-round great vibe.

Paranga

Shop 1, The Promenade, Victoria Road, Camps Bay (021 438 0404, www.paranga.co.za). **Open** 9am-10.30pm daily. **RR**. **Cocktail Bar/seafood**. **Map** p115 B3 ➐

Set on Camps Bay's platinum mile, this stylish restaurant creates a suitably swish impression with its rough-hewn stone walls, monochromatic cappuccino colour scheme and dramatic damask bolster cushions. As can be expected, there's a strong focus on seafood, with favourites including shellfish platters, the signature Patagonian calamari tubes, and baby salmon trout served with strawberry and spring-onion salsa. But with treats like Moroccan-style beef medallions and ostrich fillet basted in red wine,

Secret beaches

Beta Beach

Map p115 A4.

It's easy to miss this sandy little patch, flanked by big boulders, in the posh suburb of Bakoven, just ten minutes' drive from the city centre. From Beta Road, look out for a small walkway between houses leading to the beach.

Oudekraal

Map p115 A4.

Right next door to Beta Beach. It's a protected cove at the bottom of a steep set of stairs, surrounded by a thicket of milkwood trees. There's an R10 entrance fee. Take the first signposted right turn after passing the Twelve Apostles Hotel on Victoria Road.

Smitswinkelbaai

Look out for a tiny gravelled parking area by the side of the road between Simon's Town and the Cape of Good Hope Nature Reserve. Park, cross the road and take a 15-minute amble down the overgrown footpath until you reach the unspoilt, isolated Smitswinkelbaai.

Tietiesbaai

Part of the Cape Columbine Reserve, two hours' drive north of the city. From Paternoster, take a left at the four-way stop and go straight on until you see the Tietiesbaai signpost.

These secluded beaches are not immune to crime. Always go in a group and never leave your valuables unattended.

Roundhouse

meat eaters won't feel left out either. A favourite with the city's beautiful people who come out for cocktails dressed to impress.

Pepper Club

Shop 2A, The Promenade, Victoria Road, Camps Bay (021 438 9551, www.pepperclubonthebeach.co.za). **Open** Noon-11.30pm daily. **RR**. **Cocktail bar**. Map p115 B3 ❽
With a slew of classic cocktails to choose from, this smart seafront restaurant and cocktail bar is a favourite among Camps Bay's styled-to-a-tee bar hoppers. It's a sin not to sit on the canopied deck overlooking the Atlantic if the sun's out, but when the south-easterly wind starts up, you can still enjoy the stunning sea view from indoors. Seafood and sushi are definitely at the top of the list when it comes to food, with meaty mains like the venison hunter's pot, herb-crusted ostrich and rosemary-and-red-wine lamb shank coming in close second.

Roundhouse

Kloof Road, The Glen, Camps Bay (021 438 4347, www.theroundhouserestaurant.com). **Open** Noon-3pm Wed-Sun; 6-9pm Tue-Sat. **RRRR**. **Haute cuisine**. Map p115 B2 ❾
Set in a renovated hunting lodge in The Glen up above Camps Bay, the gun room now serves as the entrance hall to this culinary hotspot. Evenings see Chef PJ Vadas pull out all the stops with his award-winning French fare. Hits include a 24-hour roasted pork belly with white bean cassoulet and calvados jus, and warthog fillet with roast pumpkin and chocolate jus. For dessert, expect the likes of passion fruit soufflé with coconut ice-cream, and quince tarte tatin with spiced ice-cream. In summer, the outside dining area, the Rumbullion, is a lively alfresco space dotted with people enjoying their baskets stuffed with a choice of homemade pickles, freshly baked bread, cheese and charcuterie.

Sandbar

31 Victoria Road, Camps Bay (021 438 8336, www.sandbar.co.za). **Open** 9.30am-10pm (last rounds at 11pm) daily. **RR**. **Cocktails bar/café**. Map p115 B3 ❿
The light, cheery pavement café and cocktail bar, with its white tables overlooking the ocean, sets the seaside mood. Relaxed Balearic beats and the famous jam-jar-mixed cocktails add to the summertime vibe. Breakfasts – encompassing everything from eggs benedict to vegetarian omelettes – are a big draw for sustenance after a beach walk, while popular main courses include spinach and spicy chicken salad and ostrich burger topped with rocket, onion rings, pineapple and tomato salsa.

Tuscany Beach Restaurant

41 Victoria Road, Camps Bay (021 438 1213, www.tuscanybeachrestaurant.com). **Open** 8am-10pm daily. **RR**. **Cocktail bar/Italian**. Map p115 B3 ⓫
The red interior of this popular Camps Bay cocktail joint entices passers-by to take a seat, order a cocktail and wait for the sun to set over the Atlantic. The epic menu has an Italian slant and pleases most, with plenty of safe bets like salads, sushi platters, seafood, pastas, pizzas and meat dishes. A great place to stop for oysters and champagne after the beach.

Shopping

Martine's on the Bay

7 The Promenade (021 438 2325). **Open** 10am-6pm Mon-Fri, 10am-6pm Sat 12-6pm Sunday. **Map** p115 B3 ⓬
It's been around for 15 years and still this bastion of great style and ladies' fashion continues to surprise, with its concentrated seasonal collections. You'll find a slew of local designers like Maya Prass and Desray, both of whom excel in easy-to-wear, style-driven garments, while international labels such as Metallicus and Desigual also stand out as leading brands to browse.

Rainbow swimwear

2 The Promenade Camps Bay, Victoria Road, Camps Bay (021 438 2087). **Open** 9am-6pm daily. **Map** p115 B3 ⑬

Looking for something that'll turn heads on the beach? Visit this cult store that stocks brands like the ever-popular Love Water Love. Board shorts and bikinis (as well as flattering full pieces) and all the beach paraphernalia are their game.

Nightlife

Karma Lounge

Victoria Road, Camps Bay (021 438 7773, www.karmalounge.co.za). **Open** 9pm-2am Fri-Sun. **Admission** R50-R100. **Map** p115 B3 ⑭

These days locals tend to avoid Camps Bay in the summer, finding it overpopulated with tourists, but there are good reasons for that – the beach is beautiful and our own sunset strip is crammed with restaurants for pavement eating and drinking. And then there is Karma for the more serious business of partying the night away. It's upmarket for an over-23 clientele and embraces a wide range of music styles, from house to Latino, hip hop to electro.

La Med

Glen Country Club, Victoria Road, Clifton (021 438 5600/www.lamed. co.za). **Open** 11am-late Mon-Fri; 9am-late Sat-Sun. **Map** p115 A2 ⑮

With the ocean on one side and the magnificent Table Mountain and Twelve Apostles on the other, La Med has to have one of the best locations in Cape Town. In summer, it's easy to go from beach to bar, and in winter the place transforms into a warm cosy venue with roaring fires and comfy lounges, where rugby is the sport of choice on TV. Enjoy delicious pizzas, DJs playing sundowner sets and an all-round great vibe at this popular hangout.

Sapphire

The Promenade, Victoria Road, Camps Bay (021 438 1758, www.sapphirecocktailbar.com). **Open** 5pm-2am Mon-Thur; noon-2am Fri. **Map** p115 B3 ⑯

Overlooking the ocean and its spectacular sunset views Sapphire offers the perfect setting for a laid-back cocktail from the extensive menu, which blends seamlessly into an entertaining night out. From the bar you can order champagnes, cap classiques, premium beers and red or white wines, and to snack on there are various platters and light meals. Live acts and DJs set the party mood.

Arts & Leisure

Dizzy's

41 The Drive, Camps Bay (021 438 2686, 021 438 7328, www.dizzys.co.za). **Open** noon-4am daily (no live bands Mon). **Map** p115 B3 ⑰

Local landmark Dizzy's dishes up the best of both worlds – excellent burgers and seafood fare in their restaurant, and an adjacent space for experimental ska, acoustic and rock bands, from the Rudimentals to muchl oved local band Bed on Bricks to Checkered Zebra. And if you happen to lose all inhibition there's karaoke too, which all makes for a welcome relaxation of Camp's Bay's usual posh pretensions.

Theatre on the Bay

1 Link Street, Camps Bay (021 438 3300, www.theatreonthebay.co.za). **Map** p115 B3 ⑱

You'll find this popular theatre beneath swooping seagulls and a cheesy concrete-curtained façade. This brain child of theatre impresario Pieter Toerien is a legend on the Camps Bay strip and produces a variety of musicals, comedy and cabaret, with the odd drama to spice up the pot. Broadway hits (like *Evita*, *Hair* and *Chess*), starring local actors, are especially popular.

Hout Bay

Hout Bay & Southern Peninsula

Hout Bay

The small seaside town of **Hout Bay** is accessible via the beautiful, winding Chapman's Peak Drive, which is carved out of the mountain, or the equally picturesque Constantia Nek pass. It boasts a kilometre-long family-friendly beach and picturesque harbour.

Sights

Boat Trips to Seal Island
Hout Bay Harbour
Circle Launches *(021 790 1040, www.circlelaunches.co.za).* **Trips** 8.45am (pre-booked), 9.30am, 10.15am, 11.10am (pre-booked) daily; longer hours Sat-Sun. **Tickets** R42.50 adults; R15 under-13s.
Nauticat Charters *(021 790 7278, www.nauticatcharters.co.za).* **Trips** 8.45am, 9.45am, 11am, 12.30pm, 2.30pm, 3.30pm daily (weather permitting). **Tickets** R60 adults; R30 under-12s.

Drumbeat Charters *(082 658 7055, 021 791 4441, www.drumbeatcharters. co.za).* **Trips** 8.30am (min 15 people), 9:15am, 10am, 10:45am (min 15 people). **Cost** R60 adults; R25 children (2-14 years). **No credit cards**.
Head to Hout Bay harbour if you're keen on the least expensive and most easygoing options for getting out to sea. Stock up on some fish and chips at Mariner's Wharf bistro for an on-board feast while your progeny play below deck, glueing themselves to the glass window to see the underwater performance from the Cape Fur seals off Duiker Island. There's no better way to see the Sentinel, a majestic peak jutting out from the water, with sheer cliff face reaching for the sky. The boats have on-board cash bars.

Chapman's Peak Drive
Between Hout Bay & Noordhoek (021 790 9163, www.chapmanspeak drive.co.za). **Toll** from R30.

World of Birds

One of the most stunning coastal drives in the world. Wind along for nine kilometres above the deep-blue southern Atlantic between Hout Bay and Noordhoek and be sure to stop at more than one of the many picnic spots and lookout points on the sea-facing side of the road. The small toll fee pays for all the metal nets that keep falling boulders off your car.

Hout Bay Beach
Beach Road, Hout Bay.
Spanning from the beginning of Chapman's Peak Drive to the harbour, Hout Bay Beach's kilometre-long expanse means that there's space for all and sundry. Equestrians and dog walkers are allocated special times when they can frolic in the surf with their four-footed friends.

ImiZamo Yethu Township Tours
7263 Mandela Road, ImiZamo Yethu, Hout Bay (083 719 4870, www.sued afrika.net). **Tours** by advance booking only 10.30am, 1pm, 4pm daily. **Tickets** R75. **No credit cards.**
Hout Bay's Township ImiZamo Yethu offers visitors the opportunity to experience life there. Local resident and registered guide Afrika Moni's two-hour tours are just the ticket for a gentle introduction to the townships. You'll get to meet residents, enjoy sorghum beer at a shebeen, sample some local dishes and even consult a traditional healer.

World of Birds
Valley Road, Hout Bay (021 790 2730, www.worldofbirds.org.za). **Open** 9am-5pm daily. *Monkey Jungle* 11.30am-1pm; 2pm-3.30pm daily. **Admission** R65, R39-R50 concessions.
Expect walk-through aviaries and over 3,000 birds and small animals (400 different species) here. Most memorable are the mammoth martial eagles, the talking cockatoos, the acrobatic macaws, kleptomaniac squirrel monkeys and doe-eyed alpacas. Kids will love it.

Eating & drinking

Chapmans Peak Hotel
Chapmans Peak Drive, Hout Bay (021 790 1036). **Open** noon-10pm Mon-Sat; noon-9pm Sun. **RR**. **Seafood/grills**.
When in the mood for some serious seafood, Capetonians head for this local icon, arguably the home of the best calamari and prawns in town. A Portuguese flavour is evident – order your chorizo and calamari pan to start or perhaps a pan of spicy *trinchado* if you're after something other than seafood. The sea view is lovely and there's a great weekend vibe, but be warned, they don't take bookings.

Dunes
1 Beach Road, Hout Bay (021 790 1876, www.dunesrestaurant.co.za). **Open** 9am-late Mon-Fri; 8am-late Sat, Sun. **RR**. **Café/grills**.
Another one that's right on the beach, Dunes has spectacular views of the ocean, the harbour, Chapman's Peak and the Sentinel. It's very family friendly and casual, whether you're stopping for a meal or relaxing and whiling away a lazy weekend afternoon with a few cold ones and some live music.

Kitima at the Kronendal
Kronendal Estate, 140 Main Road, Hout Bay (021 790 8004, www.kitima. co.za). **Open** 5.30pm-10.30pm Tue-Sat; noon-3.30pm Sun. **RRR**. **Asian**.
Enjoy a drink in the main bar or the Raj Lounge before making your way to your table where a pan-Asian journey awaits – from sushi, satays and dim sum to start to pad Thai, red, yellow and green curries, wok and noodle dishes and steamed ginger fish specialities for mains. Sophisticated presentation and a superior wine list finish off the culinary experience. Don't forget to try the amazing cocktails.

Pure
Hout Bay Manor, Baviaanskloof, off Main Road, Hout Bay (021 790 0116,

www.houtbaymanor.com). **Open** 6.30pm-10.30pm Tue-Sat; noon-2.30pm Sun. **RRR**. **Modern European**. This smart, design-centric restaurant housed in a refurbished manor house hotel boasts a menu that's brimming with European influence. A seasonal menu, sophisticated plating and ambitious flavour pairings ensure a memorable dining experience.

Trattoria Luigi

Main Road, Hout Bay (021 790 1702, www.luigis.co.za). **Open** 6-10.30pm Mon; noon-3pm, 6-10.30pm Tue-Sun. **RR**. **Italian**. Like your pizza and/or pasta served with a generous dash of authenticity? Then this trattoria, bedecked with red-and-white tablecloths, is perfect. The food here is tasty as can be – which explains the weekend crowds. Try the salmon angel-hair pasta or the gorgonzola gnocchi. If you're lucky, the owner (who bought the place from Luigi years ago) may break into song.

Wild Woods

Main Road, Hout Bay, next door to the Chapmans Peak Hotel (021 791 1166, www.wildwoods.co.za). **Open** 6-10.30pm Tue-Fri; noon-3pm, 6pm-10.30pm Sat, Sun. **RRR**. **Contemporary global**. Celeb chef Pete Goffe-Wood's eaterie is as down to earth as he is – with the unassuming interiors belying a seriously tasty and pedigreed menu. Soul food with a mod twist reigns supreme – from mussels in a spiced cream or caramelised butternut *involtini* to start to steaks with béarnaise or perhaps a thick tuna steak seared just so, and of course, Pete's famous slow-roasted pork belly. Lunch is served at weekends, and slow-food Sundays feature platters of food passed from table to table.

Southern Peninsula

To the south of Hout Bay is **Noordhoek** and **Kommetjie**, both with stunning beaches. Muizenberg,

Fish Hoek, Kalk Bay and Simon's Town dot the Main Road that hugs the coast on the other side of the peninsula. **Muizenberg** is a popular surfing beach prettied up with a parade of renovated art deco and Victorian buildings.

The harbour village of **Kalk Bay** sees hip crowds enjoying the host of coffee shops, restaurants, antique stores and art galleries or buying freshly caught fish from local fishmongers at the harbour.

Fish Hoek is famous for its family-friendly beach, a favoured spot for sheltered swimming. As these waters are known for shark activity, there are always shark spotters on duty (see p127).

Simon's Town is home to Cape Town's only naval base and the town centre is set around the harbour. It features a small shopping centre and a host of tourist-oriented stores. The small, secluded **Boulders Beach** forms part of the Table Mountain National Park and is home to a large colony of jackass penguins. In an effort to curb the crowds, an entry fee is charged.

The route comes to an end at **Cape Point**, which is often mistaken for the southernmost point of Africa. The **Cape Point Reserve** is located here and is a very beautiful and popular tourist destination.

Sights

Boulders African Penguin Colony

Kleintuin Road, Simon's Town, parking area in Seaforth Road (021 786 2329, www.tmnp.co.za). **Open** Dec-Jan 7am-7.30pm daily. Feb-Mar 8am-6.30pm daily. Apr-Sept 8am-5pm daily. Oct-Nov 8am-6.30pm daily. **Admission** R35 adults; R10 children.

Previously called Jackass Penguins due to their donkey-like bray, these

Kitima at the Kronendal p123

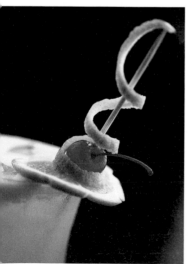

African penguins (as they're now known) attract visitors keen on a rare opportunity to see them up close in their natural environment. The large colony is accessible by boardwalks, allowing visitors to get up close without disturbing the birds.

Boyes Drive

Turn onto Boyes Drive just before entering Muizenberg (in Lakeside) or from Kalk Bay Main Road.

Offering the best vantage points from which to appreciate the beauty of False Bay, watch the succession of breaks roll in under the watchful eye of the local shark-spotter in his sun shelter. If it's not too hazy you'll also spot Seal Island in the distance – the dark-coloured parts are actually huge clusters of the 75,000-strong seal colony. You'd also do well to pull over closer to Kalk Bay to get the lie of the land, or see what conditions are like down on Danger Beach. Several signboards on the side of the road point out where you might make a start on a hike. The mountain above Kalk Bay is especially promising for the novice caver, but the numerous caves up there aren't signposted so you'd be advised to bring along a local guide.

Cape Point

Cape Point (021 780 9010, www.cape point.co.za). **Open** Oct-Mar 6am-6pm daily. Apr-Sept 7am-5pm daily.
Admission R75 adults; R10 under-12s.
The recently rebuilt funicular that ferries the reluctant hiker to the lookout point just below the lighthouse is aptly named the Flying Dutchman, after the ghost ship that is said to haunt these shores. The restaurant serves good, satisfying food at reasonable prices, while the views cannot be beaten. Cape Point is home to a lively nature reserve with eland, zebra, red hartebeest, bontebok and baboons in residence, as well as 40km of unspoilt coastline. There are endless walks and points of historic interest – if you've got the day, visit the

Buffelsfontein Visitor's Centre near the entrance to the reserve for more info on the reserve's attractions.

Cape Point Ostrich Farm

Plateau Road, property number 1051, off the M65, opposite entrance to Cape Point (021 780 9294, www.capepoint ostrichfarm.com). **Open** 9.30am-5.30pm daily. **Admission** free; R40 guided tours; R20 6-16s. *Ostrich platter* R100. *Pre-booked ostrich braai from R160 (11am-4pm).*

Buy a packet of feed and let these big birds peck away at from your palm. Between August and March the chicks hatch and you can tour the incubators.

Casa Labia

192 Main Road, Muizenberg (021 788 6068, www.casalabia.co.za). **Open** 10am-4pm Tue-Sat.

Once the seaside home of one of Cape Town's most illustrious Italian families, the magnificently renovated residence is now a museum that plays host to the family's collection of antiquities and art, African gift store and sun-splashed café where light and lovely Italian-influenced eats and visually arresting salads are the order of the day. Afternoon tea is a treat too – be sure to factor in time to take in the remarkable Rococo-esque interiors.

Danger Beach

Along the shoreline between Muizenberg and St James.

Dangers, as its known locally, has its loyal regulars who seem annoyingly assured that the nine-to-five routine is no way to live. They are attracted by great chances of good breaks for both body surfers and the guys with boards. You can wade out through the low tide and find yourself standing in knee-deep water at the edge of the reef further out, a fascinating and sometimes scary spot for snorkelling. The beach isn't visible from the road, so if you're coming from Muizenberg, pass St James's train station and park in the lot

Shark tactics

A dedicated crew of spotters protect surfers.

The tight-knit Muizenberg surfing community took matters into their own hands when Great White sharks started to take a particular liking to False Bay back in 2005. After a spate of sightings and a near-tragic attack on a local lifesaver, local surfer Greg Bertish, owner of True Blue Surf and Adventure Travel, gave car guard Patrick 'Rasta' Davids and lifeguard Monwabisi Sikiya some binoculars and appointed them as the country's first shark spotters. With Rasta manning the beach and Monwa standing on Boyes Drive, the picturesque mountain road with superb views of the beach and surf break, they kept a steady lookout from 8am to 6pm and alerted surfers to the presence of sharks with air horns and frantic waving.

These vallant early efforts have now turned into a well-oiled predator spotting machine, with a distinctly more sophisticated set-up thanks to cash injections from the City of Cape Town and World Wildlife Fund. Rasta and Monwa are still scoping out the shark scene, but they're now joined by an additional 12 permanent staff manning the shark stations, and the air horns have made way for a hi-tech remote-controlled alarm and colour-coded flag system. Fish Hoek and St James have also followed suit and now boast their own protectors on the mountain and road above the beach.

Stop off at the little sun sheltered enclosure about halfway along Boyes Drive and check out the choppy waters below alongside one of these eagle-eyed heroes. And for more information visit www.sharkspotters.org.za.

Clue up on the colour code

Green flag There's a shark spotter on duty, visibility is good and no sharks have been spotted.

Black flag There's a shark spotter on duty, but visibility is very poor.

Red flag A shark has been spotted in the last two hours.

White flag with black shark A shark is currently in the area.

that borders the tennis court. Then look for the subway tunnel that leads under the train tracks – when you find it you'll be glad you bothered. When conditions are right, this is possibly the best swimming spot in Cape Town. However, be aware that it's called Dangers for a reason – there's the occasional rip current.

Fish Hoek & Clovelly Beaches

Fish Hoek. Enter at the boom on the Fish Hoek end or park at the parking area as you enter Fish Hoek on the Clovelly side.

With an indoor/outdoor restaurant, a takeaway kiosk, a play park and clingy sand that's perfect for future architects, Fish Hoek beach is a firm favourite for folks of a kid-friendly persuasion. The beach is about 2.5km long and quite flat (perfect for a jog), and the bay is protected from the stronger surf in the rest of False Bay, so little ones can enjoy some splashing about in safety.

Heritage Museum

Amlay House, King George Way, Simon's Town (021 786 2302, www.simonstown.com). **Open** 11am-4pm Tue-Thur, Sun. **Admission** R5. **No credit cards.**

An interesting museum if you're curious about Malay culture before the forced removals of the Group Areas Act in the apartheid era. Zainab 'Patty' Davidson is the beating heart of this small collection, filled with artefacts, family memories and oral histories. Displays trace the history of Muslim culture and of the town's former residents, but it is Davidson's oral tour that makes for a memorable experience.

Het Posthuys

180 Main Road, Muizenberg (021 788 7972). **Open** 10am-2pm Mon-Fri by appointment only. **Admission** by donation.

Flanked by two cannons, you can't miss this anachronistic little cottage as

you drive along Main Road in Muizenberg, The oldest building in the country, it has white-washed walls and a thatched roof and has been everything from an inn to a toll-keeper's house to a naval storage space. Inside are interesting titbits about the history of the area, including photos depicting Muizenberg as a Victorian seaside resort for the Cape's well-heeled. It also offers an engaging history of the famous Battle of Muizenberg.

Imhoff Farm

Kommetjie Road, Kommetjie (021 783 4545, www.imhofffarm.co.za). **Open** 9am-5pm Tue-Sun (some shops open Mon). **Admission** free.

This charming family spot has a host of rural attractions, from a free-range farm shop to the Higgledy Piggledy Animal Farm, where you can teach your tot the difference between a goat and a sheep or pet a few tame rabbits. There's a snake park, camel rides, a Belgian chocolate shop, a toy and children's clothing boutique, and the Blue Water Café, which has a wonderful outdoor section with gorgeous views and a large lawn and swings.

Jaeger Walk

Between Fish Hoek Beach & Sunny Cove.

It's like a scene from *Cocoon* on the Fish Hoek side of this lovely walkway, as fit- and nimble-looking pensioners sizzle away on the concrete benches or cool off in the clear, gentle (albeit shark-frequented) waters of the bay. This is the perfect stretch for some snorkelling, with tiny underwater caves and eerie kelp forests.

Kalk Bay Harbour

Off Main Road, Kalk Bay.

Pretty fishing boats bob lazily on the waters of this charming harbour. If you like your fish so fresh they're still flopping, check the horizon for the next boat. Once you've selected your catch, get one of the ladies working at the concrete cleaning tables to gut and portion your yellowfin or kingklip. If you prefer your fish deep-fried, the no-frills Kalky's does a good job of it, or else opt for the more upmarket Polana or Harbour House for seafood and cocktails with superb views. This is also a nice spot for a post-prandial stroll along the pier, provided it's merely balmy and not blowing a gale (there are freak waves from time to time).

Kommetjie Beach

Follow the sign from Kommetjie Road.
After a storm this beach can become something of an olfactory hazard due to piles of washed-up kelp. But for most of the year it's one of the most beautiful beaches in the 'Deep South', great for walking or surfing. From here you can also see the back of Table Mountain. Insider's tip: in summer the water here is frigid, if not lethal, but on a warmer day in winter you'll find it refreshing, even manageable.

Miller's Point

About 2km south of Simon's Town, look for the signs off Main Road after the Black Marlin restaurant.
This is one of those hidden gems, a stunning picnic destination for a fish *braai* on a sunny, windless day. Partly a camping site with washing facilities, there are also numerous concrete fire pits to choose from, and gorgeous 360-degree views. Best of all, it has a large, deep tidal pool, one of the few where you can tread crystal-clear water without touching the white-sand bottom. The terrain, with the tiniest nearby harbour, is ideal for youngsters to explore, while a couple of sandy coves complete the picture. A submerged wreck off Miller's Point is a popular draw card for scuba divers.

Mineral World Topstones & Scratch Patch

Dido Valley Road, Simon's Town (021 786 2020, www.scratchpatch.co.za).
Open 8.30am-4.45pm Mon-Fri; 9am-5.30pm Sat-Sun. **Admission** free.

Scratch patch R14 for a small bag. **Mine Adventure** R20 adults; R15 children (only open on weekdays).
This is the perfect distraction for kids, from shark teeth found in the sands of Morocco, to fascinating fossils ranging from big and beautiful to small but significant, you're likely to leave with an ammonite or a few minerals. Precious and semi-precious stones sparkle at you, with reasonable price tags attached. Outside, a cave-like venue keeps young and old in a trance as they pick and pan through a sea of semi-precious pebbles to take home. This is also one of the world's largest gemstone factories and you can watch the workers polish and cut the stones to artistic perfection for their jewellery shop. Don't miss a trip down the mine shaft below the factory – the kids will love it.

Muizenberg Beach

Muizenberg, from Main Road turn into Atlantic Road. Pass under the bridge. Take the 2nd right to park at the mountain end or continue straight to the parking area.
Muizenberg holds the Guinness World Record for the most surfers on a single wave, thanks to the longest break in the Cape peninsula (about 1.5km). This is also a beach where beginners find their feet; a number of nearby surf shops arrange lessons and rent out surfboards and wetsuits. A short stroll from all the surfing action is a putt putt range and a public pool complete with waterslide to keep the younger ones occupied.

Noordhoek Beach

Some of the first scenes of director David Lean's classic *Ryan's Daughter* are set on Noordhoek beach, and include a shot of the wreck of the *Kahapo*. The iron wreck is still there, and in much the same condition, but the only way you'll find this out is if you ride there, unless you really like walking. The vast expanse of Noordhoek beach really is ideal for going at full gallop. Phone Sleepy Hollow Horse Riding

(021 789 2341, 083 261 0104, www.
sleepyhollowhorseriding.co.za), the
Imhoff Equestrian Centre (082 774
1191, www.horseriding.co.za), or Dunes
Kakapo Horse Trail (021 789 1723).

Rhodes Cottage

*246 Main Road, Muizenberg (021 788
1816, 072 482 6131).* **Open** 10am-
4pm Mon-Wed; 10am-2pm Thurs-Sun
(times can vary). **Admission** donation.
No credit cards.
'God is an Englishman and he is making the world a better place by colonis-
ing it,' insisted Cecil John Rhodes, who
left a legacy in South Africa, having
been prime minister of the Cape Colony
and founder of De Beers Consolidated
Mines. This little museum traces his
life from boyhood to deathbed and his
final words: 'So much to do, so little
done'. In fact, this is the very cottage
where he died.

Silvermine

*Ou Kaapse Weg (021 780 9002,
www.tmnp.co.za).* **Open** *May-Aug* 8am-
5pm daily. *Sept-Apr* 7am-6pm daily.
Admission R20 adults; R10 children .
Mountain biking R30. **No credit cards**.
The Silvermine reservoir is a memorable, beautiful spot for a picnic or a
braai, with a wheelchair-friendly
boardwalk and the option of a swim in
the clean, tannin-coloured water. There
are several rewarding walks that start
from here: you can fairly easily access
the forested mountain ridge above
Tokai, or continue further to
Elephant's Eye Cave. Alternately hike
all the way to Chapman's Peak for picture perfect views of Hout Bay.

Simon's Town Boat Trips

*The Town Pier, in front of Simon's
Town Waterfront Centre, Simon's
Town (083 257 7760, www.boat
company.co.za).* **Trips** daily. *Spirit
of Just Nuisance* (40 mins) R40 adults;
R20 under-12s. *Cape Point* (2 hrs)
R350 adults; R200 under-12s. *Seal
Island* (1.5 hrs) R250 adults; R150
under-12s. *Whale Watching* (2.5 hrs)
R750 adults; R500 under-12s.

Guided Sea Kayak Tours *(082 501
8930, www.kayakcapetown.co.za).*
Penguin Trip R250. **No credit cards**.
The options here are more expensive
than the gentle boat cruises from Hout
Bay harbour, but False Bay promises
more bang for your buck, with a number of adventurous options from the
pier at Simon's Town Waterfront
Centre. Book a sunrise cruise to Seal
Island to see great whites pirouette
from the water while in hunting mode.
You'll see some ocean caves on the
Cape Point cruise, while the Spirit of
Just Nuisance tour is more about man's
engagement with the ocean, with stories about the town's naval heritage.
Sea kayaking is another enjoyable, if
energetic, way to see the coast.

Slangkop Lighthouse

*Lighthouse Road, Kommetjie (021 783
1717).* **Open** 10am-3pm Mon-Fri.
Admission R16 adults; R8-R10
concessions. **No credit cards**.
At the end of the pretty seaside village
of Kommetjie stands the lone white
lady that keeps ships out of danger.
This is the tallest lighthouse on the
South African coast, and when vertigo
hits you on the balcony, rest assured
that it's also the strongest, thanks to its
cast-iron construction. She's been
blinking into the night since 1919.

Tidal Pools

St James Tidal Pool *Park near St
James Station, then go through the
tunnel running under the railway line.*
Dalebrook *Stop in the parking lot just
as you enter Kalk Bay, then go through
the tunnel under the railway line.*
Both Admission free.
If you prefer your sea 100% shark-free
and child-safe, choose one of these two
tidal pools on the False Bay coast. St
James is well patronised by the under-
sevens who can get remarkably excited
when waves crash over the sea wall at
high tide. The collection of brightly

Café Roux p132

coloured Victorian-style bathing boxes (beach huts) is possibly the most common image of Cape Town in travel guides. A paved coastal footpath runs from here to Muizenberg. Dalebrook tidal pool lies in the other direction.

Eating & drinking

The Annex

Majestic Village, 124 Main Road, Kalk Bay (021 788 2453). **Open** 7am-9pm daily; closed Sun evenings. **RR. Café.**
This extension to the Kalk Bay Book Shop has a suitably hushed atmosphere, along with wood-clad walls, trompe l'oeil decorations and a fireplace for the colder winter months. It's a popular breakfast spot, and the lunch and dinner menu, which varies according to season and availability of produce, is modern Mediterranean.

Black Marlin

Main Road, Millers Point, Simons Town (021 786 1621, www.black marlin.co.za). **Open** noon-10pm Mon-Fri; 8am-10m Sat, Sun. **RR. Seafood.**
Although the magnificent fish for which this restaurant is named is no longer served here, there are plenty of other seafood choices. Along with shellfish, seafood lovers will find everything from curries to grills, oysters and crayfish. The view across False Bay (and of the whales in winter) is a joy. Sunday crayfish *braais* are an institution.

Bombay on Beach

43 Atlantic Road, Muizenberg (078 088 8880). **Open** 12.30pm-10pm Tues-Sun. **R. No credit cards. Indian.**
If real-deal Indian without a hefty price tag is your thing, then look no further than this Muizenberg gem. Starters are limited to samosas and the like, but there's a huge range of vegetarian main courses (you'll consider swearing off meat for keeps, they're that good). You'll also find a suitably punchy lamb rogan josh and the always outstanding coriander-infused *kadai* chicken.

Home-made naan and fragrant sambals finish things off perfectly. Sunday night buffet specials offer serious value for money.

Brass Bell

Main Road, Kalk Bay (021 788 5455, www.brassbell.co.za). **Open** 11am-11pm Mon-Fri; 9am-11pm Sat, Sun. **RR. Seafood, grills, pizza.**
The Brass Bell is right on the train station in Kalk Bay, and you can't get much closer to the ocean unless you walk right up to the water itself. The view of the harbour and fishing boats is lovely. This is a classic stalwart filled with locals. Salty seadogs and those who've made a sunny-day pilgrimage to this Kalk Bay institution jostle for attention from the staff, who are kept busy ferrying pints of ice-cold beer and seafood platters. The battered fish and chips is the real deal, perfectly crispy, and their calamari is great too. Pizzas, burgers and Greek salad are also worth a mention.

Café Roux

Noordhoek Farm Village (021 789 2538, www.caferoux.co.za). **Open** 8.30am-5pm daily. **RR. Global/South African.**
Bring the children and the dogs to this perennially popular local haunt, where hearty global and Cape cooking fills the gap. It's supremely social on the weekends, when you'll rub shoulders with the regulars who meet up for late lunches and live music care of resident talent Dan Green. Outside of breakfast and lunch hours they also serve tea and cakes.

Cape to Cuba

165 Main Road, Kalk Bay (021 788 1566, www.capetocuba.com). **Open** 11.30am-10.30pm daily. **RR. Cuban-inspired.**
This harbourside eaterie is known for its lightheartedly opulent decor, with candelabras galore. The kitchen serves Cuban-inspired eats in the form of

prawns, fresh linefish and steaks. The adjoining 'beach bar' is a popular haunt on the weekends when they do a roaring trade in mojitos.

Casa Labia Café

192 Main Road, Muizenberg (021 788 6068, www.casalabia.co.za). **Open** 10am-4pm Tue-Sat. **RR**. **Italian**.
Once the home of one of the senior members of the illustrious Labia family, this magnificent building overlooking the sea in Muizenberg has been restored to its former glory. Palazzo-like interiors provide a sense of occasion while the sun-splashed café boasts a menu peppered with Italian-style offerings. Expect light and lovely pastas, prettified salads and daily specials like roast guinea fowl and seasonal risotto.

The Foodbarn

Noordhoek Farm Village, Village Lane, Noordhoek (021 789 1390, www.thefoodbarn.co.za). **Open** noon-2.30pm daily, 7pm-9pm Wed-Sat. **RR**. **French bistro**.
Chef-patron Franck Dangereaux marries his desire for a laid-back and welcoming restaurant with his passion for superbly prepared food. Dishes are many and varied – from the *avo tian* with prawn tempura to an outstanding tartare, open ravioli with mushrooms, ricotta and truffle sauce and the always-superb seared sweetbreads. Expect a finely tuned balance of flavours and superior sauces. The Foodbarn is a must-do dining destination in this part of the world – even more so for the winter specials and cooking demonstration evenings.

Harbour House

Kalk Bay Harbour (021 788 4133, www.harbourhouse.co.za). **Open** noon-4pm, 6pm-10pm daily. **RRR**. **Seafood**.
You'd be hard pressed to find a restaurant that's closer to the ocean than this Kalk Bay spot. Expect Cape Cod meets Kenyan coast interiors and a menu that's filled with seafood specials –

from line fish prepared a variety of ways to spiced calamari, along with some meaty choices. It's a romantic dinnertime spot but just as delightful on a sun-splashed afternoon.

Live Bait

Kalk Bay Harbour (021 788 5755, www.harbourhouse.co.za). **Open** noon-10pm daily. **RR**. **Seafood/café**.
Get into the holiday spirit at this Med-inspired taverna-style restaurant, complete with blue-and-white mosaics and whitewashed wooden furniture – and a killer ocean view. Seafood specialities are big news here; sushi platters fly out of the kitchen, while old-school fish and chips and spiced turmeric calamari are hugely popular too. Try the heaped seafood platter. Be warned, though, the service can be slow.

Olympia

Main Road, Kalk Bay (021 788 6396). **Open** 7am-9pm daily. **RR**. **Café**.
Situated opposite Kalk Bay harbour this ever-busy leader of the café pack has a daily-changing menu for breakfast, lunch and dinner. You'll find the likes of kidneys on toast for breakfast, just-caught seared tuna and mash for lunch and mussels or liver if you're lucky on the supper menu. Regular staples include soft and cheesy polenta, a good steak sandwich, robust linguini del mare and a roasted catch of the day with veggies. Great real-deal café fare.

Rioja Restaurant & Birocca Lounge

Solole Game Reserve, 6 Wood Road, Sunnydale (021 785 5123, www.rioja. co.za). **Open** noon-3pm, 5pm-10pm Tue-Sat; noon-3pm Sun. **RR**. **Global**.
Enjoy your lunch or dinner in the heart of this urban nature reserve where buffalo once did roam. The menu ventures from comfort staples like shepherd's pie and a gourmet burger to more globally inspired offerings such as Portuguese sardines and Cape Malay curry.

Brass Bell p132

Sorrento Trattoria

10 & 11 Westlake Lifestyle Centre, Westlake Drive, Westlake (021 702 49030). **Open** noon-3pm, 5-10pm Tue-Sun. **RR. Italian**.

Though this eaterie in a small strip mall is nothing to look at from the outside, once you get inside, you'll find a reliable, family-friendly Italian restaurant that serves excellent pizzas (the Dominique is a winner) and traditional specialities. Kids are well taken care of, thanks to the nearby play area, and the staff are the kind who remember your favourites. A good South Peninsula bet.

The Toad In The Village

16 Noordhoek Farm Village, Village Lane, Noordhoek (021 789 2973). **Open** 11.30am-11pm daily. **RR. Pub food/pizzas**.

There's live music on Mondays, Wednesdays and Thursdays, quiz nights on Tuesdays and, of course, sport over the weekends at the cosy Toad. And as well as TV screens you'll find lawns for the kids to play on too. Food is souped-up pub grub. Start with hearty, robust offerings like chicken livers with garlicky slivers of toasted baguette. Main courses are of the usual pizza, burger and steak variety.

Trattoria Antonio

56 Main Road, St James (021 788 7788). **Open** noon-3pm, 6-10.30pm Mon-Wed; 6pm-10.30pm Thur-Sun. **RR. Italian**.

This new venue is the sister restaurant to Luigi's in Hout Bay. The interior is pure trattoria – red-and-white checked tablecloths, candles in Chianti bottles, Eros Ramazotti soundtrack … The menu is crammed with pizzas, pastas, veal and seafood.

Shopping

Big Blue

82 Main Road, Kalk Bay (021 788 2399). **Open** 9am-6pm daily.

Mens' and ladies' fashions by in-house brand Holmes Bros take pride of place, although a variety of other local stars shine too. The quirky gifts are superb – think wind-up toys, magic 8 balls and '70s-style clocks.

Kalk Bay Books

124 Main Road, Kalk Bay (021 788 2266, www.kalkbaybooks.co.az). **Open** 9am-5pm Mon, Thur, Sun; 9am-7pm Fri.

This charming wood-panelled bookstore is a much-loved local fixture, with a plethora of carefully chosen local and foreign titles, and a good selection of travel tomes too.

Kalk Bay Modern

1st Floor Olympia Buildings, 136 Main Road, Kalk Bay (021 788 6571, www.kalkbaymodern.com). **Open** 9am-5pm daily.

This gallery and gift store gives you a flavour of local arts, ceramics and collectibles (look out for the fabrics available by the metre). You'll find it by walking through the blue door to the left of Olympia Café and up the stairs.

The Kalk Bay Trading Post

71 Main Road, Kalk Bay (021 788 9571). **Open** 9am-5pm daily.

This dusty store has everything from old printer's trays to battered suitcases, seascape prints of the local coastline, vintage postcards and the like. A treasure trove for those with an eye for collectibles.

Mythology & Co

100 Main Road, Kalk Bay (021 788 3387). **Open** 9.30 am-5pm daily.

This delightfully feminine store on Kalk Bay's main shopping drag is crammed with rail upon rail of local fashion wares as well as enticing displays of locally made knick knacks.

Quagga Rare Art & Books

84 Main Road, Kalk Bay (021 788 2752, www.quaggabooks.co.za). **Open** 9.30am-5pm Mon-Sat; 10am-5pm Sun.

You'll find everything from '70s Beanos to 30s annuals at this delightful old-school store. Look out for vintage copies of Mrs Beeton and a host of other interesting antiquarian books. There are also books on botany, history and art, maps, posters and more.

Polana

Kalk Bay Harbour (021 788 4133). **Open** 9am-5pm daily.

By day a café complete with a laidback menu and a spectacular position on the rocks, when night falls at the weekend the pace picks up with live cover bands and authentic acts. Book a table for early supper to ensure your ringside seat for later.

Railway House Decor & Collectables

23 Main Road, Kalk Bay (021 788 4761). **Open** 9am-5pm daily.

You never know what you'll find at this dusty stop, crammed with rusty, beaten and sometimes bedraggled things for the home: old Persians, kists (large wooden chests) and wonky paint-streaked tables set the tone. An on-site crêperie provides sustenance.

Nightlife

The Melting Pot

15 Church Street, Muizenberg Village (021 788 9791). **Open** 7pm-late Wed, Fri-Sun. **Admission** varies. **No credit cards**.

It's all in the name. This popular new social club offers a mix of talents from around the globe. Fresh weekly line-ups include everything from stand-up comedy to world music jam sessions to the most respected names in jazz and Afro-fusion.

Arts & Leisure

Baboon Matters

3 Cruiser Close, Sun Valley (021 785 7493, 084 821 4989, www.baboon matters.org.za). **Walks** Nov-Mar 8.30am, 3pm daily. *Apr-Oct* 9.30am-2pm daily. **Cost** R295 adults; R140 under-16s.

With Baboon Matters, you can hike into the mountains to hang out with the last remaining chacma baboons in the Cape peninsula. This is a rare opportunity to practically become part of the troop as they eat, play and socialise around you. The walks last about two hours and are suitable for people of all ages and fitness levels.

The Cape Farmhouse

Off Cape Point Road, about 3km past Scarborough (021 780 1246, www.capefarmhouse.co.za). **Open** 3-6pm Sat. Admission R50; R40 concessions.

This is definitely your best bet for live music in the Southern Peninsula. Every Saturday this family-friendly 250-year-old farmhouse, in a sheltered valley and surrounded by old oak trees, offers Saturday afternoon outdoor concerts showcasing South African musicians. The bands kick off at about 3.30pm, but come early for some alfresco dining. Expect anything from Hot Water to those popping proponents of Irish folk music Shanty, to blues master Dan Platansky.

Kalk Bay Theatre

52 Main Road, Kalk Bay (073 220 5430, www.kbt.co.za). **Open** from 6pm for pre-theatre dinner Wed-Sun. *Theatre sports* 8-9.30pm Tue.

This cute little Dutch Reformed church (1876) hasn't been privy to a Sunday sermon in quite some time. These days its toothpaste-white façade lights up with a glow come evening, when the church becomes a charming performance space. Packed around the petite stage are 78 red chairs. Upstairs, the gallery restaurants serves dishes such as pan-fried pepper steak and traditional Bo-Kaap curry and linefish goujons. Tuesday nights are reserved for Theatresports, the city's longest running theatre improv act.

Steenberg Vineyards p138

Southern Suburbs

Constantia & around

Constantia, one of the most well-heeled of the southern suburbs, is where the famed South African wine industry was established and is renowned as one of the best wine routes in the country. Many of its wine farms have award-winning restaurants on their estates.

Sights & museums

Buitenverwachting

Klein Constantia Road, Constantia (021 794 5190, www.buitenverwachting.com). **Open** 9am-5pm Mon-Fri; 10am-3pm Sat. **Tastings** free.

One of South Africa's oldest wine estates, Buitenverwachting has a five-star restaurant serving sophisticated, innovative cuisine. There's also Catharina's, a more informal garden restaurant with tapas, light meals and high teas in idyllic surrounds.

Constantia Uitsig

Spaanschemat River Road, Constantia (021 794 1810, www.constantia-uitsig.com). **Open** 9am-4.30pm Mon-Fri; 10am-4.30pm Sat, Sun. *Sales* 9am-5pm Mon-Fri; 10am-5pm Sat, Sun. **Tastings** from R20.

Some come for the wine, but most come for the food: the famous French-meets-Asian dining destination La Colombe has been hailed widely as the best restaurant in the country, and one of the best in the world. However, La Colombe is only one of three restaurants on site, and there's also an acclaimed spa, colonial-style cricket oval and pavilion, and hotel. One could almost forget that award-winning wines are this estate's actual *raison d'être* – the on site wine sales shop offers a wide selection of estate and valley wines.

Groot Constantia

Groot Constantia Road, Constantia (021 794 5128, www.groot constantia.co.za). **Open** *May-Sept*

9am-5pm daily. *Oct-Apr* 9am-6pm daily. *Manor House Museum, Cloete Cellar & Orientation Centre* 10am-5pm daily. **Entrance** *Manor House* R15 adults; R5 concessions; free under-16s. *Tastings* R30 (5 wines & international tasting glass). *Cellar tours* (on the hour 10am-4pm) R35 (includes a tasting); R6-R12 concessions. *Evening cellar tours & tasting* (pre-book; 25ppl+) R85. *Costume rates* R400 per outfit.

Groot Constantia has been producing some of the world's most sought-after wines for more than three centuries and remains one of the most popular tourist destinations in the valley. Visit the wine-tasting centre, the fascinating museum or enjoy an alfresco lunch at on-site eateries Jonkershuis and Simons. Picnics in summer.

Klein Constantia

Klein Constantia Road, Constantia (021 794 5188, www.kleinconstantia. com). **Open** 9am-5pm Mon-Fri; 9am-3pm Sat. *Tastings* free for groups of up to 5 people; R20 pre-booked tastings of 8 or more.

The wines from Klein Constantia have given its bigger brother a run for its money over the centuries, with kings and tsars fond consumers of the Cloete family's famous fortified dessert wine Vin de Constance. Even Jane Austen makes mention of it in *Sense and Sensibility* (in which Mrs Jennings raves about its curative properties), and Charles Dickens and Baudelaire were also inspired to give it mention.

Steenberg Vineyards

Corner Tokai and Steenberg roads, Tokai (021 713 2211, www.steenberg-vineyards.co.za). **Open** 8am-6pm Mon-Fri; 10am-6pm Sat. **Tastings** free. *Groups* (20+) R20pp (book in advance). Besides the professionally designed 18-hole golf course, the other big draws on this picturesque estate are Catharina's restaurant, and Bistro Sixteen82. The estate's robust red blend has won several awards, but the flagship cultivar

is sauvignon blanc. The on-site hotel and spa see a steady trade of guests soaking up the vineyard setting.

Tokai Forest

Tokai Road (021 712 7471). **Open** *picnic area* 8am-6pm (last admission 4pm) daily. **Admission** free for walkers; R5 vehicles; R25 cyclists; R35 horse-riding day passes. *Braai area* R5 adults; R2 under-11s.

The arboretum at Tokai forest, situated at the foot of the Constantiaberg mountain range, hosts hundreds of interesting (and some very old) tree species from around the world, including oaks and even Californian redwoods. It's also a good starting point for various hikes or mountain-bike rides up through the pine forests. For the fit there's the six-kilometre round trip to Elephant's Eye Cave, with spectacular views guaranteed – the large cave is the 'eye' of said elephant. If you plan to visit on a Saturday, consider stocking up on fresh and novel picnic fare at the nearby Porter Estate Produce Market between 9am and 1pm.

Eating & drinking

Buitenverwachting

Buitenverwachting Wine Estate, Klein Constantia (021 794 3522). **Open** *Season* noon-3pm, 7pm-10pm Mon-Sat. *Off-season* noon-3pm, 7-10pm Tue-Sat. **RRR. Modern European**.

A new-look interior has breathed new cool into this beloved Constantia wine estate restaurant that plays host to a Euro-influenced menu and an impressive line-up of estate and other local wines. A more relaxed courtyard menu is perfect for lazy alfresco dining, and there's gourmet picnic food too. Factor in time for a walk in the vineyards before or after lunch.

Catharina's

Steenberg Hotel, Tokai Road, Constantia (021 713 2222). **Open** 7-10.30am, noon-3.30pm, 7-10.30pm

Steenberg Vineyards

Wine country

Great wines, great food, just a step from the city centre.

The leafy southern suburb of Constantia is where South Africa's wine industry was born. Way back in 1655, intrepid Cape commander Jan van Riebeeck tried his hand at viticulture. Upon tasting his unremarkable range of tipples 30 years later, Dutch governor Simon van der Stel established Groot Constantia (see p137). The estate is still renowned for his flagship wine, Gouverneurs Reserve.

After his death in 1712, Van der Stel's vast estate was split up, creating Klein Constantia (see p138), Buitenverwachting (see p137) and Constantia Uitsig. Klein Constantia's sweet trademark tipple, Vin de Constance, was all the rage in the 18th and 19th centuries, favoured by royals like Napoleon Bonaparte and King Louis Philippe, and writers like Jane Austen and Charles Dickens.

Completing the quintet of Constantia's famous estates is Steenberg Vineyards (see p138). Established in 1862, Steenberg used to be called Swaneweide after the legions of spur winged

geese around the estate's dam, wrongly identified as swans by plucky owner Catharina Ras.

Apart from their steeped-in-history factor, the cool thing about all of these wineries is that they offer a great deal more than their delicious vino.

Wine and dine

■ **Buitenverwachting** Tuck into upmarket cuisine at Buitenverwachting Restaurant (see p138) or opt for a leisurely picnic under the oaks.

■ At **Groot Constantia** Simon's (see p142) serves international dishes, while Jonkershuis majors on authentic South African eats.

■ **Constantia Uitsig** has three excellent restaurants: River Café, Constantia Uitsig and, of course, the award-winning La Colombe.

■ At Catharina's (see p138) at **Steenberg**, executive chef Garth Almazan puts a contemporary spin on South African cuisine with offerings like springbok carpaccio, while Bistro Sixteen82 (see p142) serves lighter European dishes.

Mon-Sat; noon-3.30pm, 7-10pm Sun.
RR. Contemporary South African.
You'll encounter inspired salads, lots of interesting seafood options and a healthy smattering of chef Garth Almazan's favourite Cape Malay flavours at this striking wine estate restaurant. Meat-free Mondays showcase this chef's talent too. The setting, with glass walls letting in the views of the vines, is spectacular.

La Colombe
Constantia Uitsig Farm, Spaanschemat River Road, Constantia (021 794 2390). **Open** 12.30-1.30pm (last reservations), 7.30-8.30pm (last reservations) daily. Closed Sun night winter. **RRRR. Contemporary**.
This iconic restaurant reached a number 12 slot in the San Pellegrino Best Restaurants in the World Awards. The outstanding, ever-changing menu is a mouthwatering, modern mix of Euro-Asian flavours using the season's best. Impeccable service and pretty country surrounds complete the picture. The winter specials offer multi-course meals for an excellent price.

Constantia Uitsig
Constantia Uitsig Farm, Spaanschemat River Road, Constantia (021 794 4480). **Open** 12.30-2pm, 7.30-9pm daily. **RRR. Italian**.
Despite its smart, albeit slightly faded, sheen, this well-loved eaterie, with its beautiful estate and mountain views, is the ideal weekend lunch spot for families. It sees a steady trade of grateful diners the rest of the time too. The menu continues the Italian theme started by founder Frank Swainston, but chef Clayton Bell puts his own seasonal twist on things too.

Greenhouse at the Cellars
93 Brommersvlei Road, Constantia (021 794 2137/www.cellars-hohenort.com). **Open** 9am-5pm Mon-Fri, 9am-3pm Sat. **RRR. Contemporary South African**.

This new restaurant at the Cellars Hotel is delightfully laid-back and pays homage to the magnificent gardens it looks out on to. Chef Peter Tempelhoff's superb seasonal food is given a fine-tuned twist – the tasting menu is outstanding. The wine list and service is impressive too.

Greens
Shop 7, High Constantia, Constantia Main Road (021 794 7843). **Open** 8am-6pm Mon; 8am-11pm Tue-Sun.
RR. Contemporary café.
A Constantia institution, this busy eaterie does all-day breakfasts, keeps locals in cappuccinos from morning until night and does a steady trade in dishes ranging from creamy chicken livers to gourmet pizzas and a burger that comes with suitably enormous fried onion rings. It's a good weekend brunch spot despite its position overlooking a parking lot.

Jake's in the Village
Shop A5, Steenberg Lifestyle Centre, Steenberg Road, Tokai (021 701 3272, jakes.co.za). **Open** 11.30am-10.30pm Mon-Sat. **RR. Global**.
This large restaurant is popular with locals from the leafy suburban surrounds. Some swear by the roast duck, while others can't get enough of the lamb flatbread. The bar gets busy on Friday nights and is something of a social centre.

Jonkershuis
Groot Constantia Wine Estate, Groot Constantia Road, Constantia (021 021 794-6255). **Open** 9am-10pm Mon-Sat; 9am-4pm Sun. **RR. Contemporary South African**.
While a table inside the historical building or courtyard at this Groot Constantia Estate restaurant is lovely, in the warmer months try not to miss an opportunity to dine under the old oak trees. Service is warm and enthusiastic and the menu is peppered with light and lovely locally influenced choices.

Pastis

*Shop 12, High Constantia Centre,
Constantia Main Road (021 794 8334,
www.pastisbrasserie.co.za).* **Open** 9am-
11pm daily. **RR. Bar/bistro**.
New ownership has injected a renewed
sense of vigour into this popular bistro.
Checked tablecloths and Parisian period posters set the tone while the menu
is awash with Parisian café specialities.
A lively Friday night scene ensures the
cosy bar does good business.

Peddlars on the Bend

*Spaanschemat River Road, Constantia
(021 794 7747).* **Open** 11am-11pm
daily. **RR. Pub food**.
A popular watering hole and neighbourhood eatery. You'll find everyone
from twentysomething students hanging out before a big night out to lager-
drinking lads on a pre- or post-game
celebration and families enjoying the
pub grub. There's a large beer garden.

River Café at Constantia Uitsig

*Constantia Uitsig Farm, Spaanschemat
River Road, Constantia (021 794 3010).*
Open 8.30-11am, noon-3pm, 6.30pm-
9.30pm daily. **RR. Contemporary
South African**.
The bistro menu at this sibling eatery
to Constantia Uitsig restaurant and La
Colombe is relaxed and includes starters
such as chunky own-made quiches and
pâté. An emphasis on locally sourced,
seasonal ingredients is evident, and the
place has attracted a loyal following.

Simon's at Groot Constantia

*Groot Constantia Estate, Groot
Constantia Road, Constantia (021 794
1143, www.simons.co.za).* **Open** noon-
10pm daily. **RR. Global**.
This indoor-outdoor restaurant does a
roaring trade, especially at weekends,
when it's very popular with families.
You'll find a host of globally influenced
choices, and summer picnics add another alfresco dining option.

Sixteen82

*Steenberg Vineyards, Steenberg Estate,
Steenberg Road, Tokai (021 713 2211,
www.steenberg-vineyards.co.za).* **Open**
9am-7.30pm daily. **RR. Global**.
High design, great wines and excellent
bistro offerings are a lethal combination at this chic destination on the
Steenberg Vineyards (see p138). Well-
heeled locals and a food-loving crowd
flock here to enjoy everything from lavish breakfasts to wholesome lunches
and tasty tapas (served from early
evening until closing time).

Wasabi

*Shop 17 Old Constantia Village,
Constantia Main Road, Constantia
(021 794 6546/www.wasabi.co.za).*
Open noon-3pm, 6-10.30pm daily.
RR. Asian.
Sophisticated Asian fare is the order of
the day at this restaurant, which somehow manages to overcome its rather
dismal shopping-centre location. Sushi
keeps the punters coming, while seared
fish dishes, sophisticated wok fries and
tasty noodle choices are also well exe-
cuted and popular.

Shopping

Constantia Village

*Cnr Spaanschemat River Road and
Constantia Main Road, Constantia
(021 794 5065, www.constantia
village.co.za).* **Open** 9am-6pm
Mon-Fri; 9am-5pm Sat; 9am-1pm
Sun (Woolworths and Pick n Pay
stay open later).
It may not look like much from the outside, but this sprawling mini-mall
caters to many a Constantia housewife,
thanks to the giant Pick n Pay and the
many boutiques and lifestyle stores.

Mythology

*Shop 4, Old Village, Constantia Village,
Constantia (076 898 1227).* **Open**
9am-5pm Mon-Sat; 9am-1pm Sun.
Glam Southern Suburbs girls head for
this newish store for a high-fashion

Catharina's p138

mix of seasonal and vintage frocks, tops and pretty accessories. A selection of local names (like Michelle Ludek and the feminine in-house Mythology label) offer temptation, as do the pretty trinkets that would brighten up any boudoir.

Newlands

Newlands boasts two of Cape Town's main sports arenas, the Newlands Rugby Stadium and the cricket ground of Sahara Park Newlands. Kirstenbosch National Botanical Garden is also in the vicinity. Many visit simply to laze on the sprawling lawns.

Sights & museums

Kirstenbosch Botanical Gardens

Rhodes Drive (021 799 8783, www. sanbi.org). **Open** *Sept-Mar* 8am-7pm daily. *Apr-Aug* 8am-6pm daily. **Admission** R37 adults; R10-R25 concessions; free under-6s.

No trip to Cape Town is complete without visiting this world-renowned botanical haven, the first botanical garden in the world to be devoted to a country's indigenous flora (with 7,000 species in cultivation). Purchase a pre-packed picnic basket from the on-site restaurant and enjoy a lazy afternoon on the lawns, or explore the undulating gardens, with their memorable features such as the Cycad Amphitheatre and Colonel Bird's Bath, sometimes referred to as Lady Anne Barnard's bath. Also be sure to take in the fragrance garden, or, for a more vigorous adventure, follow the signs to Skeleton Gorge, undeniably one of the most beautiful (if strenuous) routes up the Table Mountain chain. During summer the Sunday sunset concerts are extremely popular.

Newlands Forest

Newlands Forest Station, Union Avenue (M3) (021 689 7438/9).

This is one of the best access points to the shaded sections of the mountain in the Southern Suburbs, and entry is free. Within three minutes of the easy parking at the forest station off the M3 northbound (look for the signs), you'll find yourself in a world of towering pines, indigenous forest and beautiful mountain streams. The walks winding up past the numerous contour paths are endless, and the landscape and foliage seems to change around every corner. If you're lucky (or ask a few locals out walking their dogs), you might stumble upon Paradise, a special little corner of the forest where the ruins of an old logging station have been reclaimed by nature.

SAB Newlands Breweries

3 Main Road (021 658 7511, www.sa miller.com). **Tours** 11am Mon, Tue, Thur, Fri. **Admission** R20 (proceeds go to charity); no under-18s. Booking essential (at least a week in advance); min 10 people, max 25 people, must wear closed shoes. **No credit cards**. The locals may be somewhat weary of the barley smell that emanates from here, but home brewers and others will be fascinated to see how the big guns brew the golden stuff. The tour starts with a documentary on the brewing process, after which you'll get to see (and smell) the fermentation and packing as it happens, rounding off the experience with two pints in the historic Letterstedt pub, named after Swedish brewer Jacob Letterstedt, who built this thriving factory and employed many members of the local community in the 19th century.

Eating & drinking

Caveau At The Mill

13 Boundary Road (021 685 5140, www.caveau.co.za). **Open** 8am-10.30pm Tue-Sat; 10am-3pm Sun. **RR**. **Wine bar**. Inside the national landmark of Josephine Mill, Caveau at the Mill is a restaurant, bar and function venue set in exquisite leafy surroundings, providing all the same elements as the sibling venue in the heart of the city (see p68). With a huge selection of the best local and international wines available by the bottle or glass, and bottles for sale to take home, it's a one-stop tour of the winelands.

Forrester's Arms

52 Newlands Avenue (021 689 5949). **Open** 11am-11pm Mon-Thur; 11am-midnight Fri; 10am-11pm Sat; 10am-6pm Sun. **R. Pub food.**

Almost every Capetonian has been to Forries, as it is affectionately known, at least once in their lifetime. Its location in the heart of the leafy Newlands makes it a popular hangout for students, and it's the destination of choice before or after a big cricket or rugby game at the famous Newlands grounds nearby. A good old-fashioned pub that serves a mean Sunday roast.

Square Restaurant and Sushi Bar

Vineyard Hotel, 60 Colinton Road, (021 657 4500, www.vineyard.co.za). **Open** 7am-10.30am, 12-3pm, 6-10pm daily. **RR. Contemporary global.**

This smart and contemporary space is open pretty much all day, so you can enjoy everything from scones and tea in the morning (or afternoon for that matter) to a platter of sushi at lunchtime. If you're looking for something more hearty, try any of the modern-global dishes.

Wijnhuis

Kildare Centre Main Street (021 671 9705, www.wijnhuis.co.za). **Open** 9am-late Mon-Sat. **RR. Wine bar/Italian.**

With a myriad different places to sit – from intimate lamp-lit nooks to more open expanses, this deservedly popular restaurant buzzes virtually every day of the week. The menu is mostly Italian and dishes range from pastas (with ingredients such as spinach, bacon, parmesan and pine nuts) to a superb tagliata, as well as steaks and very good calamari. As the name suggests, the wine list is just as important as the menu.

Arts & Leisure

Newlands Rugby Stadium

11 Boundary Road (021 659 4600, www.wprugby.com). Tours: Gateway to Newlands (021 686 2151/www.newlandstours.co.za). **Tours** Mon-Fri; excluding match days. Booking essential. **Tickets** R44 adults; R28-R30 concessions. **No credit cards.**

If you loved *Invictus* or, for that matter, the legendary 1995 Rugby World Cup, then you may enjoy the experience of visiting this famous venue, where you can run through the tunnel and on to the field as an imaginary 50,000 rugger fans cheer you on. Look out for weekend rugby games here in season.

Sahara Park Newlands

Cricket Ground, 146 Camp Ground Road (www.capecobras.co.za). Tours: Gateway to Newlands (021 686 2151, www.newlandstours.co.za). **Tours** Mon-Fri; excluding match days. Booking essential. **Tickets** R44 adults; R28-R30 concessions. **No credit cards.**

If you're more of a cricket than a rugby fan, then check out this well-kept pitch that's been hosting games since 1888. It was also the venue for the opening ceremony and match of the 2001 Cricket World Cup. The tour of the grounds includes the President's Suite, exclusive South Club and control rooms.

South African Rugby Museum

Sports Science Institute, Boundary Road, Newlands (021 686 2151, www.newlandstours.co.za). **Open** 8am-4.30pm Mon-Thur; 8am-4pm Fri. **Admission** Free. **Tours** (incl tour of Newlands Rugby Stadium) R58 adults; R36-R40 concessions. **No credit cards.**

CAPE TOWN BY AREA

Lunar p148

If the Newlands Rugby Stadium wasn't enough of a sports fix for you, then you'll certainly get satisfaction at this museum inside the Sports Science Institute of South Africa. Some of the items on display date back to 1891, while videos of famous tries brings things back up to date. Whether you want to learn more about the pigskin or prod the old boots of star kickers like Naas Botha and Joel Stransky, this is a shrine of all things rugby.

Rondebosch

The historic area of Rondebosch is the site where the first free burghers of the VOC (the Dutch East India Company) were granted land of their own. Its most famous historical beacons include the ivy-clad main campus of the University of Cape Town, the official presidential residency, Groote Schuur Hospital and the city's second-largest theatre, the Baxter Theatre Centre, a bastion of seventies architecture.

Sights & museums

Rhodes Memorial

Groote Schuur Estate, above UCT (www.rhodesmemorial.co.za).
Above the University of Cape Town on the slopes of Devil's Peak, Rhodes Mem, as the locals call it, is the perfect spot from which to view the Southern Suburbs; and you haven't really been here until you've clambered on to one of the bronze lions to have your picture taken. The monolithic granite memorial to mining magnate, imperialist and politician Cecil John Rhodes is arguably somewhat over the top, but its giant-sized steps and bronze lions help make the memorial a favourite spot. The 49 steps each represent a year in Rhodes's short but industrious life. The equestrian statue entitled *Energy* has a replica in Kensington Gardens in London.

UCT Irma Stern Museum

Cecil Road, Rosebank (021 685 5686, www.irmastern.co.za). **Open** 10am-5pm Tue-Sat. **Admission** R10 adults; R5 concessions. **No credit cards**.
Irma Stern was one of South Africa's major 20th-century artists. In the 1920s a local critic titled his scathing review: 'Art of Miss Irma Stern – Ugliness as a Cult'. By the 1940s, however, she had achieved enough success here that, after her death, the house her parents had bought her and in which she had lived for four decades, became a museum. Today, three of the rooms are still furnished as she arranged them; the sitting room, dining room and studio all demonstrate her eclectic taste as a collector – expect Egyptian and Greek artefacts, Coptic weavings, 14th-century European church carvings, seventh-century Chinese Tang dynasty sculptures and Japanese and Mexican masks. Upstairs is a commercial gallery used by contemporary South African artists – the everchanging exhibition space offers insight into the state of South African art today.

Nightlife

@mospheer

Corner Castor and Pollux roads, Lansdowne (082 407 5081, www. atmospheer.com). **Open** 9.30pm-4am Wed, Fri-Sat. **Admission** varies.
If there's a big international DJ in town, this is where he'll be playing. The club has a massive capacity (2,500), three bars, four VIP areas, a restaurant and in-house ATM, lots of secure and patrolled parking, state of the art lighting and sound equipment, 56 plasma screens as well as three big screens and a stage. It's all about a big night out, in every sense of the word.

Arts & entertainment

Baxter Theatre

Main Road, Rondebosch (021 685 7880/ 021 680 3989, www.baxter.co.za).

After the Artscape, this '70s-style monolith is the other major theatre in town. Within its walls lie four performance venues. Theatre-lovers can look forward to everything from dance to comedy and cutting-edge drama. The pocket-friendly Baxter Monday special is a real steal – R70 gets you a ticket to a selected show with a meal at the resident restaurant. The theatre also plays host to a bunch of annual festivals – including the Nando's Cape Town International Comedy Festival and Out the Box Festival of Puppetry and Visual Performance.

Claremont
Eating & drinking

A Tavola
1 Library Square, Wilderness Road (021 671 1763). **Open** noon-3pm, 6-10pm Mon-Fri; 6-10pm Sat. **RR**. **Italian**.
This bustling Italian restaurant is appreciated by those who know and appreciate authenticity. Quick, efficient service and a menu that includes the to-be-expected faves as well as modern-Med dishes are a winning combination and the reason the place is so popular. The zucchini frites are wonderful.

Shopping

Cavendish Square
1 Dreyer Street (021 657 5600, www.cavendish.co.za). **Open** 9am-7pm Mon-Sat; 10am-5pm Sun.
This multi-floor Southern Suburbs shopping institution crams a lot into a relatively small space – from all the national fashion names to a sizeable bookstore and a handful of independent lifestyle brands in between. It's as much a social as a shopping hub – the food options are surprisingly good and the adjoining Woolworths and Cavendish Connect add a whole other element to the experience. From 5pm onwards the place fills up with movie-goers galore.

Lunar
10 Cavendish Road (021 674 6871, www.lunarlife.co.za). **Open** 9am-5pm Mon-Fri; 10am-4pm Sat.
Local design legend Karen ter Morshuizen is a genius with classic contemporary cuts for men and women. Think raw silk tunics with slimline trousers, stupendously beautiful, lean-lined events outfits and some of the most beautiful wedding gowns in the city – perfect for the non-meringue-wearing girl about town.

The Space
LG 49, Cavendish Square (021 674 6643, www.thespace.co.za). **Open** 9am-7pm Mon-Sat; 10am-5pm Sun.
This concept store plays host to rail upon rail of inspired South African fashion – with labels by the likes of Amanda Laird Cherry and Colleen Eitzen. On-trend styles jostle for attention with classic cuts in seasonal prints and lines – from party pieces to weekend frocks and work essentials with a style-driven twist.

Studio 8
2 Cavendish Street (021 683 1666, www.studio8shop.com). **Open** 9am-5pm Mon-Fri; 9am-3.30pm Sat.
The eclectic mix of big and small imported brands reveals owner Marcelle Savage's sharp eye for creating well-conceived wardrobes for all kinds of women – from business types to socialites. You'll always find a well-cut something here, and there's a stylish selection for well-dressed men too.

Urban Degree
Shop L74 Cavendish Square (021 671 4398, www.urbandegree.co.za). **Open** 9am-7pm Mon-Sat; 9am-2pm Sun.
Weekend wear and leisure-influenced fashions in the style of Gap and Abercrombie & Fitch are the order of the day at this popular fashion brand (sibling to Vertigo and Aca Joe). You'll find lightweight knits in a slew of subdued shades, jeans, chinos and seasonal

Baxter Theatre p147

basics like the perfect denim jacket. Quality shirts in safe stripes and more out-there prints are a given.

Nightlife

Carnage

56 Main Road (entrance in Toffie Lane) (079 534 4503). **Open** 8.30pm-2am Thur-Sat. **Admission** R20.

This tucked-away spot has three bars, one being a shooter bar for all the brave souls willing to try strong shots. Chill spots are included for those who want to relax and smoke a hubbly or two. You'll also find three pool tables. A pole is provided for the sexy girls strutting their stuff to commercial beats. The two-for-one special is a major draw and the fact that you can play 'ching chong cha' (rock paper scissors) against the bartender to ensure a free drink is always a lot of fun.

Club 91

91 Main Road (021 674 9191, www.club91.co.za). **Open** 8pm-4am Tue, Thur, Fri, Sat. **Admission** R20-R50.

Southern Suburbs clubs are bigger and more lavish than those in the City Bowl. This one has three bars, a VIP lounge, table bookings, top-quality sound and lighting, and valet parking. The music is mainstream commercial house, with a bit of hip hop, old skool and electro thrown for good measure.

Tiger Tiger

The Atrium, 103 Main Road (021 683 2220, www.tigertiger.co.za). **Open** 8pm-4am Tue, Thur; 8.30pm-4am Fri-Sat. **Admission** varies.

With its proximity to the famous Newlands rugby and cricket grounds, Tiger Tiger naturally attracts sports stars and their followers, and its party nights often have sports themes. Expect big radio DJ names on the turntables. The place has no less than six bars, a spacious dance floor and the kind of sound and lighting you would expect from a club of this size.

Rondevlei Nature Reserve

Fisherman's Walk Road, Zeekoevlei, at the end of Perth Road (021 706 2404, www.rondevlei.co.za). **Open** 7.30am-5pm daily. **Admission** R10 adults; R5 concessions; free under-3s. *Fishing* R34 adults; R12 children (catch and release). **No credit cards.**

Who'd have thought that hippos are still hiding in Cape Town's suburbs? Come to this reserve and you'll get to see grysbok, porcupine, Cape clawless otter and grey mongoose as well. Settle down in one of the camouflaged bird hides and spot some of the more than 230 species who make the reserve their habitat. Observation towers with convenient mounted telescopes offer good views too. Contact Imvubu Tours (021 706 0842) for sundowner hippo-spotting boat trips and birding-by-boat day trips (Aug-Feb) as well as guided nature walks. For an unusual wild getaway in the heart of suburbia, stay overnight in the island bush camp.

Wynberg

Maynardville Open-Air Theatre

Cnr Wolfe and Church streets, Wynberg (021 421 7695, www.maynardville. co.za). **Shows** Jan-Feb. **Bookings** Computicket or Dial-a-Seat.

Popular with courting couples, this wooded open-air theatre has been putting on Shakespeare productions every summer since the 1950s. Pack a picnic and some wine and enjoy the sunset on the lawns; then make yourself comfortable for this year's take on a Shakespearean classic. Every year features a different director and interpretations vary from the boldly creative to the more traditional. Near the entrance, vendors ply coffee and nibbles, and fluffy blankets for chilly nights. The theatre also puts on an annual star-lit ballet, courtesy of Cape Town City Ballet.

Blue Peter p152

Northern Suburbs

This suburban region, predominately populated by a middle-class Afrikaans-speaking community, boasts some of the best views of the Peninsula and Table Mountain. Once a mostly rural sprawl, the suburbs here now encompass the likes of pristine **Welgemoed**, with its grassy verges and designer homes, glitzy **Panorama** and an increasing number of private estates in varying architectural styles.

Apart from the **Tygerberg** region – which houses Tygerberg Hospital, the medical campus of the University of Stellenbosch and the Tygerberg Zoo (the only one in the Western Cape) – **Durbanville** is the biggest tourist draw card thanks to its two large shopping centres (Tygervalley and Willowbridge) and Durbanville Wine Valley, a small but successful wine route encompassing nine estates and a handful of fine-dining restaurants.

Sights & museums

Blouberg Beach

Otto du Plessis Drive (M14), Blouberg.
The location that spawned myriad iconic Table Mountain-and-perfect-blue-sea postcards is best experienced first-hand, in person, in 3D. The sprawling beach is prone to high winds – capitalised on by kitesurfers and bodyboarders alike – but it remains a favoured hang-out among tan fans and dog-walkers.

Dolphin Beach

Marine Drive, Table View.
High winds rule in these parts, making Dolphin Beach a popular hangout for kitesurfers. If you're keen to catch a breeze and give your arms a serious workout into the bargain, head to a local kite shop such as Cabrinha (Shop 4, Marine Promenade, Porterfield Road, 021 556 7910, www.cabrinha.co.za), which will not only hire out a kite but give you lessons too.

Durbanville Wine Valley

Durbanville (083 310 1228,
www.durbanvillewine.co.za).
Vinophiles with a soft spot for sauvignon blanc should hit the road out to Durbanville Wine Valley. Thanks to the top-notch terroir, the other varietals aren't bad either – the cool climes associated with this hilly area make for fruity and intense reds. There are also a number of excellent restaurants to choose from. The nine estates on the route are Altydgedacht (021 976 1295, www.altydgedacht.co.za), Bloemendal (021 976 2682, www.bloemendalwines. co.za), D'Aria (021 801 6772, www.daria. co.za), De Grendel (021 558 6280, www.degrendel.co.za), Diemersdal (021 976 336, www.diemersdal.co.za), plus Durbanville Hills (021 558 1300, www.durbanvillehills.co.za), Hillcrest (021 975 2346, www.hillcrestfarm.co.za), Meerendal (021 975 1655, www.meerendal.co.za) and Nitida (021 976 1467, www.nitida.co.za).

Tygerberg Nature Reserve

Totius Street, Welgemoed, Bellville
(021 913 5695). **Open** *Winter* 7.30am-
5pm Mon-Fri; 7.30am-6pm Sat, Sun.
Summer 7.30am-6pm Mon-Fri; 7.30am-
7pm Sat, Sun. **Admission** R10; R5
reductions. No credit cards.
This area was declared a nature reserve in 1973, and today boasts a tangle of excellent hiking trails. The reserve's fauna and flora is impressive – as you amble through thickets of endemic renosterveld, you might spot anything from bontebok and bat-eared foxes to a rainbow of butterflies.

Tygerberg Zoo

Exit 39, Klipheuwel-Stellenbosch
off-ramp, N1 Highway (021 884
4494, www.tygerbergzoo.co.za).
Open 9am-5pm daily. **Admission**
R60; R40 reductions.
Great for families and home to some 200 different species, this impressive menagerie is the place to come to see rare creatures like white storks, mini

antelope, alpacas, crocodilians, snakes and chimps. Little ones keen to meet and greet some of the tamer beasts can do so at the farmyard petting zoo, while their parents relax with a brew in the pleasant tea garden.

Eating & drinking

Blowfish

1 Marine Drive, Bloubergstrand
(021 556 5464). **Open** 6.30am-
10.30am, noon-10pm daily. **RR.**
Sushi & seafood.
This Bloubergstrand darling not only showcases the blue-hued Table Mountain in its entirety, but also offers a fresh fish and seafood counter to rival the best. Choose your fish from the selection before having it grilled to perfection or join fellow sushi fiends at the conveyor belt piled with delicious just-made morsels.

Blue Peter

Blue Peter Hotel, 7 Popham Road,
Bloubergstrand (021 554 1956,
www.bluepeter.co.za). **Open** 9.30am-
10pm daily. **RR. Pub, grills**
& pizza.
The Blue Peter, with its breathtaking Table Mountain view, is divided into a laid-back, lawn-fringed lower deck and a smarter upper-deck restaurant called the Lighthouse. The latter has an award-winning wine list and is renowned for its Sunday lunches and dinner and dance evenings, while the bistro downstairs focuses on crowd pleasers like pizzas, hamburgers and fish and chips. Just a stone's throw from the beach, it's the perfect spot for post-beachcombing sustenance and a relaxed sundowner or two.

Buckley's

4 Blue Waters, Porterfield Road, Table
View (021 556 1618). **Open** noon-4am
daily. **R. Pub.**
Much like its sister venue in Durbanville, Buckley's is a chilled bar that pulls in a young, 'emo' crowd

(though it's equally popular with older drinkers looking for a relaxed vibe) with its pool and foosball tables, friendly, efficient staff (there's never too much of a wait at the bar) and music that ranges from commercial rock and radio hits to drum and bass.

Cassia

Nitida Wine Estate, Tygerberg Valley Road (M13), Durbanville (021 976 0640). **Open** noon-9.30pm Mon-Fri; 9-11am, noon-9pm Sat; 9-11am, noon-3pm Sun. **RR. Modern rustic**.
Overlooking Nitida Estate's farm dam, vineyards and surrounding mountains, this well-dressed restaurant showcases contemporary but hearty eats, like starters of rabbit and mushroom pie with citrus compôte, and mains such as slow-cooked pork belly with a pancetta and creamed bean sauce.

Doodles

110 Beach Boulevard, Blouberg Strand (021 554 1080/www.doodles.co.za).
Open 9am-late daily. **R. Beach bar**.
Whether you're a kitesurfing participant or just like to watch others in action, Doodles is perfectly located – it's just across the road from the beach. Expect all the ingredients required for a low-key night (or afternoon) out: a friendly, unpretentious crowd, plenty of seating both indoors and out, a decent bar menu, good beer on tap, big-screen sports, live music and DJs.

Poplars

Tygerberg Valley Road (M13), Durbanville (021 975 5736). **Open** 11.30am-late Mon-Fri; 9am-close Sat, Sun. **RR. Modern rustic**.
This popular venue ticks all the boxes for a satisfying country outing (if you can, go for a table on the terrace to make the most of the attractive surroundings). The bill of fare features starters such as thyme rösti topped with smoked salmon, cream cheese and a fig glaze, along with hearty mains including slow-roasted, orangey duck

Township tours

Another side of Cape Town life.

A large proportion of Cape Town's residents live in informal settlements. Many once-informal set-ups are now thriving, formalised communities, and not everyone who lives in a township does so in poverty. That said, many people live in difficult circumstances and a tour can prove very insightful.

Uthando Tours (021 683 8523, www.uthandosa.org) enable you to discover township life while doing your bit for the greater community. Uthando is a non-governmental organisation that takes visitors on tailor-made half-day trips through Cape Town's townships to check out a series of community-based, social development programmes dedicated to everything from teaching residents to grow their own food to the rehabilitation of prisoners and providing of care for HIV/Aids orphans.

Nomvuyo's Tours (083 372 9131, www.nomvuyos-tours.co.za), meanwhile, offer the opportunity to zip around Cape Town's largest township, Khayelitsha, and meet its friendly residents. During your visit, you can stock up on bargain buys at the local spaza shop (SA's version of the corner café), down an illicit tipple while playing pool at the shebeen ('pub' to the uninitiated), tuck into hearty African fare and spend the night in Cape Town's township gem, Vicky's B&B.

on mushroom risotto, and mustard-coated eisbein on sweet-potato mash.

Southpole

Ocean Square, Sunset Beach, Milnerton (021 551 5752). **Open** 6-10pm Tue-Sat. **RR. Contemporary South African.**

Located in Milnerton's ritzy Sunset Strip, you can expect gourmet fare on the Southpole's weekly tasting menus, which may include starters like grilled springbok medallions with mustard mash, and mains such as beef with spiced oats and coriander seeds with gremolata. This is a great place to sample high-quality, well-cooked South African specialities.

Ruby Bar

Crystal Towers Hotel & Spa, Century City (021 525 3888, www.africanpride hotels.com). **Open** 8am-2am daily. **RRR. Cocktail bar.**

If designer decor and swankily delicious cocktails are your thing, Ruby Bar might just be the perfect place to kick back as the sun goes down before getting stuck into a game of pool on the bright orange table. For a more intimate experience, check into one of the private lounges – each has been individually styled with relics and mementos from explorer Kingsley Holgate and singer David Kramer, both African icons in their own rights.

Shopping

Canal Walk

Century Boulevard, Century City, Milnerton (021 529 9699, www.canal walk.co.za). **Open** 9am-9pm daily.

With over 400 places to swipe your plastic, this gigantic mall is a one-stop shopping extravaganza for those in a spending – or browsing – state of mind. All the big chain stores are accounted for – from supermarkets to electronics shops, clothing specialists to furniture stores – along with a giant food court, several movie theatres, the

MTN Science Centre and holiday programmes to keep the kids occupied. You could easily lose a whole day here.

Nightlife

China White

Edward Street, Tyger Valley (021 910 2184/www.chinawhite.co.za). **Open** 7pm-4am Wed; 9pm-4am Thur-Sat; 6pm-12am Sun. **Admission** R30 (free Thur, Sun).

This spot oozes style and class, with a long bar, two dance floors, lounges, a live performance area and an exclusive VIP area, all set against a glamorous oriental backdrop.

Arts & Leisure

Grand Arena

GrandWest Casino & Entertainment World, 1 Vanguard Drive, Goodwood (021 505 7777, www.suninternational.com).

This massive 5,000-seater venue is set in the neon belly of the GrandWest Casino & Entertainment World. The space regularly plays host to headlining international acts, including bands, stand-up acts, musical tribute shows and other big-budget spectaculars. Check the regularly updated website for details of upcoming music and entertainment events.

Villa Pascal Theatre

28 Van der Westhuizen Street, Durbanville (021 975 2566, www.villapascal.co.za). **Open** 6pm-late Wed-Sun.

This pleasingly intimate venue is owned by expatriate French chanteuse Danièle Pascal. It predominately plays host to cabaret, tribute shows and musical revues, but anything goes with blues, rock 'n' roll, acoustic folk, jazz, classical, opera and even belly dancing featuring on the bill. The place really is a celebration of all things musical and good-quality productions are pretty much guaranteed.

Terroir p161

Winelands

They're only an hour's drive from Cape Town, but with rolling vineyards, towering mountains and historic wine estates, the famous Cape Winelands feel like a different world. Stellenbosch and Franschhoek are two of the area's most popular destinations.

Stellenbosch

Oak-lined Stellenbosch is South Africa's second-oldest town. Home to the University of Stellenbosch, the community is generally a wealthy one.

The **Stellenbosch Wine Route** was established in 1971 and includes several internationally renowned estates like Simonsig, Delheim and Spier. The annual Stellenbosch Wine Festival attracts many visitors, and the town and surrounding region are also renowned for their excellent restaurants.

Sights & museums

Bergkelder

Adam Tas Road, Papegaaiberg, (021 809 8025, www.bergkelder.co.za).
Open 8am-5pm Mon-Fri; 9am-2pm Sat. *Tours* 10am, 11am, 2pm, 3pm Mon-Fri; 10am, 11am, noon Sat. **Tickets** R25.
This cellar is located inside the Papegaaiberg, which has ideal conditions for storing wine. The recently revamped hour-long tour explains the wine-making process, and includes the tasting of five wines and a visit to the museum with its antique implements.

Cape Town Lion Park

Vredenheim Wine Farm, R310 (083 868 4119, www.capetownlionpark.co.za).
Open 10am-4pm daily. **Admission** R65 adults; R45 children. **Guided tours** R130 adults; R90 children.
Since blue-eyed white lions are very scarce, it's a real treat to catch them in action up close: from the gambolling cubs and mischievous teens to the

majestically maned males basking in the sun. You can stroll around on your own, but the guided tour is recommended.

Cheetah Outreach

Spier Wine Estate, R310 (021 881 3242, www.cheetah.co.za). **Open** 10am-5pm daily (6pm at weekends in high season). *Cheetah encounters* 11am-1pm, 2-5pm daily (6pm at weekends in high season). **Admission** R10 Mon-Fri; R5 Sat, Sun. *Cheetah encounters* R100-R200. **No credit cards.**

The cheetahs of this non-profit centre have been hand-reared as ambassadors for their endangered brethren, so you get the rare chance to stroke the spotted fur of the cheetah cubs and adults.

Giraffe House Wildlife Awareness Centre

Cnr of R304 towards Stellenbosch & R101 towards Paarl (021 884 4506, www.giraffehouse.co.za). **Open** 9am-5pm daily. *Animal encounters* 11am, 1pm, 3pm daily. **Admission** R45 adults; R25-R30 concessions. **No credit cards.**

This wildlife awareness centre boasts a menagerie of weird and wonderful animals and is an ideal family-friendly destination. Catch the shenanigans of vervet monkeys and meerkats, gambolling buck and perpetually grinning Nile crocodiles, before picnicking on the lawn with refreshments from the kiosk. Kids can run amok on the jungle gyms and giraffe-shaped jumping castle.

Stellenbosch American Express® Wine Routes

Information *Stellenbosch Tourism Information Bureau, 36 Market Street (021 886 4310, www.wineroute.co.za).* Stellenbosch has the oldest and largest wine route in the country. It's split into five sub-routes: Greater Simonsberg, Stellenbosch Berg, Helderberg, Stellenbosch Hills and Bottelary Hills. With over 140 wineries to choose from, you will have endless tasting opportunities, and you'll also be able to try

other products like honey, olives and cheese. There is also a burgeoning Methode Cap Classique (MCC) route where visitors trail from cellar to cellar enjoying quality sparklers.

Village Museum

18 Ryneveld Street (021 887 2902). **Open** *May-Aug* 9am-5pm Mon-Sat; 10am-1pm Sun. *Sept-Apr* 9am-5pm Mon-Sat; 10am-4pm Sun. **Admission** R25 adults; R5 children.

This quaint museum offers an authentic and fascinating walk through 150 years of history of Stellenbosch village life. Four houses from different architectural periods (1709-1850) are decorated according to their period, and even the gardens are historically accurate too. Costumed guides are on hand to give a handy explanation or two.

Vine Hopper

36 Market Street (084 492 4992, 021 882 8112, www.adventureshop.co.za). **Open** 9am-5pm Mon-Sat. **Rates** R170 1 day; R300 2 days.

Why spoil the fun for a designated driver when you can hop on or off a merry bus with other wine lovers, sampling some of the finest varieties along the way? The bus service is divided into two routes (north and south) and each stops at six different wineries.

Waterford Estate Wine Experiences

Blaauwklippen Road (021 880 0496, www.waterfordestate.co.za). **Open** by appointment only, weather dependent. **Admission** wine safari R50; chocolate and wine pairing R40.

For wine-tasting with a difference, a trip to the Provençal-inspired Waterford Estate on the slopes of the Helderberg Mountains is just the ticket. Take a wine safari, where you'll explore the estate on an open vehicle and get to taste its prized tipples among the vines. Learn about the terroir and, during harvest, see the working action for yourself. If you have a sweet tooth, give the

Stellenbosch Fresh Goods
Market p161

chocolate and wine-tasting a whirl. Master chocolatier Richard von Geusau's Belgian creations are paired with Waterford's shiraz, cab sauv and sweet wine.

Eating & drinking

Amazink
Ikhaya Trust Centre, Kayamandi (021 889 7536, www.amazink.co.za). **Open** 11am-midnight Tue-Sat; 11am-10pm Sun. **RR. Shebeen/grill.**
For a real-deal township dining and drinking experience, head for this quirky, colourful spot in Stellenbosch's oldest informal (now formal) settlement. Enjoy meats cooked over the coals and a host of traditional accompanying specialities.

Bodega Restaurant
Dornier Wines, Blaauwklippen Road off R44, Paradyskloof (021 880 0557, www.dornier.co.za). **Open** noon-4pm daily; 6-9.30pm Thur-Sat. **RR. Modern country.**
Overlooking the sculptural cellar and the impressive mountains, this colourful restaurant tucked away in a corner of Stellenbosch offers a memorable experience. Chef Neil Norman creates his farm cuisine to complement the wines of Dornier and surrounding wineries. The food is unfussy but offers a rather careful balance of tastes. Wine pairings are available.

Cupcake
Blackhorse Centre, Dorp Street (021 886 6376). **Open** 8am-5pm Mon-Fri; 8am-3pm Sat. **R. Café/cakes.**
Take a seat in the courtyard and enjoy sweet treats like French toast with cinnamon sugar or a delicious cupcake. There's also an interesting selection of gifts, especially for children.

Cuvée at Simonsig
Simonsig Wine Estate, Kromme Rhee Road, off R44 (021 888 4932, www.cuveeatsimonsig.co.za). **Open**

11am-3pm Tue-Sat; 7-10pm Fri, Sat; 11am-2pm Sun. **RRR. Contemporary South African.**
Furnished in an eclectic mix of classic wooden and funky retro, this establishment's menu takes inspiration from the Cape Dutch building in which it finds itself. The emphasis is very much on traditional Western Cape fare with a contemporary twist, in dishes like coriander-roasted Hantam lamb encased in sour-cream pastry and served with preserved green figs. The estate's wines are also a fixture in desserts such as sweet-wine sorbet.

De Akker
Corner Dorp and Herte Street (021 883 3512). **Open** 10.30-2am Mon-Sat. **R. Bar.**
A favourite among Stellenbosch's post-grad students, De Akker is one of the oldest watering holes in town. Fans of live local music can cut a rug at the upstairs Hidden Cellar.

De Oewer
Aan-de-Wagen Road (021 886 5431, www.deoewer.co.za). **Open** noon-3pm; 6.30-10pm daily. **RR. Global.**
This is the only restaurant in Stellenbosch where you can sit on the banks of the Eerste River, and this alone is reason enough to visit this food and wine garden. The menu offers seafood, meat, burgers and salads and is ideal for a lazy summer lunch.

Delaire Graff
Helshoogte Pass (021 885 8160, www.delaire.co.za). **Open** noon-2.30pm; 6.30-8.30pm daily. **RRRR. Contemporary.**
There's no denying it: this place is cool with a capital C, from the progressive David Collins-designed space, with its signature hot-orange leather seats and Stellenbosch valley view, to the contemporary-chic menu. Created by executive chef Christiaan Campbell, it features beautifully constructed mains like rabbit with olive jus and desserts such as rose geranium ice-cream.

Gino's @ De Kelder

*63 Dorp Street (021 887 9786,
www.ginos.co.za)*. **Open** noon-9.30pm
Tue-Sun. **R**. **Italian**.
Housed in an original farmhouse in
Dorp Street, this Italian eatery serves
standard Italian fare such as pizzas
and pastas alongside specialities like
oxtail, tripe stew or grills – and at good
prices too. The wine list, including various wines from the area, is well priced.
In fine weather you can eat outside
under the oaks.

Jordan Restaurant with George Jardine

*Stellenbosch Kloof Road (021 881
3612, www.jordanwines.com)*. **Open**
noon-3pm Tue-Sun; 7pm-close Thur,
Fri. **RRR**. **Contemporary global**.
Top chef George Jardine has taken his
talents to the Winelands with a new
venture at Jordan winery. This intimate restaurant has been custom-
designed with an open kitchen so
diners can watch the man at work.
Glass doors along the entire length of
the dining room open on to a generous
veranda with endless views over the
dam and mountains. On the food side,
Jardine's standards remain exception-
ally high, with locally sourced, seasonal fare, presented accessibly. The
walk-in cheese room is a delight, so
leave some space.

Moyo

*Spier Estate, Lyndoch Road, R310
(021 809 1137, www.moyo.co.za)*.
Open noon-4pm, 6-11pm daily.
RRR. **Pan African**.
A visit to the beautiful Spier estate
isn't complete without a lazy meal at
this popular restaurant. Stake out a
seat at one of the tree-top decks or in
the exotic Bedouin tent, then dip into
the bountiful Umdliva buffet table
brimming with Pan-African dishes.
The waiting staff double as face-
painters, making for a fun, interactive
dining experience. There's also live
music and dancing.

Nook Eatery

*42 Van Ryneveld Street (021 887
7703, www.nookeatery.co.za)*. **Open**
8am-4pm Mon-Fri; 6-9pm Wed; 8.30am-
1pm Sat. **R**. **Café**.
This small and nostalgia-laced eaterie
is seriously popular. Enjoy the well-
priced sandwiches (served on wooden
boards), the lunch buffet or the daily
blackboard specials. Teatime treats are
delightful, especially the coconut bread
with mascarpone and honey.

Overture

*Hidden Valley Estate, Annandale Road,
(021 880 2721, www.dineatoverture.
co.za)*. **Open** noon-2pm Tue-Sun; 6.30-
8pm Thur, Fri. *Tasting room* 10am-
5pm Mon-Fri; 10am-4.30pm Sat, Sun.
RRR. **Modern French**.
Perched high above the Annandale
Valley, with magnificent views, this top
restaurant's changing menu is small but
very exciting. Wines also change weekly to complement the classic but contemporary French cuisine. Choose between
three to five courses or the eight-course
tasting menu. Picnics are also available
to enjoy beside the dam.

Restaurant Christophe

44 Ryneveld Street (021 886 8763).
Open noon-2pm Tue-Fri; 7-9pm Mon-
Sat. **RR**. **Bistro**.
French chef Christophe Dehosse of
Klein Joostenberg Deli has finally
opened his long-awaited restaurant.
Expect a muted sage green interior and
traditional French cuisine, including
classics like poached foie gras. The
menu changes regularly. Wines are
from Burgundy or local wineries.

The Rock Room

*Blackhorse Centre, cnr Dorp & Market
Streets (021 887 3144)*. **Open** noon-
2am Mon-Sat; noon-5pm Sun. **R**. **Bar**.
Spangled walls and all, this venue rais-
es the bar for hip hang-outs in town.
Enjoy the *stoep* vibe while sipping
great cocktails (happy hour 7-8pm
Mondays and Thursdays), or eat a

Bodega Restaurant p158

gourmet burger or tapas while listening to live acoustic, blues or rock music on Friday or Saturday evenings.

Rust en Vrede Restaurant

Rust en Vrede Farm, Annandale Road (021 881 3757, www.rustenvrede.com). **Open** noon-3pm, 7pm-close Tue-Sat. **RRRR. Modern European/South African**.

This highly acclaimed restaurant, headed by chef David Higgs, offers food rooted in classical French cuisine but infused with the best South African produce. The four-course menu is joined by a six-course tasting menu, with or without wine pairing. A daily winemaker's set lunch is served outside the tasting room.

TasteBud

Skuinshuis, 44 Ryneveld Street (083 233 5537, 083 625 2301). **Open** 8am-5pm Mon-Fri. **R. French café**.

TasteBud is a relatively new kid on the block but its lunch buffet has already proved a hit. They also offer great *tartines* (open sandwiches on French country loaf) and the cheesecake is delicious. The atmosphere is very relaxed but get there early as it fills up quickly.

Terroir

Kleine Zalze Wine Estate, R44 (021 880 8167, www.kleinezalze.com). **Open** 12.30-2.30pm, 7-9.30pm Mon-Sat; 12.30-2.30pm Sun. **RRR. Contemporary French**.

Don't let the blackboard menu and bucolic surrounds fool you into thinking this is just another Winelands country café. Chef Michael Broughton's French-inspired fare has racked up a ridiculous number of awards. From his signature prawn and mushroom risotto to his superbly sauced fillet with parmesan cream, each bite is a triumph.

Tokara DeliCATessen

Tokara, Helshoogte Pass (021 808 5951, www.tokara.com). **Open** 9am-5pm Tue-Sun. **RR. Café**.

This deli is another splendid addition to Tokara, with its innovative architecture and unrivalled views of the Simonsberg Mountain. Great olive oils (available for tasting), delicious cakes and freshly baked bread, preserves and charcuterie are all on offer, along with a weekend buffet. Children will enjoy the designer jungle gym.

Volkskombuis

Aan-de-Wagen Rod (021 887 2121, www.volkskombuis.co.za). **Open** noon-3pm, 6.30-10pm daily. **RR. Traditional South African**.

This restaurant is a Stellenbosch institution. The interior hints at traditional Cape Dutch, with copper implements on the walls and yellow wood furniture. You can also expect traditional Cape cuisine, with dishes like *bobotie* and Meraai's chicken pie. The menu offers some wine-pairing suggestions.

Shopping

Oom Samie se Winkel

82/84 Dorp Street (021 887 0797). **Open** 8.30am-5.30pm Mon-Fri (winter from 9am); 9am-5pm Sat, Sun.

This shop captures the essence of the 18th-century general dealer. The air is filled with the aroma of tobacco, *bokkoms*, biltong and *mebos* (made of dried peaches or apricots). It's all mixed with a bit of touristy stuff, wine and other memorabilia not easily found elsewhere. Like shopping in a time warp.

Stellenbosch Fresh Goods Market

Oude Libertas, cnr Adam Tas and Oude Libertas streets (072 416 4890, www.slowmarket.co.za). **Open** 9am-2pm Sat. **No credit cards.**

Set in the sunken, oak-dappled courtyard of the Oude Libertas, this slow-food market has become quite the Saturday-morning institution amongst Stellenbosch's foodies. The stalls have the continents covered, proffering everything from schwarmas and tacos to *spanakopita* and *apfelstrudel*. Add in a soothing soundtrack of world music and a few glasses of artisan beer, and you've got yourself a party.

Arts & Leisure

Endler Concert Hall

University of Stellenbosch Conserve, cnr Victoria Avenue and Neethling Street (021 808 2343, www.sun.ac.za, music). Bookings Computicket (083 915 8000, www.computicket.com).

Showcasing the University of Stellenbosch's symphony orchestra, brass band and choir, this concert hall boasts great acoustics and a famous Marcussen organ. Students perform mainly during university semesters but great international musicians are also often on the programme. The International Chamber Music festival during winter is a highlight.

Oude Libertas Amphitheatre

Oude Libertas Centre, cnr Adam Tas and Oude Libertas Road (021 809 7473, www.oudelibertas.co.za). Bookings Computicket or box office (083 915 8000, 021 809 7380).

This amphitheatre has a reputation for great productions under the stars featuring local and international artists. Shows run from November to March and cover plays, music (classic to rock), and many a genre in between. Bring your own picnic and laze on the lawns during the Sunday sunset concerts.

Franschhoek

Franschhoek is famous for both its wine and its award-winning restaurants, as well as its food-related festivals.

The Franschhoek Valley Wine Tram is set to open in late 2010, offering a hop-on hop-off service between Franschhoek and Paarl. Two vintage trams will run along the 28-kilometre line, with stops at wine estates along its route. Ask at the tourist information office for more information (021 876 3603, www.franschhoek.org.za).

Sights & museums

Franschhoek Motor Museum

L'Ormarins Wine Estate, off R45 (021 874 9000, www.fmm.co.za). **Open** *July-Apr* 10am-5pm Tue-Fri; 10am-3pm Sat, Sun. *May-June* 10am-5pm Mon-Fri; 10am-3pm Sat, Sun. **Admission** R60 adults; R30-R50 concessions.

Petrolheads will drool with envy at this private car collection of industrial magnate Johann Rupert. Eighty cars from Rupert's 200-car collection are on display at any one time, including legendary wheels like the first Model-T Ford to drive in South Africa, and a ridiculously expensive Ferrari Enzo.

Eating & drinking

Bistro Allée Bleue

Allée Bleue Wine Estate, junction R45 & R310 (021 874 1021, www.alleebleue.com). **Open** 8am-5pm daily. **RR. Bistro**.

This is a delightful country bistro on an estate tucked well away from the hubbub of central Franschhoek; expect a small, well-chosen menu. The striking Mediterranean decor works well on grey wintry days, or bag a table with vineyard views in summer. Wine-tasting is available at the tasting room across the gum-tree-lined avenue.

Le Bon Vivant

22 Dirkie Uys Street (021 876 2717, www.lebonvivant.co.za). **Open** noon-3pm, 7-9.30pm Mon, Tue, Thur-Sun. **RR. Global/South African**.

A classy art-filled restaurant that spills onto a wonderful shaded terrace. The discreet open kitchen allows you to keep an eye on Dutch-born chef/patron Pierre Hendricks while he whips up dishes that balance Asian and

European flavours with fabulous local produce. Excellent value for the gourmet artistry on offer.

Bread & Wine

Môreson Wine Farm, Happy Valley Roda (021 876 3692, www.moreson. co.za). **Open** noon-3pm daily. **RR**. **Bistro**.

Languid summer afternoons are the best time to sample the famous charcuterie platters at this laid-back courtyard restaurant. Neil Jewell's legendary artisan-style charcuterie takes pride of place, but there are other lovely dishes too, as well as his equally talented wife Tina's own-baked breads. Wines from the estate are all available by the glass. Stock up on meats, cheeses and own-made bread at the deli on the way out.

Dutch East

42 Huguenot Street (021 876 3547). **Open** 11am-4pm, 7-9pm daily. **RR**. **Contemporary café**.

Franschhoek regulars might notice that the old Burgundy's restaurant has been given a new lease of life. Exposed brick walls, rustic tables and chandeliers set the scene for a spot that looks likely to become a local favourite. The tuna starter is excellent.

Elephant & Barrel Village Pub

Huguenot Square, 48 Huguenot Street, (021 876 4127, www.elephantand barrel.co.za). **Open** 11am-2am (kitchen closes 10pm) daily. **R**. **Pub food**.

This English-style pub is as unpretentious as they come. Tuck into pub grub of bangers and mash or chicken curry outside in the courtyard, but when there's a game on, the flatscreen TVs are where you'll find the action. Look out for regular live music too.

Essence Restaurant & Coffee bar

Shop 7, Huguenot Square, Huguenot Street (021 876 4135). **Open** 7am-6pm daily. **R**. **Café**.

Style bank

Good food, great wine and upmarket shopping have turned the once sleepy student town of Stellenbosch into a thriving tourist hub.

The **De Oude Bank** precinct, on the corner of Church and Bird streets, is a new arrival on the Stellenbosch scene, now home to a number of bustling shops, cafés, restaurants and galleries.

Star of the show here is the **De Oude Bank Bakkerij** (021 883 2187). Marrying rural charm with urban cool, this wood-clad café serves up artisan-style breads with meats, cheeses and other accompaniments. Open until 3pm from Tuesday to Saturday, it's also open on Wednesday and Saturday nights for wood-fired pizzas and music.

Just across the stone courtyard is **Crystal** (021 887 2173), a showroom for hand-blown glassware from famous brand Bohemia – you'll find everything from curvaceous carafes to elegant decanters and wine and whisky glasses. **Die Dorpstraat Gallery** (021 887 2256, www.dorpstraat gallery.co.za) is one of the best-loved galleries in town, stocking a heady mix of contemporary art, photography, sculpture, objets d'art and jewellery. Also, be sure not to miss the permanent **Dylan Lewis Exhibition** (021 887 3976). The 3.7metre-high bronze sculpture outside the exhibition space is a fitting hallmark. Wander indoors and marvel at the magnificent half-men, half-mythical creatures created by this legendary South African sculptor.

Tables in this quaint café spill out on to the pavement, making it a great place to watch the world go by while you tuck into the menu of light meals, sandwiches and salads. The coffee is good and there's Wi-Fi on offer, so it's a good spot to catch up on your emails.

Fizz Affair

Shop 2, Place Vendôme Lifestyle Centre, Huguenot Street (021 876 2580). **Open** noon-10pm daily. **RRR.** **Wine/champagne bar.**

This glamorous champagne and wine bar is a good bet for a pre-dinner drink, or a celebration. You'll find a good mix of local Méthode Cap Classiques (often labelled MCC) as well as French champagnes to frighten your credit card. The service can be slack, so settle in at one of the terrace tables.

Franschhoek Station Pub & Grill

4 Huguenot Street (021 876 3938). **Open** 11am-2am Tue-Sun. **R.** **Pub food.**

This delightfully unpretentious eaterie in the old railway station has become a firm favourite with local families. The menu is unashamedly pub grub, with well-priced dishes paired with a small selection of local wines. Tables (with blankets for chilly days) are scattered on the station platform, and kids will love the boules court laid out between the railway tracks.

Fyndraai

Solms-Delta Wine Estate, off R45, Groot Drakenstein (021 874 3937, www.solms-delta.co.za). **Open** noon-5pm daily. **RR.** **South African.**

The tables under the oaks are some of the prettiest in the valley, great for a fine summer's day. Food – a selection of Cape favourites – matches the views. Picnic baskets are also available, to be enjoyed at a private spot on the riverbank. Also, pay a visit to the estate's Museum van de Caab, which explores the history of the valley from the

Stone Age, through the eras of slavery and apartheid to the present day.

Genot

Klein Genot Estate, Valley Road (021 876 2729, www.kleingenot.com). **Open** noon-3pm, 6-9.30pm Tue-Sat; noon-3pm Sun. **RR.** **European.**

Despite the chic interiors, there's an old-school comfort to the menu at this restaurant whose name, suitably, means 'delight'. Expect classic or retro dishes like Caesar salad and garlic snails to start, before a mains menu that's heavy on dependable grills. The wine list proudly promotes local estates, including Klein Genot wines.

The Grillroom

Heritage Square, 9 Huguenot Street (021 876 2548). **Open** noon-3pm, 6.30-10pm daily. **RR.** **Grills.**

Exposed brick walls and plush banquettes give this classy steakhouse a New York feel, while an open kitchen lets you watch the chefs at work. Matthew Gordon (of Haute Cabrière fame) is in charge here, so the meat-heavy menu, with interesting daily specials, doesn't disappoint.

Haute Cabrière

Cabrière Estate, Franschhoek Pass (021 876 3688, www.hautecabriere.com). **Open** *Summer* noon-3pm, 7pm-9pm daily. *Winter* 7pm-9pm Mon-Fri; noon-3pm, 7pm-9pm Fri, Sat. **RRR.** **Bistro.**

Achim von Arnim's Saturday morning cellar tours have become legendary in Franschhoek, thanks in no small part to the gregarious cellar master's deft hand at the art of sabrage (opening champagne with a sword). Swords and corks aside, Matthew Gordon's acclaimed cellar restaurant is as much of a reason to visit. Dishes are available in half portions, and food and wine pairing is a must.

Kalfi's Restaurant

17 Huguenot Street (021 876 2520).

Oom Samie se Winkel p161

Open 8am-9.30pm daily. **R. Café**.
A welcome break from the foams and infusions at Franschhoek's upmarket eateries, this laid-back spot offers more rustic fare, with a menu as approachable as the service. Expect generous, no-frills favourites like toasted sarmies, *bobotie* and old-fashioned chicken pie.

Lecca Il Gelato
Shop 4, Village Centre, Main Road, (021 876 2636, www.leccailgelato.co.za). **Open** 9am-5pm Mon-Thur; 9am-6pm Fri-Sun. **R. No credit cards**.
Ice-cream.
You won't want to share your dark chocolate and orange ice-cream with anyone else, but luckily there are around 70 other flavours for them to choose from at what is easily one of the best ice-cream shops in the Cape. Grab a cone to enjoy as you stroll along the Main Road, or stop and enjoy at the tables outside.

Mange Tout
Mont Rochelle Hotel & Mountain Vineyards, Dassenberg Road (021 876 2770/www.montrochelle.co.za). **Open** *Summer* 7-8.30pm daily. *Winter* 7-8.30pm Wed-Fri; 12.30-2.30pm, 7-8.30pm Sat, Sun. **RRR. Modern European**.
The best views in Franschhoek? The jury's out, but this hilltop hotel restaurant is certainly in the running. A subtle balancing act of traditional and modern is reflected in both the decor and the menu. Executive chef Ryan Smith makes the most of the region's local produce.

Mont Rochelle Country Kitchen
Mont Rochelle Hotel & Mountain Vineyards, Dassenberg Road, (021 876 2770/www.montrochelle.co.za). **Open** 10am-9.30pm Mon, Tue; 10am-7pm Wed-Sun. **RR. Modern country**.
A relaxed way to enjoy the great views from Mont Rochelle is to eat at the country kitchen next door to the estate's wine-tasting tables. The chalkboard menu has a distinctly Mediterranean

slant, with great vegetarian options. Gourmet picnics can also be ordered to enjoy at designated picnic spots.

La Petite Ferme
Franschhoek Pass Road (021 876 3016, www.lapetiteferme.co.za). **Open** noon-4pm daily. **RRR. European**.
Franschhoek's gourmet reputation was kick-started by this family-owned restaurant with panoramic views. Continental culinary influences marry with local produce to offer a menu of adventurous comfort food. Helpful pairings match estate wines to each dish.

The Restaurant at Grande Provence
Grande Provence Estate, Main Road (021 876 8600, www.grandeprovence. co.za). **Open** noon-2.30, 7-9.30pm daily. **RRRR. Global**.
There's a strong Asian influence on the menu at this historic wine estate, where diners are can create their own menu from a selection of 20 or so choices. This is fine dining made fun, with the likes of duck and rabbit gateaux. Enjoy it at delightful tables under the oaks. The estate is home to a leading contemporary art gallery, and there's local art and sculpture in the garden too.

Reuben's
19 Huguenot Strete (021 876 3772, www.reubens.co.za). **Open** noon-3pm, 7-9pm daily. **RRR. Modern global**.
Award-winning chef-patron Reuben Riffel needs no introduction in the village, and his expanded restaurant continues to draw diners from far and wide. Asian influences abound, and the crisp pork belly is a house specialty not to be missed. The impressive wine list offers something for every pocket and palate.

Rickety Bridge Restaurant in the Vines
Rickety Bridge Wine Estate, off R45, (021 876 3650, www.rickety bridge.com). **Open** noon-4pm daily. **R. Country**.

Wonderful vineyard views come as standard at this unassuming restaurant where the focus is firmly on hearty country fare. Picnic baskets are a good option in summer, and the boules court among the vines is a great way to work off lunch. Don't forget your beret!

The Riverside

R45, just before Berg River Bridge (021 874 2058, www.theriverside.co.za). **Open** 8am-5pm Wed-Sun. **R**. **South African**.

This family-friendly spot is decidedly laid-back, with a safe children's play area so parents can relax and enjoy the restaurant's legendary *bobotie* or chicken pie. There are also braai-equipped riverside picnic spots and spacious lawns for tossing a Frisbee.

Salmon Bar at The Yard

The Yard, 38 Huguenot Street (021 876 4591, www.salmonbar.com). **Open** *Summer* 8am-7pm daily. *Winter* 8am-5pm daily. **RR**. **Salmon dishes**.

The perfect place to soak up the sun with the Saturday papers, this quiet courtyard offers a variety of fish dishes, from piquant gravadlax to light and fluffy salmon scrambled eggs. There's freshly smoked local trout and delicious breads to take away if you're planning a picnic.

Tasting Room at Le Quartier Français

16 Huguenot Street (021 876 2151/ www.lequartier.co.za). **Open** 7-9pm daily. **RRRR**. **African-inspired contemporary**.

Margot Janse's kitchen artistry has seen this venue voted one of the world's top 50 restaurants. Creative menus use local ingredients in strikingly original combinations: coffee roasted warthog loin, served with potato fondant, garlic purée, bone marrow and currant vinaigrette, say; or whipped Kimilili Farm tulbagh blue cheese, with mustard pear and pistachio sable. In addition to the regular five-course menu, there's a nine-course

'surprise menu' of African-inspired dishes. The adjoining bistro, iÇi, offers a more relaxed, and cheaper, option.

Le Verger

Le Franschhoek Hotel & Spa, Excelsior Road (021 876 8900, www.lefranschhoek.co.za). **Open** noon-2.30pm Tue, Sun; noon-2.30pm, 6.30-10pm Wed-Sat. **RRR**. **Global**.

For once, a Franschhoek destination that's not all about the vines. Here, it's the orchards that provide the backdrop. A 'market-place' buffet offers everything from Asian stir-fry to wood-fired pizza, but the real delight is the tables: individual greenhouses set among the fruit trees.

Shopping

Huguenot Fine Chocolates

62 Huguenot Stree (021 876 4096, www.huguenotchocolates.com). **Open** 8am-5.30pm Mon-Fri; 9am-5pm Sat, Sun.

This old-style chocolatier comes alive at Easter, but any day of the week you'll find a crowd here picking out their favourites from among the homemade goodies. Real chocoholics should sign up for the half-hour Chocolate Experience (R25), which tells the story of chocolate and ends with a demonstration and tasting.

Arts & leisure

Franschhoek Wine Bus

Departs from Rickety Bridge Wine Estate (021 859 1989, www.adventure winetours.co.za). **Tours** *Winter* 10am, 2pm Mon-Fri; 11am Sat, Sun. *Summer* 9.30am, 2.30pm Mon-Fri; 11am Sat, Sun. **Rates** R350 (Champagne tour); R550 (Adventure tour).

A new way to wander between wineries, the off-road 'wine bus' whisks you through vineyards and over mountains, tasting some of the valley's best wines and meeting winemakers along the way. Booking is essential, as each tour can only accommodate ten people.

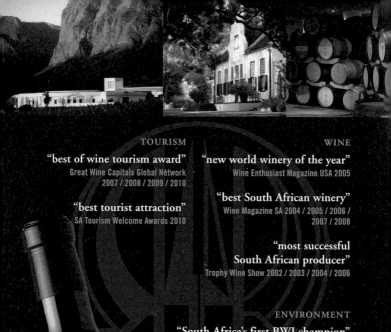

Essentials

Mount Nelson Hotel p175

Hotels

There's no shortage of superb hotels and places to sleep in South Africa's 'pretty city'. From glamorous five-star establishments housed in centuries-old buildings to sexy new boutique operations, visitors are spoilt for choice.

The local scene

The Mother City's best-known hotel is the **Mount Nelson** (see p175), as loved for its pretty pink exterior as its mix of modern amenites within an old property. For superior service look no further than the impressive **Cape Grace** (see p178), with her prime V&A Waterfront position, local flavour and signature restaurant menu. New on the buzzing Waterfront is the **One & Only Resort Hotel & Spa** (see p179), a favoured celeb haunt. For quirkiness, though, it's hard to beat the perenially popular **Daddy Long Legs** (see p174), an art hotel with attitude. Meanwhile, there are some ultra-stylish boutique guesthouses dotted throughout the city, among them the **Cape Cadogan** (see p173).

Classification

We've divided hotels by area and included an indication of price in the listings. For deluxe hotels (RRRR) expect to pay in excess of R1,500 for a double room; expensive (RRR) ranges from R900 to R1500; moderate (RR) runs between R450 and R850 and budget (R) ranges from around R150 to R400.

City Bowl

15 On Orange

Cnr of Grey's Pass and 15 Orange Street, Gardens (021 469 8000, www.15onorange.com). **RRRR**.

The decor here is super sleek, in both public spaces and guest rooms. All the latter are spacious, with luxury touches like in-room DVD players and rain-showers. There's also a sexy rooftop pool, family-friendly double rooms, and the Murano Bar is a smart venue for cocktails. The location – squeezed between Long Street, Kloof Street and the Company's Garden – is ideal.

An African Villa

19 Carstens Street, Tamboerskloof (021 423 2162, www.anafrican villa.co.za). **RR**.
This cosy choice comprises three historic Victorian terrace houses in a peaceful suburban street. Decor is neo-African. Some rooms have street-facing balconies, while others boast views of the city's favourite mountain. It's owner-run and intimate.

Ashanti Lodge

11 Hof Street, Gardens (021 423 8721, www.ashanti.co.za). **R**.
Only five minutes' walk from the Company's Garden and the CBD, this hotel has a swimming-pool area with a row of loungers, a travel desk and a cute little café with a pool table and sundeck that serves up pizzas, burgers and breakfasts. Also available is a speck-sized, sandy campsite that, while not exactly a camper's paradise, will appeal to travellers counting every rand.

The Backpack & African Travel Centre

74 New Church Street, Tamboerskloof (021 423 5555, www.backpackers. co.za). **R**.
Flashpackers will love this boutique backpacker's, boasting very clean dorms and doubles, each with wooden floors, tea and coffee making facilities, hot water bottles and crisp, white bed linen adorned with shweshwe-print cushions. The on-site café has courtyard seating for balmy summer nights and its own pizza oven. Best of

S H O R T L I S T

Best newcomers
- Crystal Towers (see p181)
- 15 on Orange (see p170)
- Taj Cape Town (see p175)

Best spa splurge
- Constantia Uitsig (see p176)
- Lanzerac Hotel & Spa (see p182)
- Onc&Only (see p179)
- Vineyard Hotel & Spa (see p176)

Best breakfasts
- Steenberg Hotel & Spa (see p178)
- Winchester Mansions (see p181)

Best high tea
- Cape Grace (see p178)
- Mount Nelson (see p175)

Best budget
- Ashanti (see left)
- Cape Diamond (see p173)
- Long Street Backpackers (see p175)

Best historical
- Cape Heritage Hotel (see p173)
- Hout Bay Manor (see p176)

Best views
- The Bay (see p178)
- Mont Rochelle (see p182)
- Pepper Club (see p175)
- Twelve Apostles (see p178)

Style stops
- Cape Cadogan (see p173)
- Dutch Manor Antique Hotel (see p174)
- Kensington Place (see p175)

Luxe stays
- Cellars Hohenort (see p176)
- Dock House (see p178)
- Lanzerac Hotel & Spa (see p182)

ESSENTIALS

One&Only
Cape Town

Reuben's at One&Only Cape Town

One&Only Cape Town is now home to one of South Africa's most loved and award-winning chefs, Reuben Riffel. Reuben's serves deceptively simple, wholesome bistro fare, with fresh flavours, generous portions and beautifully-plated dishes. The restaurant has a sophisticated, but unfussy, brasserie feel and the food provides an exciting combination of local flavours.

To make a reservation at Reuben's,
call 021 431 4511 or email
restaurantreservations@oneandonlycapetown.com

Reuben's
restaurant & bar

all, it's within walking distance of the centre of the city and there's a pool.

Cape Cadogan

5 Upper Union Street, Gardens (021 480 8080, www.capecadogan.com). **RRR**.

Housed in a Georgian and Victorian building, Cadogan' Park has a chic mix of contemporary and antique decor and furnishings, themed, the hotel says, around the life of Oscar Wilde. Each room has a balcony or patio and the hustle of Kloof Street, with its many cafés, restaurants and shops, is just around the corner.

Cape Diamond Hotel

Cnr Parliament and Longmarket Streets, City Centre (021 461 2519, www.capediamondhotel.co.za). **R**.

Rooms are individually decorated at the Cape Diamond and there's a cosy resident restaurant, Patat, serving local favourite dishes. Also on site is a speck-sized theatre café, mostly featuring Afrikaans music and cabaret acts, while a jacuzzi and barbecue on the roof beckon guests on sunny days. A transport service is available for tours and the hotel also has three self-catering apartments.

Cape Heritage Hotel

90 Bree Street (021 424 4646, www.capeheritage.co.za). **RRR**.

Set in a historic square containing a cluster of some of Cape Town's earliest Dutch and Georgian houses (circa 1771) this hotel is a charmer. Rooms are modern with old-world touches – like high-beamed teak ceilings, sash windows and 200-year-old Cape yellow-wood floors. Amenities include in-room massages, babysitting and picnic baskets for day trips.

Cape Milner

2A Milner Road, Tamboerskloof (021 426 1101, www.capemilner.com). **RR**.

The luxury rooms and suites here boast foot spas, filter coffee machines,

iPod docking stations, mammoth baths and 42-inch swivelling plasma screens.

Cape Town Backpackers

81 New Church Street, Tamboerskloof (021 426 0200, www.capetown backpackers.com). **R**.

This squeaky clean gem comprises two atmospheric Victorian houses with gleaming wooden floors. Management keeps guests entertained with regular themed nights – quiz nights, curry nights, traditional Xhosa dinner nights, summer braais, themed parties and sundowner excursions to Signal Hill among them. Hotel amenities for backpacker budgets.

Cat & Moose Backpackers

305 Long Street, City Centre (021 423 7638, www.catand moose.co.za). **R**.

Although a tad grungy, this is a good choice for folks who want to be in the thick of things. At the top of the Long Street strip, with a host of great restaurants, cafés, bars, clubs and indie clothing boutiques on your doorstep, you'll never be far from the action.

Coral International Cape Town

Corner Buitengragt and Wale Street (021 481 3700, www.coral-capetown.com). **RRR**.

Bringing some Arab hospitality to the Mother City, this hotel oozes ritzy Middle Eastern style. Rooms and suites feature views of either the mountain or the charming candy-coloured cottages of Cape Town's Malay quarter, the Bo-Kaap. Guests are welcomed with dates, Arabian coffee and lemon mint tea, and the hotel – South Africa's first dry hotel – also has male and female prayer rooms. On-site eateries include an atmospheric poolside shisha lounge, where you can relax in your own cushioned private nook, smoking hubbly bubbly or enjoying a light meal under a romantic overhanging lantern.

Hot beds

Hit the pillow at one of these hip city sleeps.

When it comes to cool Cape Town hotels, the **Grand Daddy** (see right) really is the granddaddy of them all. Rooms are stylish, with zany touches like plastic grass and quirky lampshades printed with South African town names; the pimped out Daddy Cool bar has blingy rapper-style chains hanging from the ceiling. And on the roof is the only rooftop trailer park on the planet. Seven shiny vintage Airstream trailers each have themed decor by different local artists: they include a *Stepford Wives*-inspired trailer and a baby-blue polka dotted Dorothy-style pad (complete with red shoes).

Just up the street is the original **Daddy Long Legs** (see right), which spawned the Grand Daddy; it also has themed rooms by various artists. The Emergency Room, complete with nurse's outfit, is for living out those doctor/nurse fantasies, while artist Kim Stern's creation is a karaoke singer's dream, with five microphones, including one in the shower.

The perfect place for adrenalin junkies is the fun-filled **Protea Hotel Fire & Ice** (see right), with attractions like themed elevators (a shark-diving cage and cable car) and a climbing wall on the building's exterior. The bar's themed toilets cause a giggle: 'Temptation' has a naked couple gracing the wall. Move the towel covering up their naughty bits and a loud buzzer informs everyone you're a Peeping Tom.

Daddy Long Legs
134 Long Street (021 422 3074, www.daddylonglegs.co.za). **RRR**.
See box left.

Dutch Manor Antique Hotel
158 Buitenchragt, Bo-Kaap (021 422 4767, 072 847 5239,www.dutchmanor. co.za). **RR**.
This house has been lovingly restored to its former elegance, with damask curtains, Persian carpets, four-poster beds and high ceilings: furniture here dates from the late 17th and 18th centuries. Hugging the cobbled streets of the Bo-Kaap, it offers a culturally enriching experience that evokes a strong sense of yesteryear.

Grand Daddy
38 Long Street (021 424 7247, www.granddaddyhotel.co.za). **RRR**.
See box left.

Hippo Boutique Hotel
5-9 Park Road, Gardens (021 423 2500, www.hippotique.co.za). **RRR**.
This hip little hotel is situated in the middle of buzzing Kloof Street. Evocative black and white photographs line the walls in the lounge, while loft-style guest rooms, each with their own kitchenette and computer, show off modish decor and furnishings. For a real treat, splash out on one of the massive suites, featuring mezzanine level bedrooms, open-plan bathrooms, fully fitted kitchens and funky style.

Holiday Inn Express
101 St George's Mall, City Centre (021 480 8300, www.hiexpress.com). **RRR**.
This hotel suits travellers looking for a neat, clean, no-frills pocket-friendly stay; a great location in the centre of the city is another major advantage. An added draw for families is that rooms where kids can stay for free are available too.

ESSENTIALS

Kensington Place

38 Kensington Crescent, Higgovale (021 424 4744, www.kensington place.co.za). **RRR**.
A peaceful spot, hidden away in leafy Higgovale. Chic rooms have private balconies and city views. Charming extra touches include baskets with sarongs and sunscreen next to the pool, in-room laptops, free Wi-Fi, Skype phones, iPod docking stations, in-room spa treatments and free gym membership for guests.

Long Street Backpackers

209 Long Street, City Centre (021 423 0615, www.longstreetbackpackers. co.za). **R. No credit cards**.
This is the place to be if you're planning on getting merry. Set around a leafy courtyard, it used to be an apartment block. These days each flat boasts a dorm or two, a bathroom and smallish double/twin or single room. On Sundays guests are treated to a long-standing tradition – the owner's famous veggie *potjie* (traditional South African stew made on the fire) – while adrenaline junkies will love the stack of activities offered by the travel centre.

Mandela Rhodes Place Hotel & Spa

Cnr Wale and Burg Streets, City Centre (021 481 4000, www.mandelarhodes place.co.za). **RRR**.
This central spot fuses the comfort of a self-catering apartment with the amenities of a hotel. Think 24-hour in-room dining, a laundry service, under-floor heating, heated towel rails, a gym, spa and the like. Apartments have fully equipped kitchens and spectacular views over the Mother City. Choose a studio, one-bedroomed, two-bed-roomed or penthouse flat.

More Quarters

2 Nicol Street, Gardens (021 487 5660, www.morehotels.co.za). **RRR**.
This extension of the Cape Cadogan consists of a cluster of swish one- and two-bedroom apartments. The white, airy interiors are pristinely appointed with modern furnishings, including fully equipped kitchens and dreamy bathrooms decorated with polished river stones.

Mount Nelson Hotel

76 Orange Street, Gardens (021 483 1000, www.mountnelson.co.za). **RRRR**.
Situated in a leafy garden in the heart of the city, this pink colonial-style hotel has been welcoming the well-heeled since 1899. The Nellie, as the locals have dubbed her, is famous for her fabulous high tea spread. It's also well known for its child-friendly stance amid the sophistication.

Pepper Club

Cnr of Loop Street and Pepper Street (021 812 8888, www.pepperclub.co.za). **RRR**.
This chic spot boasts views of the entire city and beyond. The penthouse suite – with crystal chandeliers, shiny black baby grand piano, walk-in wine cellar, wrap-around balcony, floor-to-ceiling windows, personal sauna with a view and rooftop pool – is fit for royalty (one or two having actually stayed here). Otherwise, guests can choose between stylish apartments with full kitchens and rooms with kitchenettes. The hotel has its own spa, gym and a cinema.

Protea Hotel Fire & Ice

Cnr New Church & 198 Bree streets (021 488 2555, www.protea hotels.com). **RRR**.
See box left.

Taj Cape Town

Wale Street, City Centre (021 423 3000, www.tajcapetown.co.za). **RRRR**.
The plush rooms here come with big-screen TVs, fluffy bathrobes, mini bars and city views. You have the option of dining on-site at Bombay Brasserie, with its wood-panelled walls and lush armchairs, or Mint, which spills out on

to the cobbled pavement outside. The hotel bar, Twankey, is popular with the city's jet set who flock here for champagne, Guinness and oysters.

Westin Grand Cape Town
Convention Square, 1 Lower Long Street, City Centre (021 412 9999, www.westin.com). **RRRR**.
Standing tall on the foreshore, the five-star Westin is popular with business travellers (thanks to its nose-to-nose proximity to the Cape Town International Convention Centre). Executive Club rooms have access to a private restaurant and lounge on the top floor with floor-to-ceiling windows and jaw-dropping views over the city. Also on the 19th floor you'll find a gym and spa.

Southern Suburbs

The Cellars-Hohenort
93 Brommersvlei, Constantia, Cape Town (021 794 2137, www.cellars-hohenhort.com). **RRRR**.
Country-style rooms boast views of the hotel's gardens and vineyards. The lengthy list of amenities includes fine restaurants, a spa, hair salon, tennis court, three swimming pools, a Gary Player-designed nine-hole chipping and putting green, petanque, boules, and bicycles to explore the estate.

Constantia Uitsig
Spaanschemat River Road (021 794 6500, www.constantia-uitsig.com). **RRRR**.
Wine lovers and foodies will enjoy this vineyard-flanked hotel, with its award- winning restaurant and 16 garden rooms. Don't forget the swish spa, with a signature treatment massage and scrub consisting of the components of the estates fine wines, crushed with vine bark.

The Vineyard Hotel & Spa
Colinton Road, Newlands (021 657 4500, www.vineyard.co.za). **RRR**.

A lush hotel housed in an impressive manor house sporting two fine restaurants and a spa. Accommodation is great value for money and overlooks beautiful gardens. If you prefer to cook your own, book the self-catering garden cottage. The on-site Angsana Spa is a haven of Zen.

Hout Bay & South Peninsula

Chapman's Peak Hotel
Chapman's Peak Drive, Hout Bay (021 790 1036, www.chapmanspeak hotel.com). **RR**.
Lying along one of the world's most beautiful coastal roads, a stone's throw from the beach, this decently priced hotel has glorious beach and mountain views. Family run, you can expect great service dished up with a smile.

Hout Bay Manor
Baviaanskloof, off Main Road, Hout Bay (021 790 0116, www.houtbay manor.com). **RR**.
Wooden floors, freestanding baths and chandeliers add to the ambience at the Hout Bay Manor, built in 1871, but it has a cool, modern edge too. Rooms all have African names. The Sotho has its own garden terrace hideaway and romantic outdoor shower.

Simon's Town Boutique Backpackers
66 St George's Street, Simon's Town (021 786 1964, www.capepax.co.za). **R**.
This welcoming hostel offers spacious, clean rooms with wooden floors, crisp linen and fresh rolled towels waiting at the foot of your bed. It's close to the beach and there's also a sprawling, chill-out balcony overlooking the harbour, a bar and a travel desk.

Southern Right Hotel
12-14 Glen Road, Glencairn (021 782 0315, www.southern righthotel.com). **RR**.

Steenberg Hotel & Spa p178

Twelve Apostles Hotel & Spa p178

Mont Rochelle p182

ESSENTIALS

Clean but basic rooms have wooden floors, thick walls and deep-set windows with either ocean or mountain views. The place is kid-friendly (there's a dedicated play area) and an English breakfast is included in the rate.

Steenberg Hotel & Spa

10802 Steenberg Estate, Tokai Road, Constantia (021 713 2222, www. steenberghotel.com). **RRRR**.

You'll find lush vineyards, an 18-hole golf course and a five-star boutique hotel and spa in historic buildings on the Steenberg Estate. Rooms, some with private patios, are peppered with 17th-century-style furnishings. The stunning heritage suites in the historic Jonkershuis have fireplaces and butlers; each room is themed to reflect a different part of the farm's history. Catherina's restaurant (see p138) serves award-winning contemporary Cape cuisine.

Clifton & Camps Bay

The Bay

69 Victoria Road, Camps Bay (021 430 4444, www.thebay.co.za). **RRRR**.

The beach beckons just across the road and rooms (with either private patios or balconies) have serene natural elements, such as zen-style wooden headboards. There are swimming pools for chilling, frolicking and sunning, a hair salon, florist, restaurant, deli, cocktail bar and cigar lounge. And for guests needing somewhere to chill or freshen up outside check-in/check-out times, there are change rooms or day rooms (with shower, day bed and television).

Twelve Apostles Hotel & Spa

Victoria Road, Camps Bay (021 437 9000, www.12apostleshotel.com). **RRRR**.

Wedged between the mountain and ocean and surrounded by fynbos (shrubland) is this stunner of a hotel.

Rooms have either mountain or sea views. Each offers unashamed luxury, from 400-thread-count sheets to private balconies. There's also a 16-seater cinema and fine-dining restaurant with a fynbos-infused menu.

V&A Waterfront & Green Point

Avatara Guesthouse

5 Leinster Road, corner of York Road, Green Point (087 808 6930, www.avatara.co.za). **RR**.

Nestling at the foot of Signal Hill, this cosy guest house has individually decorated rooms, where contemporary decor is fushed with touches of India inspired by the travels of its owner.

Cape Grace

West Quay Road, V&A Waterfront (021 410 7100, www.capegrace.com). **RRRR**.

This award-winning hotel has world-class personalised service, sweeping views over the harbour and marina, and gorgeous Cape-chic deco. Antiques are offset with modern pieces, and there are various artful touches, such as the hotel's spectacular selection of chandeliers: assembled from salvaged bits and pieces from driftwood and whalebones to old cutlery and crockery, they tend to fascinate guests. The swanky resident restaurant boasts cosy booths and Cape contemporary cuisine while the nautically themed Bascule whisky bar has the largest collection of whiskies in the southern hemisphere, and its own whisky sommelier.

Dock House

Portswood Close, Portswood Ridge, V&A Waterfront (021 421 9334, www.dockhouse.co.za). **RRRR**.

A lavish little five-roomed hotel looking over the Waterfront, featuring spruced-up antique furniture and contemporary creature comforts, lending a chic, new-Victorian look. Upstairs rooms have wonderful harbour views, while all enjoy 24-hour butler-style service and duck-down pillows.

One&Only Cape Town

Dock Road, Victoria & Alfred Waterfront (021 431 5800, www.oneandonlyresorts.com). **RRRR**.
This swisher-than-swish Waterfront hotel and resort has seen its fair share of celeb guests since its opening in 2009. The spa and resort sections are set in lush gardens on two man-made islands, while the hotel towers over the Waterfront. Private balconies have magical views of Table Mountain and rooms have all sorts of special touches, like pillow and scent menus. A Nobu restaurant is on the premises. The hotel also has an impressive onsite art gallery.

Romney Park All Suite Hotel & Spa

Corner of Hill Road and Romney Road, Green Point (021-439 4555, www. romneypark.co.za). **RR**.
Romney Park has apartment-style accommodation with full kitchens, balconies and sea views (ground floor suites have petite private gardens instead). Apartments are luxuriously furnished with deep-buttoned upholstery, crystal chandeliers, Venetian-cut mirrors, velvets and swish linen. The atmospheric bar, the George, has plush couches in royal colours with trophies and vintage hard covers lining the walls. The bar space spills out on to a sexy poolside veranda with daybeds.

Southern Sun Waterfront

1 Lower Buitengragt (021 409 4000, www.southernsun.com). **RRR**.
Popular with businessmen and within walking (or water taxi) distance of the V&A, this moderately priced hotel offers fuss-free accommodation with all the amenities you'd expect from a hotel. Stand-out touches include complimentary juice, water and bowls of sweets at reception in the afternoons; a

cosy lounge with board games and magazines; a spacious gym with overhead television screens, a hair salon, connecting family rooms, and shoe shines and babysitting on request.

Villa Zest

2 Braemar Road, Green Point (021 433 1246, www.villazest.co.za). **RRR**.
This hotel was built in the Bauhaus style, with minimalist clean lines – lots of glass, stainless steel and light – with a splash of '70s fun. Rooms have names like Warhol, American Graffiti and Barbarella and the decor is brightened up with retro quirks like zany patterned wallpaper. The pool area features a cushion-scattered Bedouin-tented chill-out area with white-pebbled gas-fireplace, perfect for whiling away summer days.

Three Anchor Bay to Bantry Bay

Ashanti Lodge Greenpoint

23 Antrim Road, Three Anchor Bay (021 433 1619, www.ashanti.co.za). **R**.
Sparkling clean, and stylish to boot – this option is a flashpacker's dream. Sister to the same-named spot in Gardens, this Green Point sibling features gorgeous rooms with gleaming wooden floors, but without the other's party scene. Great for those looking for a chic but cheap stay.

New Kings Hotel

94 Regent Street, Sea Point (021 430 5580, www.newkingshotel.co.za). **RRR**.
This trendy Sea Point spot is built around a bustling piazza where the suburb's sexy set gather daily to nurse lattes or wield chopsticks. Rooms are hip industrial-style affairs with Italian furnishings, laminated wooden floors, 42-inch TVs and iPod docking stations.

O on Kloof

92 Kloof Road, Bantry Bay (021 439 2081, www.oonkloof.co.za). **RRR**.

ESSENTIALS

DIY beds

Cape Villas

For modern self-catering accommodation right in the thick of things on Long Street, try the **Daddy Long Legs Self-Catering Apartments** (021 424 1403/ www.daddylonglegs.co.za). The airy loft-style flats have wooden floors, exposed brick walls and open ceiling beams.

If you're after something more swanky, the **Newmark Villa Collection** (www.newmarkhotels. com), has luxury penthouses, apartments and other properties across the city.

Alternatively, if you're in the mood for some Camps Bay swish and a taste of the Atlantic Seaboard lifestyle, try **Cape Villas** (021 438 9384/www.capevillas.com) or the smart **Sea & Rock Villa** (1A Rontree Avenue, Camps Bay; 084 306 8635, www.seaandrock.com). Another option is the **Village and Life Group** (021 438 3972, www.village andlife.com), which has scores of stylish, serviced apartments, houses and villas in the V&A Waterfront, Mouille Point, De Waterkant and Camps Bay.

Further along the coast, why not kick back in boho fishing village Kalk Bay at the architect-designed

Bishop's View (1 Upper Quarter Deck Road, Kalk Bay; 021 701 5149/074 203 4151, www.cape villarental.co.za) or stay in the sea-view stunner **Phi** (60 Boyes Drive; 08326887, www.theone andonly.co.za).

If you're in a group, **Villa St James** (36 Main Road, St James; 082 784 8000, www.villast james.com), once home to the Greek Royal Family and legendary South African statesman Jan Smuts, sleeps up to 20 guests. **Icon Villas** also has an impressive selection of villas across the Peninsula (021 424 0905/ www.icape.co.za).

Village and Life Group

A staircase suspended over an azure water feature leads you into this hip urban sanctuary. Rooms (overlooking the sea or Lion's Head) are super luxurious, with percale linen, under-floor heating, fruit baskets and DVD players. Book a suite and you'll be treated to your own private balcony, with an alfresco jacuzzi and loungers for sunning. Both the trendy bar, serving cocktails and smoothies, and the outdoor breakfast nook have sea views.

Winchester Mansions

221 Beach Road, Sea Point (021 434 2351, www.winchester.co.za). **RRR**.
This magical vintage dame, with her balcony-style, bougainvillea-clad walkways on upper floors, used to be an apartment block. Rooms, still sporting old-school brass doorbells, have a vintage feel; the top-floor loft suites have a more modern look. Sea-facing rooms look out over the promenade. The green, felt-lined walkways between rooms with putt-putt holes (stick and ball attached to the wall) at the end of the corridors are a zany touch that will enthrall children.

Northern suburbs

Crystal Towers Hotel & Spa

Century City (021 525 3888, www. africanpridehotels.com). **RRR**.
On driving by the Crystal Towers, your attention is immediately grabbed by the glass-framed green-lit cube that is the swimming pool. When it comes to decor, think massive wooden cubes that double as couches, a snaking geometric red lounger, a hip bar with sci-fi style pendant lights, and fun-themed private lounges. There's also an on-site restaurant, sushi bar, pastry shop, spa and poolside rooftop bar with daybeds and a canopied deck. Rooms are spacious affairs with floor-to-ceiling postcard-perfect views of the city and its mountain, LCD screens that pop up from the foot of the bed at the push of

a button, the latest magazines, designer furniture, DVD players with DVDs, complimentary snacks and a futuristic pod-shaped shower in the centre of the room.

Protea Hotel Colosseum

Cnr Century Way & Century Boulevard, Century City (021 526 4000, www.proteahotels.com). **RR**
This smart hotel is popular with business travellers. A show-stealing technicolor chandelier dangles over the foyer, where a bar with beckoning foosball table serves cocktails. Accommodation consists of spacious suites, with fabulous floor-to-ceiling views, kitchenettes, electronic safes big enough for a laptop (with nifty plug points inside to charge your laptop and phone), plasma televisions, modish decor and bathrooms featuring round, freestanding baths and black glass washbasins.

Saltycrax Backpackers and Surfers Lodge

20 Briza Road, Table View (021 556 9369, www.saltycrax.com). **R**.
A stone's throw from the world-kiting surfing mecca of Kite Beach, Saltycrax is a hot choice for adventure junkies. The beach is a great spot to learn how to surf, kitesurf, windsurf, skydive, sandboard or scuba, while indulging in all sorts of other hair-raising activities on the side, from shark cage diving to abseiling. Rooms at the Lodge comprise a range of doubles, triples, family rooms, en suites and dorms (private rooms have fridges, heaters, fans and linen is included). Facilities include a cheery bar, jacuzzi, TV lounge, bonfire area and zen garden.

Winelands

De Hoek

7-9 Drostdy Street; corner Church and Drostdy streets, Stellenbosch (021 886 9988, 084563 5329, www.dehoek manor.co.za). **RR**.

What makes this spot special is the location – just a stroll away from Stellenbosch's many characterful cafés, shops, art galleries and other attractions and overlooking the town's regal-looking Mother Church and its gorgeous gardens. Each of the five en-suite rooms in this beautifully restored Cape Dutch home has sparkling wooden floors and country-chic decor, with amenities like underfloor heating and Wi-Fi.

Lanzerac Hotel & Spa

Lanzerac Estate, Stellenbosch (021 887 1132, www.lanzerac.co.za). **RRRR**.
Set on a 300-year-old Cape Dutch estate, this intimate hotel is heaven for history buffs. It's also indulgently luxurious. Most rooms and suites have their own private patios overlooking vineyards, gardens and mountains. If you've got the dosh to splurge, then book a night or two in the Royal Pool Suite, which comes with its own private swimming pool.

Mont Rochelle

Dassenberg Road, Franschhoek (021 876 2770, www.mont rochelle.co.za). **RRR**.
Memories of the sprawling views of the Franschhoek Valley and surrounding mountains here will stay with you forever. The 22 luxurious rooms and suites are super-spacious and all have vistas. There's an on-site fine-dining restaurant, while adventures like horse-back wine-tasting trips, stomping grapes with your feet and bottling and labelling your own wine can also be arranged (in season). Don't want to drive all the way to the Winelands? Then make use of the hotel's helicopter pad.

Le Quartier Français

16 Huguenot Road, Franschhoek (021 876 2151, www.lequartier.co.za). **RRRR**.
This fine hotel has luxurious rooms, set around the winding pathways of a rambling country garden. Each has its own fireplace, and some even have their own pool. Amenities include a spa treatment room and a cosy cinema playing classics and arthouse films. But the main event has to be the resident restaurant, the Tasting Room, one of South Africa's best.

Rusthof Country House

12 Huguenot Street, Franschhoek (021 876 3762, www.rusthof.com). **RR**.
A location on Franschhoek's quaint main drag means you're only a short walk away from the town's many shops, galleries and restaurants. The place is owner-run, the service is personal, and the eclectic colonial country-style rooms are individually decorated with contemporary and antique pieces. The intimate on-site restaurant, Ryan's Kitchen, is a new addition, headed up by chef Ryan Smith, which serves South African favourites with a twist, such as ostrich *bobotie* with apple and truffles and Elgin chicken, roasted Cape Malay style. There's a shiny show kitchen where you can watch your food being whipped up in front of you.

Spier Resort Management

R310 Lynedoch Road, Stellenbosch (021 809 1100, www.spier.co.za). **RR**.
A resort-style hotel that's great for families with kids and packed with all sorts of fun things to do. Village-style accommodation is set in leafy gardens, with twinkling walkways and golf carts to drive yourself to your room. These have all the amenities you need for a comfortable stay – including extra-fluffy bathrobes. The entertainment roster is full and varied: activities range from visiting a cheetah outreach programme to chilling at the resort's spa and ogling some of the fine art on display (Spier is a big patron of the arts), going horse-riding or sitting down at one of the estate's many restaurants.

Getting Around

Arriving & leaving

The Mother City is pretty easy to find your way around and to get to know, especially since most of it can be explored on foot. Just watch out for the informal taxis that stop as and where they will (though from a passenger's point of view they are actually very convenient).

If, during your wanderings, you find yourself lost, don't panic. Just look to your surrounds for guidance: if you're in the inner city, Table Mountain lies to your south, and the Atlantic Ocean to the north. Still confused? Give the **Cape Town Tourism Bureau** (021 487 6800) a call. They'll put you on the right track in no time.

By air

Cape Town International Airport was recently given a much-needed facelift by the the Airports Company of South Africa (ACSA – 021 937 1200, 086 727 7888, www.airports.co.za). The facility now features a 2,000-car park, as well as a retail mall and swanky new terminal building

Cape Town International is approximately 22 kilometres from the city centre, when taking the N2 highway. It should take you about 30 minutes to drive there outside peak hours, but unexpected road maintenance can sometimes throw a spanner in the works. Rush hour is between 7am and 9am and 4.30pm and 6pm.

International airlines connecting directly to Cape Town include **South African Airlines** (SAA), **British Airways** and **KLM**, while domestic carriers include **SAA**

(www.flysaa.com), **SA Airlink** (www.saairlink.co.za) and **British Airways** (www.ba.co.za).

Local flights can cost anything from R800-R2,500 for a return ticket, depending on the season and how far in advance you book. Cheap flights are regularly up for grabs, so check the websites regularly. ACSA's three low-cost airlines, **Kulula.com** (www.kulula.com), **1Time** (www.1time.co.za) and **Mango Air** (ww5.flymango.com) are an unfussy, affordable way to make your way from A to B.

At arrivals, make your way to the city with one of the airport's shuttle services like **Way2Go** (0861 929 246,www.way2go.co.za), **Magic Bus** (021 505 6300,www.magicbus.co.za) or **City Hopper** (021 386 0077,www.citihopper.co.za). A **MyCiti** (0800 656 463) airport shuttle bus departs every 20 minutes taking people to a central terminus in the city (see p184).

Alternatively, get a cab from the airport-authorised **Touch Down Taxis** (021 919 4659), or hire your own car from on-site agencies like Avis, Hertz and Budget.

By bus

Bus travel is a pretty reliable, affordable option. Major Cape Town bus services include **Greyhound** (083 915 9000, www.greyhound.co.za), **Translux** (021 449 6209) and **Intercape Mainliner** (0861 287 287, www.intercape.co.za).

Get yourself ready for a long haul if you're going to travel to Johannesburg, since it takes around 19 hours. But for a pittance of R500 (during off-peak times), it's worth arriving in the city of gold a bit rumpled.

If you're up for an adventure, try **Baz Bus** (021 422 5202, www.baz bus.co.za). It's similar to Europe's hop-on hop-off bus services, and makes convenient pit stops at inexpensive backpackers between Cape Town and Jo'burg for between R2,900 and R3,500. There's also a return ticket option available for around R4,600.

By road

The **N1** connects Cape Town to Johannesburg, and the trek can take up to 16 hours, while the **N2** connects the Mother City to Port Elizabeth, with a journey that'll take around 10 hours. For more on driving in South Africa, *see p185*.

You have to be over 25 and in possession of an international driver's licence to hire a car. There are myriad rental agencies, with top performers including **Avis** (021 927 8800, www.avis.co.za) and **Hertz** (021 935 4800, www. hertz.co.za). Rates are calculated according to kilometres travelled. If budgeting is imperative, go for 'no frills' options like **Value Car Hire** (021 386 7699, www.value carhire.co.za) and **Budget** (021 418 5232, www.budget.co.za).

By train

The **Cape Town Railway Station** (Adderley Street, City Centre, 021 449 2991, 021 449 4597) is the main hub of travel in the Western Cape and offers routes to all of South Africa's main destinations. Long-distance trains have dining cars and trolleys, with loos proving a bit hit or miss, so best opt for the first class section. For ticket prices and timetables,

contact **Shosholoza Meyl** (086 000 8888, 011 744 4555, www. shosholozameyl.co.za).

If travelling by regular train isn't for you, climb aboard one of the swish railway options like the **Blue Train** (021 449 2672, www.bluetrain.co.za) or **Rovos Rail** (021 421 4020, www.rovos.co.za).

In town

By bike

If you're keen to feel the wind through your hair, you can hire a bicycle from **Downhill Adventures** (021 422 0388, www.downhilladventures.com), or a hardcore Harley from **Harley-Davidson Cape Town** (021 446 2999, www.harley-davidson-capetown.com).

By bus

Golden Arrow buses (021 937 8800, www.gabs.co.za) are ubiquitous in the city and surrounding suburbs. The 'Bus for Us' is for everyday Joes, so don't go expecting something flashy. It does, however, take you from point A to B in the Cape metropolis for a negligible sum – expect to pay between R10 and R15 for a one-way journey. Look out for the new **MyCiti** (0800 656 463) Rapid Bus Transit services in and around the city. Well-priced and reliable, they'll get you around the city efficiently. There's also a quick to and from the airport shuttle service that runs every 20 minutes, and like all other MyCiti routes departs from the central terminal Hertzog Boulevard.

If you're feeling touristy, climb aboard the **City Sightseeing Bus** (021 511 6000, www.city

sightseeing.co.za), which traverses the southern peninsula on the Blue Route, and the City Bowl on the Red Route. The first bus departs from the bus stop at the Two Oceans Aquarium at 9am, continuing every hour thereafter until 5pm. Hop-on-hop-off day tickets cost around R120.

By car

The city is small and well signposted, which makes it a breeze to explore by car. Driving is on the left. Capetonians can seem pretty casual in their approach to driving, and road safety statistics aren't much to shout about here, with drink driving and speeding the biggest cause of accidents, particularly at Christmas.

South Africa's roads are variable: pristine on some stretches and pockmarked to within an inch of their lives in others.

Speed limits vary between 60km/hr in urban areas and 120km/hr on highways, and the legal blood alcohol limit for someone over 70kg is two glasses of wine. If you feel like partying, it's best to appoint a designated sober driver for the evening, or travel by taxi.

Finding a parking space can be a bit of a hassle. The ubiquitous neon-bibbed traffic wardens, or car guards as they're known, are another factor when deciding where to park. Some are official, with meters, but others are chancers, who will expect alms when you come to leave. If you aren't keen to contend with them, find a parking lot or underground garage. Never leave your car on a red or yellow line during the day as it will be clamped, or worse, towed, resulting in a painfully tedious and expensve (up to R1,000) recovery process. Remember to park in a

well-lit, populated area if you can't find an official parking lot when you're going out at night.

For car hire, see p184.

By taxi

Locally, 'taxi' can either mean a sedan taxi with a running meter or minibus vehicles with drivers who apparently got their licences via correspondence course.

The latter is the preferred mode of transport for many during the day, since it's cheap and quick. You really need only linger a moment too long in one spot, and nine out of ten times, a taxi will sound its horn for you to jump in. Make sure you've got enough spare change for the fare, which will be collected by the taxi guard between destinations.

If the minibus option freaks you out a tad, there are plenty of sedan taxis around the streets – at R12 per kilometre, they're a lot more expensive, though. Try **Unicab** (021 486 1610) or **Excite** (021 418 4444, www.excitetaxis.co.za), or make a free call to **Rikkis Taxis** (0861 745547, www.rikkis.co.za) from any of the Rikki phones dotted about the city.

By rail

Cape Town's railway service is the **Metrorail** (0800 656 463, 021 449 6181, www.capemetrorail.co.za). The **Cape Town Railway Station** is situated in Adderley Street and is the centre of all train networks in the Western Cape. Railway crimes have been a problem in off-peak hours, so make sure you travel between 7am and 9am, and 4pm and 6pm, use first class, and leave your valuables at home. In the event of a crime, phone Metrorail Protection Services (021 449 4336).

ESSENTIALS

Resources A-Z

Accidents & emergencies

In case of an emergency call:
Emergency Services 10177
Netcare 911 (Private EMS) 082 911
ER24 (private EMS) 084 124
General emergencies 107 from a landline and 112 from a cellphone
Mountain Rescue Services 021 948 9900
Poison Crisis Centre 021 931 6129
Police 10111
National Sea Rescue Institute 021 449 3500
See also p187 **Hospitals** and p188 **Police**.

Credit card loss

Lost or stolen credit cards can be reported to the following 24-hour services:
American Express 0800 991 021.
Diners Club 0860 34377.
MasterCard 0800 990 418.
Visa 0800 990 475.

Crime

There are a few effective crime deterrents like CCTV, and mounted and vehicular police patrols, but despite this, petty crimes like pickpocketing and muggings are still a common occurence.

Park your car in well-lit places, draw money (but not too much) in populated areas and don't drive around the sticks in the small hours.

Unfortunately, Cape Town's breathtaking natural surrounds aren't crime-free, either, and muggings have been known to occur on hiking trails and deserted beaches. Never go hiking or to a deserted beach on your own. Leave your valuables at home, and let someone know when to expect you back. A hard blow on an old-fashioned whistle is an effective way to let passers-by know that you're in trouble.

Disabled

Most of Cape Town's hotels, shopping centres and attractions are disabled-friendly. If you're disabled and planning to fly somewhere, pre-arrange with your airline to come and get you at the entrance, and to make the necessary arrangements for you on board.

Reputable car hire companies have hand-control vehicles for disabled drivers. For additional information, phone the **Association for the Physically Disabled** (011 646 8331/www. apd.org.za), based in Johannesburg, or the SA National Council for the Blind (012 452 3811/www.sancb. org.za) in Cape Town.

Electricity

The power supply in South Africa is 220/230 volts AC. The standard plug is the 15-amp round-pin, three-prong variety. European- and US-style two-pin plugs, and UK-style three-pin plugs, can be used with an adaptor, available at supermarkets. Most hotels have 110-volt outlets for electric shavers.

Embassies & consulates

British Consulate General
Southern Life Centre, 8 Riebeek Street, City Centre (021 405 2400).

ESSENTIALS

Canadian Consulate General
*19th Floor, Reserve Bank Building,
60 St George's Mall, City Centre
(021 423 5240).*
French Consulate *78 Queen Victoria
Street, Gardens (021 423 1575).*
**German Consulate General
& Embassy** *19th Floor, Safmarine
House, 22 Riebeek Street (021 405
3000).*
**Consulate General of the
Netherlands** *100 Strand Street,
cnr Buitengragt, City Centre
(021 421 5660).*
**New Zealand Honorary Consulate
General** *345 Lansdowne Road,
Lansdowne (021 696 8561).*
US Consulate *2 Reddam Avenue,
Westlake, Tokai (021 702 7300).*

Health

Even though there's no difference
in the medical expertise offered by
state and private hospitals, tourists
are advised to go the private route,
since the doctor-patient ratio is
much lower. Take out travel
insurance before leaving.

Contraception & abortion

Government hospitals and clinics
offer free mother-and-child services
like family-planning counselling,
pregnancy tests and abortions to
South Africans and tourists.
Contraceptive pills and condoms
are also available free from clinics.
Over-the-counter pregnancy tests
are available from most chemists
and Clicks outlets and cost around
R30, while 'morning after' pills can
be anything from R40 to R90.
Cape Town Station Clinic *Cape
Town Railway Station (021 425 2004).*
Open 7am-3.45pm Mon-Thur; 7am-
3.30pm Fri.
Chapel Street Clinic *Cnr Chapel
and Balfour streets, Woodstock (021
465 2793).* **Open** 7.30am-4pm
Mon-Fri.

Marie Stopes Clinic *91 Bree Street,
City Centre (021 422 4660).* **Open**
8.30am-4.30pm Mon-Fri; 8.30am-
12.30pm Sat.

Doctors & dentists

The **Talking Yellow Pages**
(10118) and **Cape Town Tourism
Bureau** (021 426 5639/www.
tourismcapetown.co.za) can supply
you with a list of registered medical
practitioners and dentists in your
area. If you're a tourist wanting to
visit a doctor or dentist you might
have to pay your bill up front.
Doctors and dentist consultations
generally cost about R400.

   Netcare Travel Clinic
(www.travelclinic.co.za) is a
national network of specialised
mobile medical centres offering
services to locals and tourists.
Services include immunisations,
pre- and post-travel examinations,
malaria pills and the supply of
first-aid travel kits.

Hospitals

Cape Town Medi Centre *21 Hof
Street, City Bowl (021 464 5555,
www.capetownmc.co.za).*
Groote Schuur Hospital *Main
Road, Observatory, Southern Suburbs
(021 404 9111. www.gsh.co.za).*
Somerset Hospital *Beach Road,
Sea Point (021 402 6911).*

HIV & AIDS

The statistics for HIV infection
and AIDS in South Africa are
alarmingly high. As a consequence,
millions of rands have been
invested into AIDS research
and educational programmes, and
establishing first-rate treatment
facilities. Phone the **National
AIDS Helpline** (0800 012 322,
www.aidshelpline.org.za) if you
think you might have contracted

the virus, for assistance and to find out where you can get anti-retroviral treatment. Also try **New Start HIV Counselling and Testing Centre** (Shop 11, Lower Ground Floor, 58 Strand Street; 021 425 5843).

Late-night pharmacies

Clicks Glengariff Pharmacy *2 Main Road, Sea Point (021 434 8622)*. **Open** 8am-10pm Mon-Sat; 9am-9pm Sun.
Lite-Kem *24 Darling Street, City Centre (021 461 8040)*. **Open** 8am-11pm Mon-Fri; 9am-11pm Sat, Sun.
M-Kem Medicine City *Cnr Durban and Raglan roads, Bellville (021 948 5707)*. **Open** 24hrs daily.

Internet

Wireless internet is available at most hotels in Cape Town. If the hotel you're staying at doesn't have access, it should be able to point you in the right direction. Even though internet cafés have become a bit outdated, there are still several dotting the city centre. Several coffee shops such as Vida e Caffè (www.caffe.co.za) and Mugg and Bean (www.muggandbean.co.za) also offer Wi-Fi services.

If you're planning on an extended stay, it's best to open an account with a local service provider like Polka.co.za (0860 00 4455/www.polka.co.za), M-Web (0860 032 000/www.mweb.co.za) or iBurst (www.iburst.co.za).

Opening hours

Shops in the City Bowl and City Centre normally open between 9am and 5pm on weekdays, staying open until 1pm on Saturdays. Shops on certain touristy stretches of Kloof and Long streets stay open for longer on Saturdays.

Shopping centres open between 9am and 9pm daily. Sundays and public holidays see things starting about an hour later. Banks open between 9am and 3.30pm on weekdays and 8.30am and 11.30pm on Saturdays. Muslim-owned businesses may close for prayers between noon and 1pm on Fridays.

Lost property

If you've left any valuables behind on the plane or are missing any luggage, phone **Cape Town International Airport** (021 937 1200).

If you've lost something in the city, report it to the police station, or place an ad in the classifieds section of a local newspaper like the *Cape Times* (www.capetimes.co.za), the *Cape Argus* (www.capeargus. co.za) or free newspaper the *Cape Towner* (021 488 4624).

Police

The police's national emergency number is **10111**. Ask for the officer's name and rank, as well as a case number. When reporting a crime after the event, it's best to phone your nearest police station (find their number in the blue section of the telephone directory, or call directory inquiries on 1023).

Other useful contacts include:
Cape Town Charge Office 021 467 8000.
Cape Town International Airport Police Station 021 934 0707/0218.
Metro Protection Service 021 449 4336.
Consumer Protector 0800 007 081.

Postal services

Sure, in an era where most people's digits are glued to iPhones and Blackberries, sending postcards and packages to your loved ones is a bit passé, but if you're enamoured with antiquities, you can still head to your local post office. To prevent your letter, postcard, care package or important documentation getting lost in the nothingness, send it by registered mail, and make use of the tracking option from the **South African Post Office** (0860 111 502/ www.sapo.co.za).

You can also go the registered post route, or courier it with a shipping company such as **Fedex** (08000 33339/www.fedex. com/za), **UPS** (021 555 2745/www. ups.co.za) or **TNT** (0860 12 2441/ www.tnt.com).

Sending a postcard overseas costs around R3, while letters in standard envelopes are about R5. The post office also offers a 24-hour door-to-door service between the major centres in South Africa.

Most post offices open 8.30am to 4.30pm weekdays and 8am and noon on Saturdays. Stamps are available from post offices, news-agents and some retail outlets.

Tickets

Book events, concerts, theatre shows, festival tickets and exhibitions through **Computicket** (083 915 8000/www.computicket.co.za).

Telephones

Make a phone call in South Africa by dialling the area code followed by the number, even if your call is local. Cape Town's code is 021. To phone overseas, dial 00 before the phone number. If you don't have a telephone directory at the ready, phone Directory Enquiries (1023), Yellow Pages (10118) or try iFind (www.ifind.co.za/34600), a mobile directory service that you can call or SMS (text message) to find the numbers of local shops and services in your area.

Public phones are still in abundance. Green public phones work with cards, which can be bought at post offices, newsagents and Telkom offices, while the blue ones are of the old-fashioned coin-operated variety.

Most new mobile phones will operate in South Africa, provided they're unlocked and enabled for roaming. SIM cards for the four national networks, Cell C (www.cellc.co.za), Vodacom (www.vodacom.co.za), MTN (www.mtn.co.za) and Virgin Mobile (www.virginmobile.co.za), can be bought at airports, supermarkets, retail stores and newsagents.

Time

South Africa is two hours ahead of GMT, seven ahead of Eastern Standard Winter Time and ten ahead of Pacific Standard Time. There is no daylight saving time during the summer.

Tipping

When eating out, you should add a gratuity of between 10 and 20 per cent to your bill. Taxi drivers usually get about ten per cent, porters up to R10 a bag, and pump attendants between R5 and R10. Unofficial car guards will settle for around R5, depending on how long they 'looked after' your car.

Tourist information

Situated on the corner of Castle and Burg streets, the **Cape Town Tourism Visitor Centre** (021 426 4260) offers plenty of maps, brochures and tour options, and will let you know about events.

A smaller visitor centre, the **Cape Town Tourism Office** (021 405 4500), is located in the Clock Tower at the V&A Waterfront.

ESSENTIALS

Index

ESSENTIALS

ESSENTIALS

The travel apps city lovers have been waiting for...

Apps and maps work offline with no roaming charges

Search for 'Time Out Guides' in the app store

timeout.com/iphonecityguides

AGUA RESTAURANT: 101tl; AISA, Barcelona: 1c, 11c, 30tl, 30tr, 30c, 31bl, 31tr, 31cr, 31br, 118c; ALAMY IMAGES: ICSDB 131tr; Melvyn Longhurst 61bl; BARCELONA TURISME: 61tr; 110c; Espai d'Imatge 64c; 65b; Jordi Trullas 64t; BUBO: 75tr; CAL PEP: 79t; CASA ALFONSO: 108tr; CASA CALVET: 109tl; CINC SENTITS: 44tl; CLUB CATWALK: 100tl; COMERÇ 24: 44tr. DK Images: Ian Aitken 85tl; Steve Gorton 134tr; DANIEL CAMPI: 146tl. EGO GALLERY: 84tl; EL PIANO: 114tr; ELEPHANT CLUB: 46ca, 46tc; FUNDACION JOAN MIRO: Pagès Català al cla de Luna Joan Miró © Sucession Miró/ADAGP, Paris and DACS, London 2006 22bl; Tapis de al Fundacio Joan Miró © Sucession Miró/ADAGP, Paris and DACS, London 2006 22–3c; Home i Dona Davant un Munt d'Excrement Joan Miró © Succession Miró/ADAGP, Paris and DACS, London 2006 23tr; GALERIA DELS ANGELS: 84tl; GETTY IMAGES: Tony Stone/Luc Beziat 48c. HOTEL OMM: 107tr; MANUEL HUGUET: 128–9. IMAGE-STATE: AGE-Fotostock 141tr; Courtesy of CAIXA CATALUNYA: 137tl; JAMBOREE: 47tr, 77tr; LA MANUAL ALPARGATERA: 75tc;

LIKA LOUNGE: 107tl; MON DE MONES: 114tl; MUSEU NACIONAL d'ART DE CATALUNYA: 18b; 19tl; 19tr; 19ca; 19b; 92–93; MUSEU d'ART CONTEMPORANI: 28tl; 28cl; 28–29c MUSEU PICASSO: Hombre con Boina Pablo Picasso © Sucession Picasso/DACS, London 2006 24b; La Espera Pablo Picasso © Sucession Picasso/DACS, London 2006 24–5; El Loco Pablo Picasso © Sucession Picasso/DACS, London 2006 25t; Sketch for Guernica Pablo Picasso © Sucession Picasso/DACS, London 2006 25cr; Las Meninas Pablo Picasso © Sucession Picasso/DACS, London 2006 25b; MIRIAM NEGRE: 44tr; 46bl; 58bl; 114l; 144r; 112b; 113t; 117; 139r; PARC ZOOLOGIC: 16bl; FRANCISCO FERNANDEZ PRIETO: 76tl; 76tr; PRISMA, Barcelona: 66b; 125t; 126t; RAZZMATAZZ: Albert Uriach 47cl; 100tr; RENFE: 132tr; SALA BECOOL: 46bl; SIDECAR FACTORY CLUB: Moises Torne (motobi@terra.es) 77tl; TEXTIL CAFE: 42bl; XOCOA: 78tr; ZELIG: 86tl; ZENTRAUS: 86tr.

All other images are © Dorling Kindersley. For further information see www.dkimages.com.

English-Catalan Phrase Book

In an Emergency

Help!	**Auxili!**	ow-**gzee**-lee
Stop!	**Pareu!**	**pah**-reh-oo
Call a doctor!	**Telefoneu un metge!**	teh-leh-fon-**eh**-oo oon **meh**-djuh
Call an ambulance!	**Telefoneu una ambulància!**	teh-leh-fon-**eh**-oo oo-nah ahm-boo-**lahn**-see-ah
Call the police!	**Telefoneu la policia**	teh-leh-fon-**eh**-oo lah poh-lee-**see**-ah
Call the fire brigade!	**Telefoneu els bombers!**	teh-leh-fon-eh-oo uhlz boom-**behs**
Where is the nearest telephone?	**On és el telèfon més proper?**	**on**-ehs uhl tuh-leh fon mehs proo-**peh**
Where is the nearest hospital?	**On és l'hospital més proper?**	**on**-ehs looss-pee-tahl mehs proo-**peh**

Communication Essentials

Yes	**Sí**	see
No	**No**	noh
Please	**Si us plau**	sees plah-oo
Thank you	**Gràcies**	**grah**-see-uhs
Excuse me	**Perdoni**	puhr-**thoh**-nee
Hello	**Hola**	**oh**-lah
Goodbye	**Adéu**	ah-they-**oo**
Good night	**Bona nit**	**bo**-nah neet
Morning	**El matí**	uhl muh-**tee**
Afternoon	**La tarda**	lah **tahr**-thuh
Evening	**El vespre**	uhl **vehs**-pruh
Yesterday	**Ahir**	ah-**ee**
Today	**Avui**	uh-voo-ee
Tomorrow	**Demà**	duh-**mah**
Here	**Aquí**	uh-**kee**
There	**Allà**	uh-**lyah**
What?	**Què?**	keh
When?	**Quan?**	kwahn
Why?	**Per què?**	puhr keh
Where?	**On?**	ohn

Useful Phrases

How are you?	**Com està?**	kom uhs-**tah**
Very well, thank you.	**Molt bé, gràcies.**	mol beh **grah**-see-uhs
Pleased to meet you.	**Molt de gust.**	mol duh **goost**
See you soon.	**Fins aviat.**	feenz uhv-**yat**
That's fine.	**Està bé.**	uhs-**tah** beh
Where is/are . ?	**On és/són?**	ohn ehs/sohn
How far is it to.?	**Quants metres/ kilòmetres hi ha d'aquí a ...?**	kwahnz meh-truhs/kee-**loh**-muh-truhs yah dah-**kee** uh
Which way to ...?	**Per on es va a ...?**	puhr **on** uhs **bah** ah
Do you speak English?	**Parla anglès?**	**par**-luh an-**glehs**
I don't understand	**No l'entenc.**	noh luhn-**teng**

Useful Words

Could you speak more slowly, please?	**Pot parlar més a poc a poc, si us plau?**	pot par-**lah** mehs pok uh pok sees plah-oo
I'm sorry.	**Ho sento.**	oo **sehn**-too
big	**gran**	gran
small	**petit**	puh-**teet**
hot	**calent**	kah-**len**
cold	**fred**	fred
good	**bo**	boh
bad	**dolent**	doo-**len**
enough	**bastant**	bahs-**tan**
well	**bé**	beh
open	**obert**	oo-**behr**
closed	**tancat**	tan-**kat**
left	**esquerra**	uhs-**kehr**-ruh
right	**dreta**	**dreh**-tuh
straight on	**recte**	**rehk**-tuh
near	**a prop**	uh **prop**
far	**lluny**	**lyoon**yuh
up/over	**a dalt**	uh **dahl**
down/under	**a baix**	uh **bah**-eeshh
early	**aviat**	uhv-**yat**
late	**tard**	tahrt
entrance	**entrada**	uhn-**trah**-thuh
exit	**sortida**	**soor**-tee-thuh
toilet	**lavabos/ serveis**	luh-**vah**-boos sehr-**beh**-ees
more	**més**	mess
less	**menys**	**men**yees

Shopping

How much does this cost?	**Quant costa això?**	kwahn kost ehs-**shoh**
I would like ...	**M'agradaria ...**	muh-**grah-thuh-ree**-ah
Do you have?	**Tenen?**	**tehn**-un
I'm just looking, thank you	**Només estic mirant, gràcies.**	noo-mess ehs-teek mee-**rahn grah**-see-uhs
Do you take credit cards?	**Accepten targes de crèdit?**	ak-**sehp**-tuhn tahr-**zhuhs** duh **kreh**-deet
What time do you open?	**A quina hora obren?**	ah **keen**-uh **oh**-ruh **oh**-bruhn
What time do you close?	**A quina hora tanquen?**	ah **keen**-uh oh-ruh **tan**-kuhn
This one.	**Aquest**	ah-**ket**
That one.	**Aquell**	ah-**kehl**
expensive	**car**	kahr
cheap	**bé de preu/ barat**	beh thuh preh-oo/bah-**rat**
size (clothes)	**talla/mida**	**tah**-lyah/**mee**-thuh
size (shoes)	**número**	**noo**-mehr-oo
white	**blanc**	blang
black	**negre**	**neh**-gruh
red	**vermell**	vuhr-**mel**
yellow	**groc**	grok

158

English	Catalan	Pronunciation
	verd	behrt
	blau	blah-oo
...ue store	antiquari/	an-tee-kwah-ree/
	botiga	boo-tee-gah/dan-
	d'antiguitats	tee-ghee-tats
...ry	el forn	uhl forn
	el banc	uhl bang
...store	la llibreria	lah lyee-bruh-ree-ah
...her's	la carnisseria	lah kahr-nee-suh-ree-uh
...y shop	la pastisseria	lah pahs-tee-suh-ree-uh
...nist's	la farmàcia	lah fuhr-mah-see-ah
...nonger's	la peixateria	lah peh-shuh-tuh-ree-uh
...ngrocer's	la fruiteria	lah froo-ee-tuh-ree-uh
...r's	la botiga de queviures	lah boo-tee-guh duh keh-vee-oo-ruhs
...dresser's	la perruqueria	lah peh-roo-kuh-ree-uh
...ket	el mercat	uhl muhr-kat
...sagent's	el quiosc de premsa	uhl kee-ohsk duh prem-suh
...office	l'oficina de correus	loo-fee-see-nuh duh koo-reh-oos
...e store	la sabateria	lah sah-bah-tuh-ree-uh
...ermarket	el supermercat	uhl soo-puhr-muhr-kat
...cconist's	l'estanc	luhs-tang
...el agency	l'agència de viatges	la-jen-see-uh duh vee-ad-juhs

...ghtseeing

...gallery	la galeria d'art	lah gah-luh-ree-yuh dart
...edral	la catedral	lah kuh-tuh-thrahl
...rch	l'església	luhz-gleh-zee-uh
	la basílica	lah buh-zee-lee-kuh
...en	el jardí	uhl zhahr-dee
...ry	la biblioteca	lah bee-blee-oo-teh-kuh
...eum	el museu	uhl moo-seh-oo
...tion office	l'oficina de turisme	loo-fee-see-nuh thuh too-reez-muh
...n hall	l'ajuntament	luh-djoon-tuh-men
...ed for	tancat per	tan-kat puhr
...day	vacances	bah-kan-suhs
...station	l'estació d'autobusos	luhs-tah-see-oh dow-toh-boo-zoos
...way	l'estació de tren	luhs-tah-see-oh thuh tren
...tion		

...ying in a Hotel

...you have	¿Tenen una habitació	teh-nuhn oo-nuh ah-bee-tuh-see-oh
	room?	
double	habitació	ah-bee-tuh-see-oh
room with	doble amb	doh-bluh am
double bed	llit de matrimoni	lyeet de mah-tree-moh-nee
twin room	habitació amb dos llits/ amb llits individual	ah-bee-tuh-see-oh am dohs lyeets/ s am lyeets in-thee-vee-thoo-ahls
single room	habitació individual	ah-bee-tuh-see-oh een-dee-vee-thoo-ahl
room with a bath	habitació amb bany	ah-bee-tuh-see-oh am bahnyuh
shower	dutxa	doo-chuh
porter	el grum	uhl groom
key	la clau	lah klah-oo
I have a reservation	Tinc una habitació reservada	ting oo-nuh ah-bee-tuh-see-oh reh-sehr-vah-thah

Eating Out

Have you got a table for...	Tenen taula per...?	teh-nuhn tow-luh puhr
I would like to reserve a table.	Voldria reservar una taula.	vool-dree-uh reh-sehr-vahr oo-nuh tow-luh
The bill please	El compte, si us plau.	uhl kohm-tuh sees plah-oo
I am a vegetarian	Sóc vegetarià/ vegetariana	sok buh-zhuh-tuh-ree-ah buh-zhuh-tuh-ree-ah-nah
waitress	cambrera	kam-breh-ruh
waiter	cambrer	kam-breh
menu	la carta	lah kahr-tuh
fixed-price menu	menú del dia	muh-noo thuhl dee-uh
wine list	la carta de vins	ah kahr-tuh thuh veens
glass of water	un got d'aigua	oon got dah-ee-gwah
glass of wine	una copa de vi	oo-nuh ko-pah thuh vee
bottle	una ampolla	oo-nuh am-pol-yuh
knife	un ganivet	oon gun-ee-veht
fork	una forquilla	oo-nuh foor-keel-yuh
spoon	una cullera	oo-nuh kool-yeh-ruh
breakfast	l'esmorzar	les-moor-sah
lunch	el dinar	uhl dee-nah
dinner	el sopar	uhl soo-pah
main course	el primer plat	uhl pree-meh plat
starters	els entrants	uhlz ehn-tranz
dish of the day	el plat del dia	uhl plat duhl dee-uh
coffee	el cafè	uhl kah-feh
rare	poc fet	pok fet
medium	al punt	ahl poon
well done	molt fet	mol fet

Menu Decoder

l'aigua mineral	lah-ee-gwuh mee-nuh-**rahl**	mineral water
sense gas/	sen-zuh gas/	still
amb gas	am gas	sparkling
al forn	ahl **forn**	baked
l'all	**lahl**yuh	garlic
l'arròs	lahr-**roz**	rice
les botifarres	lahs **boo**-tee-fah-rahs	sausages
la carn	lah **karn**	meat
la ceba	lah **seh**-buh	onion
la cervesa	lah-sehr-**ve**-sah	beer
l'embotit	lum-boo-**teet**	cold meat
el filet	uhl fee-**let**	sirloin
el formatge	uhl for-**mah**-djuh	cheese
fregit	freh-**zheet**	fried
la fruita	lah froo-**ee**-tah	fruit
els fruits secs	uhlz froo-**eets** seks	nuts
les gambes	lahs **gam**-bus	prawns
el gelat	uhl djuh-**lat**	ice cream
la llagosta	lah lyah-**gos**-tah	lobster
la llet	lah **lyet**	milk
la llimona	lah lyee-**moh**-nah	lemon
la llimonada	lah lyee-moh-**nah**-tuh	lemonade
la mantega	lah mahn-**teh**-gah	butter
el marisc	uhl muh-**reesk**	seafood
la menestra	lah muh-**nehs**-truh	vegetable stew
l'oli	**loll**-ee	oil
les olives	luhs oo-**lee**-vuhs	olives
l'ou	**loh**-oo	egg
el pa	uhl **pah**	bread
el pastís	uhl pahs-**tees**	pie/cake
les patates	lahs pah-**tah**-tuhs	potatoes
el pebre	uhl **peh**-bruh	pepper
el peix	uhl **pehsh**	fish
el pernil	uhl puhr-**neel**	cured ham
salat serrà	suh-**lat** sehr-**rah**	
el plàtan	uhl **plah**-tun	banana
el pollastre	uhl poo-**lyah**-struh	chicken
la poma	la **poh**-mah	apple
el porc	uhl **pohr**	pork
les postres	lahs **pohs**-truhs	dessert
rostit	rohs-**teet**	roast
la sal	lah **sahl**	salt
la salsa	lah **sahl**-suh	sauce
les salsitxes	lahs sahl-**see**-chuhs	sausages
sec	**sehk**	dry
la sopa	lah **soh**-puh	soup
el sucre	uhl-**soo**-kruh	sugar
la taronja	lah tuh-**rohn**-djuh	orange
el te	uhl teh	tea
les torrades	lahs too-**rah**-thuhs	toast
la vedella	lah veh-**theh**-lyuh	beef
el vi blanc	uhl **bee** blang	white wine
el vi negre	uhl **bee** neh-gruh	red wine
el vi rosat	uhl **bee** roo-**zaht**	rosé wine
el vinagre	uhl bee-**nah**-gruh	vinegar
el xai/el be	uhl **shah**ee/uhl beh	lamb
la xocolata	lah shoo-koo-**lah**-tuh	chocolate
el xoriç	uhl shoo-**rees**	red sausage

Numbers

0	zero	**seh**-roo
1	un (masc)	oon
	una (fem)	**oon**-uh
2	dos (masc)	**dohs**
	dues (fem)	**doo**-uhs
3	tres	**trehs**
4	quatre	**kwa**-truh
5	cinc	**seeng**
6	sis	**sees**
7	set	**set**
8	vuit	**voo**-eet
9	nou	**noh**-oo
10	deu	**deh**-oo
11	onze	**on**-zuh
12	dotze	**doh**-dzuh
13	tretze	**treh**-dzuh
14	catorze	kah-**tohr**-dzuh
15	quinze	**keen**-zuh
16	setze	**set**-zuh
17	disset	dee-**set**
18	divuit	dee-voo-**eet**
19	dinou	dee-**noh**-oo
20	vint	**been**
21	vint-i-un	been-tee-**oon**
22	vint-i-dos	been-tee-**doh**
30	trenta	**tren**-tah
31	trenta-un	**tren**-tah oon
40	quaranta	kwuh-**ran**-tuh
50	cinquanta	seen-**kwahn**-
60	seixanta	seh-ee-**shan**-
70	setanta	seh-**tan**-tah
80	vuitanta	voo-ee-**tan**-ta
90	noranta	noh-**ran**-tah
100	cent	**sen**
101	cent un	**sent** oon
102	cent dos	**sen** dohs
200	dos-cents (masc)	dohs-**sens**
	dues-centes (fem)	doo-uhs **sen**-tuhs
300	tres-cents	**trehs**-sen
400	quatre-cents	**kwah**-truh-se
500	cinc-cents	**seeng**-senz
600	sis-cents	**sees**-senz
700	set-cents	**set**-senz
800	vuit-cents	**voo**-eet-senz
900	nou-cents	**noh**-oo-cenz
1,000	mil	**meel**
1,001	mil un	**meel** oon

Time

one minute	un minut	oon mee-**noo**
one hour	una hora	oo-nuh **oh**-ru
half an hour	mitja hora	**mee**-juh oh-r
Monday	dilluns	dee-**lyoonz**
Tuesday	dimarts	dee-**marts**
Wednesday	dimecres	dee-**meh**-kruh
Thursday	dijous	dee-**zhoh**-oos
Friday	divendres	dee-**ven**-druhs
Saturday	dissabte	dee-**sab**-tuh
Sunday	diumenge	dee-oo-**men**-j